ERASMUS AND THE NEW TESTAMENT:
THE MIND OF A CHRISTIAN HUMANIST

ERASMUS AND THE NEW TESTAMENT: THE MIND OF A CHRISTIAN HUMANIST

by
ALBERT RABIL, JR.

Associate Professor of Humanities
State University of New York
College at Old Westbury

Trinity University Press 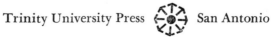 San Antonio

Copyright © 1972 by Trinity University Press
Library of Congress Card Catalog Number 71-184768
Printed in the United States of America
Printed by Von Boeckmann-Jones Co.
Bound by Custom Bookbinders
SBN # 911536-45-0

This book is dedicated to

WILHELM PAUCK

*a scholar through whom the sixteenth
century began to live for me
a teacher whose deep feeling for the
men, women, and ideas he sought to
interpret has deepened my own feeling
for all of life
a friend whose warmth and charm have
enriched my personal life*

ERASMUS AND THE NEW TESTAMENT:
THE MIND OF A CHRISTIAN HUMANIST

PREFACE

There have been a number of attempts to describe Erasmus' intellectual development and to measure his greatness, but none has thus far succeeded in analyzing that development and greatness in a way consistent with all the source material on which such an interpretation must be based. The range of interpretations has been very great, from Albert Hyma's insistence that Erasmus' training in the worldly mysticism of the Brethren of the Common Life is the key to understanding his life[1] to Augustin Renaudet's notion that Erasmus was a "humanist," that is, a man whose primary allegiance was to classical literature and the philological method, for whom religion was subordinate to morality, and who professed an orthodox creed from self-serving more than from sincere motives.[2] I shall disagree with these interpretations, as with a host of others in between, but I want to agree here to the extent of affirm-

---

[1] *The Youth of Erasmus* (2nd ed., enl.; New York: Russell & Russell, 1968).

[2] "Erasme, sa Vie et son Oeuvre jusqu'en 1517 d'àpres sa correspondance," *Révue Historique,* CXI (1912), 225-62; CXII (1913), 241-74; *Etudes Erasmiennes* (Paris: Droz, 1939), ch. 4; *Erasme et l'Italie* (Geneva: Droz, 1954); *Humanisme et Renaissance* (Geneva: Droz, 1958), ch. 9.

ing that religion and humanism are the proper poles in relation to which Erasmus' intellectual development must be understood.[3] Almost from the beginning of his writings —whether letters, poetry, or prose treatises—tension between his religious heritage and his love for Latin letters is evident.

My point of view is forward rather than backward. I shall not speculate on the origins of Erasmus' religion or his humanism before he becomes visible as a writer, nor on the psychological factors which led him in one direction or another.[4] Rather, I believe, and I shall attempt to demonstrate, that Erasmus' intellectual development was at every turning point, from his first poem in 1483 until he achieved a maturity of outlook in his edition of the Greek New Testament in 1516, dependent upon some self-conscious resolution of the conflict between a vaguely felt childhood religion and an adolescent love of Latin literature. The outcome of this analysis requires a modification of the judgment of Huizinga in his penetrating portrait of Erasmus,[5] that "his character was not on a level with the elevation

[3]A number of writers understand these as the important poles of tension in Erasmus. See, for example, Paul Mestwerdt, *Die Anfänge des Erasmus: Humanismus und 'Devotio Moderna'* (Leipzig: Haupt, 1917); Rudolf Pfeiffer, *Humanitas Erasmiana* (London: Warburg Institute, 1933); and "Erasmus und die Einheit der klassischen und der christlichen Renaissance," *Historisches Jahrbuch*, LXXIV (1954), 175-88; Lewis Spitz, *The Religious Renaissance of the German Humanists* (Cambridge: Harvard University Press, 1963), pp. 199, 203. What I shall attempt here is to unfold the stages by which this fusion took place in order to characterize its precise meaning for Erasmus.

[4]James D. Tracy, *Erasmus: The Growth of a Mind* (Ph.D. dissertation, Princeton University, 1966), despite flashes of insight, fails to clarify Erasmus' intellectual development through his effort to isolate character traits (freedom, simplicity, sincerity) and to illustrate the influence of these through Erasmus' writings and the events of his life. When, for example, he says that freedom (*libertas*) deserves a special place in interpreting Erasmus because "the specific reforms he called for usually entailed some kind of liberation from restraint" (pp. 426-27), he explains nothing. The same is true of all religious reforms, including especially that of Luther and Calvin with whom Erasmus was in explicit disagreement. The texts often say too little or too much when they are made to serve some a priori idea which comes from elsewhere. See further, below, ch. II, n. 132; ch. III, n. 7.

[5]Johan Huizinga, *Erasmus and the Age of Reformation* (New York: Harper Torchbooks, 1957), chs. 12-14.

of his mind."[6] Instead of our having "to see of that great Erasmus as much as the petty one permits,"[7] we should begin to see that his own self-consciousness renders these very categories inappropriate.

The text will be confined to detailed proof of this thesis through analysis of Erasmus' writings. Agreements and disagreements with other scholars will be confined largely to the footnotes. No bibliography is appended to this study. The notes mention in context most of the significant literature related to the areas with which the book deals. Up-to-date bibliographies of the growing literature on Erasmus are available from a number of sources.[8]

My debts have increased as the book has grown from conception to fulfillment. I would like to express my thanks to The Society for Religion in Higher Education which, through the award of one of its cross-disciplinary fellowships, made possible a year of study (1968-69) in the classical background of Erasmus' humanism. During that year I received generous assistance from Professors William S. Anderson and Ralph Johnson of the Department of Classics, University of California at Berkeley. Professor Anderson especially shared many hours out of a busy schedule. I am also indebted to my students at The Chicago Theological Seminary with whom I struggled through initial formulations of ideas

[6] *Ibid.*, p. 117.

[7] *Ibid.*, p. 129.

[8] General bibliographies are to be found in many recent books on Erasmus. Two that are readily available are E.-W. Kohls, *Die Theologie des Erasmus* (Basel: Reinhardt, 1966), II; and R. H. Bainton, *Erasmus of Christendom* (New York: Charles Scribner's Sons, 1969).

For more complete bibliographies the work of J.-C. Margolin, who has compiled a nearly exhaustive list of publications on Erasmus between 1936 and 1961, is indispensable: *Douze années de bibliographie érasmienne, 1950-1961* (Paris: Vrin, 1963); *Quatorze années de bibliographie érasmienne, 1936-1949* (Paris: Vrin, 1969). Professor Margolin will be extending his work in subsequent volumes. Annual bibliographies which include publications on Erasmus are available from 1965 in *Bibliographie internationale de l'Humanisme et de la Renaissance* (Geneva: Droz). Annual bibliographies are also published in the journal *Studies in Philology*. An informative discussion of recent literature on Erasmus, including the plethora of publications marking the quincentenary of his birth, is C. Reedijk, "Erasmus in 1970," *Bibliothèque d'Humanisme et Renaissance*, XXXII: II (May, 1970), 449-66.

presented here and achieved greater clarity in the process; and to the seminary for providing clerical assistance in completing an earlier draft of the manuscript. I owe a special thanks to Professors Roland H. Bainton, Wilhelm Pauck, and John B. Payne who read an earlier draft of the manuscript and offered suggestions which have increased its accuracy and quality. Professor Pauck, to whom the volume is dedicated, first excited my interest in Erasmus, as he did in many aspects of sixteenth-century European culture. It goes without saying, however, that I am responsible for any errors of fact or interpretation that remain. Finally, I would like to thank Ms. Isabelle McKeever, State University of New York at Old Westbury, who typed the final manuscript for publication.

    Westbury, N. Y.   Albert Rabil, Jr.

    July 9, 1971

ABBREVIATIONS

The following abbreviations are used in the notes:

EE   *Erasmi Epistolae,* eds., P. S. Allen, H. M. Allen, and H. W. Garrod, 12 vols., Oxford, 1906-1958

EOO, I.1   *Erasmi Opera Omnia,* I.1, Amsterdam, 1969

EOO, I.2   *Erasmi Opera Omnia,* I.2, Amsterdam, 1971

Himelick   *The Enchiridion of Erasmus,* ed., Raymond Himelick, Bloomington, 1963

Holborn   *Desiderius Erasmus Roterodamus Ausgewählte Werke,* ed., Hajo Holborn, Munich, 1933

LB   *Erasmi Opera Omnia,* ed., LeClerc, 10 vols., Leiden, 1703-1706

Nichols   *The Epistles of Erasmus,* ed., F. M. Nichols, 3 vols., London, 1901-1918

Pauck   *Luther: Lectures on Romans,* ed., Wilhelm Pauck, Philadelphia, 1961

PG   *Patrologiae cursus completus, series Graeca,* ed., J.-P. Migne, 162 vols., Paris, 1857-1866

PL   *Patrologiae cursus completus,* series Latina, ed., J.-P. Migne, 217 vols., Paris, 1844-1855

TABLE OF CONTENTS

I. ERASMUS' INTELLECTUAL DEVELOPMENT: RELIGION AND HUMANISM— EITHER/OR: 1467-1499

In January, 1518, two months after he had published the first edition of his *Paraphrase of Romans*, Erasmus wrote to the man to whom he was later to dedicate his *Paraphrase of Corinthians* that "in me there is nothing to be seen; or if there is, it is represented by my books. The best part of me is there, and the rest would not sell for a nickel."[1] But "the best part of me" was indeed a great deal. He had by that time established a reputation as an educator, theologian, satirist, and scholar.

He was known first (1500) as an educator, primarily through his collections of adages from the writers of Greece and Rome (and in later editions, from Christian writers as well). In subsequent years he published formal treatises on education to assist teachers *(On the Right Method of Instruction,* 1511) and students *(On Copia of Words and Ideas,* 1512). At length he even wrote for the edification of future rulers *(The Education of a Christian Prince,* 1516).

In 1501 Erasmus wrote his first work of theology, *Handbook of a Christian Soldier* (published, 1503), a treatise whose ideas found their way, after a long process of develop-

[1]EE, III, 194, lines 15-17; Nichols, III, 218.

ment, into Erasmus' paraphrases of the New Testament (1517 and following).

Satire came full-blown from the head of a mature thinker in the form of *The Praise of Folly* (1509, published 1511). It was followed by a number of essays and dialogues in which Erasmus castigated the powerful for their waywardness and called them back to responsibility.

The scholar in Erasmus is evident not only in the various editions of the adages but in the preparation in languages and manuscript study that accompanied them and led finally to his New Testament (1516 and following) and editions of the Christian classics (1520 and following).

How did it happen that Erasmus began as an educator of children and youth and by 1516 was educating princes? Or that his obscure *Handbook of a Christian Soldier* was translated into thousands of pages of published commentary that was to influence decisively the religious revolution of his time? How did it come about that his criticism of individual vice became social satire directed at men in high places, and that his scholarship developed from a preoccupation with pagan classics to a passion for uncovering the sources of the Christian tradition? What kind of unity is discernible in all these transformations? How is one to explain the internal movement from obscure beginnings to international acclaim?

Erasmus' casual statement emerges as a perplexing question. What precisely was "the best part of me"?

Literature and Religion in Tension: The Monk as Poet

Erasmus[2] was born in Rotterdam on October 27 or 28, probably in 1467.[3] He was the second illegitimate son of Gerhard, a priest, and Margaret, the daughter of a physi-

[2]He was named Herasmus by his father. The earliest authentic use of Erasmus is 1503. Desiderius he adds himself in 1497. Roterodamus first appears in 1504. The full form, Desiderius Erasmus Roterodamus, occurs first in a reissue of the *Adagia* in 1506. (See EE, I, 72, first note.)

[3]The year of Erasmus' birth has long been debated by scholars. The favorite candidates have been 1466 and 1469. These were the years selected in the most recent debate on the issue by E.-W. Kohls and R. R. Post

cian.⁴ He spent his early childhood (1475-1478) in Gouda, attending the school of the Brethren of the Common Life, a group of largely (though not exclusively) lay men and women who emphasized Christ as example and companion and who stressed heartfelt inwardness (over against formal ceremonial observance) as the essence of true religion. They sought a deepening of Christian commitment in the world and to this end devoted themselves to copying religious texts for widespread use, by which also they supported themselves.

(Bibliothèque d'Humanisme et Renaissance, XXVI [1964]), 489-509; *Theologische Zeitschrift*, XXII: II [1966], 96-121; XXII: V [1966], 317-33, 347-59). Kohls argues for 1466, Post for 1469. The arguments of both have been superseded, in my opinion, by A. C. F. Koch, *The Year of Erasmus' Birth*, tr. E. Franco (Utrecht: Haentjens Dekker & Gumbert, 1969), who demonstrates that by correlating Erasmus' statements (that he was fourteen when he left Deventer and that when he left, the bridge over the Ijssel River had not yet been completed) with town records of the construction of the bridge and the coming of Alexander Hegius to Deventer as headmaster of the school, 1467 emerges as the year of his birth. He demonstrates further that the discrepancies in Erasmus' statements about his age during the later years of his life were made during "climacteric years," that is, during the seventh or ninth year after he passed the age of 49. Koch writes: "Exceptionally critical was the 49th year, being the square of seven, and more dangerous yet the 63rd, a multiple of both nine and seven and for this reason termed 'the grand climacteric.' Also dangerous were the 70th year (10 times 7) and the 81st (9 times 9). It was the custom in Germany to send special good wishes to anyone who happily completed a 'Stufenjahr'." (pp. 41-42) Erasmus tended to add a year to his life every six years after he reached age 49. Why? In order to flee a climacteric year. Koch writes: "When he transferred prematurely in 1528, from the 63rd to the 64th year, he was fleeing from an imaginary climacteric. The same can be said of his attempt, shortly before the end of his life, to smuggle in yet an additional year during his (imaginary) seventieth year." (p. 43)

It may strike us as curious that Erasmus should have had such anxiety about climacteric years. But the evidence makes this explanation much more plausible than the earlier explanation of Preserved Smith and others that Erasmus was attempting in his later life to set his age further and further back in order to clear his father of the charge of illicit intercourse while ordained a priest. This explanation would be without reason, since no one at that time could have determined when his father was ordained. Koch's is the first explanation of the matter which most plausibly accounts for the most accurate information we have and which also explains the discrepancies in Erasmus' later testimony about his age. This is as close to unraveling the mystery surrounding the year of Erasmus' birth as we have ever come.

⁴In his *Compendium vitae* (EE, I, 46-52; Nichols, I, 5-13; also J. C. Olin,

Their mystical piety, expressed most beautifully in Thomas à Kempis' *Imitation of Christ,* spread from Holland throughout Europe during the latter half of the fourteenth century, largely through schools, of which they founded a great number.[5] But in 1478 Erasmus moved with his mother from Gouda to Deventer, where he attended St. Lebwin's School— not under the control of the Brethren. During two of the next eight years, however, he attended the choir school at Utrecht, so that at the end of his stay in Deventer he had completed only six grades. In 1485 his mother and father both died from the plague. Erasmus was sent by the three guardians appointed by his father to a Brethren school at Bois-le-Duc rather than to a university which he desired very much to attend, for they wanted to devote him to religion. One of the guardians died; the other two had apparently not managed well the money left behind by Erasmus' father for the education of his two sons. They arranged for the two

Christian Humanism and the Reformation [New York: Harper Torchbooks, 1965], pp. 22-30), Erasmus reports that his father left Margaret while she was pregnant because of family harassment. He went to Rome where he earned a living as a copyist. The family sent word that Margaret had died; Gerhard assumed holy orders out of grief. He remained faithful to his vows even after discovering the deception upon his return. (Charles Read based his novel, *The Cloister and the Hearth* [1862] on this story in the *Compendium vitae.*) In this account, Erasmus makes no mention of his older brother, Peter. He seems concerned to prove that his father was not in holy orders when he was conceived. But in 1523 he had no reason for such a deception, since he had been freed from the disabilities of his illegitimacy in 1517, and, in addition, as pointed out in the preceding note, no one could have determined at that date when his father had been ordained.

Doubt about the authenticity of the *Compendium vitae* has been raised by Roland Crahay, "Recherches sur le *Compendium vitae* attribué à Erasme," *Bibliothèque d'Humanisme et Renaissance,* VI (1939), 7-19, 135-53. Allen regards it as genuine (EE, I, 575-78).

[5]On the Brethren of the Common Life and the *Devotio Moderna,* see Albert Hyma, *The Christian Renaissance: A History of the 'Devotio Moderna'* (2nd ed.; Hamden: Archon Books, 1965); and R. R. Post, *The Modern Devotion: Confrontation with Reformation and Humanism* (Leiden: Brill, 1968).

There are many translations of *The Imitation of Christ,* one of the most widely read of Christian devotional classics. The edition I cite below is that of Harold C. Gardiner, *The Imitation of Christ* (Doubleday: Image Books, 1955).

boys to enter the monastery of Sion at Delft. The boys agreed between themselves that they would resist the wishes of the guardians and remain in school for the next few years. When this decision was communicated to the guardians, however, pressure was brought upon the boys to change their minds. Peter soon yielded to this pressure and became a monk. Erasmus continued to resist the guardians. But his head was turned toward another monastery, that of Steyn, by William Herman, a friend of Erasmus' from Deventer schooldays who now resided there.[6] William painted a glowing picture of the freedom, abundance of books, and leisure for study afforded by this particular monastery. Erasmus was persuaded and entered Steyn in 1487.[7] He remained there for six years. In 1492 he was ordained and in 1493 left the monastery in the service of the Bishop of Cambrai, never to return as a permanent resident.

We know from later statements that Erasmus was strongly critical of his treatment in the school of the Brethren, and that with respect to curriculum, he regarded them as "barbarous."[8] No more than conjecture is possible, how-

[6]William Herman (1466-1510) had been a pupil of Winkel at Gouda and had studied under Hegius at Deventer, remaining there longer than Erasmus did. Hence, the two knew each other from early childhood. He and Erasmus were together at Steyn from 1487 until 1489, when William was transferred to Haarlem. But he had returned before Erasmus left the monastery. The first extant correspondence between them dates from 1493. Letters written during the Paris years (1495-1499) reveal much about their early life together. Erasmus was responsible for the publication of William's poetry in Paris in 1496 (see EE, I, 160-61). After 1501 the relationship between the two became less cordial, or at least less intense. (For further biographical details see EE, I, 128.)

[7]The most authentic account by Erasmus of his early life is to be found in his "Letter to Grunnius," written to the pope in 1516 requesting dispensation from his vows (EE, II, 291-312; Nichols, II, 339-70). Events unfolded in the letter are accurately represented, so far as we can tell. What is questionable, however, is Erasmus' attempt to portray his stay in the monastery as coerced from the very beginning. This might have strengthened his case with the pope, but it is not a true recording of his experience in the monastery. His early letters and treatises reveal, as we shall see below, that he was quite content during his first years there.

[8]See the letter cited in the note above (EE, lines 97-146; Nichols, 342-44) on the school at Bois-le-Duc. In the *De pueris instituendis* (*On the Education of Children*), written initially around 1500, revised between 1506

ever, regarding his intellectual development prior to en-
trance into the monastery at Steyn. But from that period we
possess some works from his own pen; notably, a few letters
to his peers, a number of poems, an *Oration on Peace and
Discord* (1488), paraphrases on the *Elegantiae* of Lorenzo
Valla (1488), an *Oration at the Funeral of Bertha de Heyen*
(1489), a treatise *On the Contempt of the World* (1489),
and a work begun in the monastery but cast in its present
form only after he had left Steyn, *Against the Barbarians*
(1494). What can we learn from these of his intellectual development before and just after he left the monastery?

On his youth Erasmus wrote in later life that "some
secret natural impulse drove me to good literature. Discouraged even by my masters, I stealthily drank in what I could
from whatever books came to my hand; I practised my pen;

and 1509, but not published until 1529, Erasmus gives an account of a
flogging he received at the hands of one of his teachers who deliberately
charged him with an offense and then punished him for it (W. H. Woodward, *Des. Erasmus concerning the Aim and Method of Education* [New
York: Columbia Teachers College, 1964], pp. 205-6; also in Nichols, I, 19).
In all that he later wrote about education, Erasmus was consistent in
extolling kindness and persuasion as the proper methods for exciting a
love of learning. "Masters who are conscious of their own incompetence,"
he said in the same treatise, "are generally the worst floggers. What else,
indeed, can they do? They cannot teach, so they beat." (Woodward, p. 206;
see 210-11) The *De pueris instituendis* was published in a critical edition
with a French translation by Jean-Claude Margolin (Geneva: Droz, 1966),
and again by the same editor in EOO, I.2, 1-78. There is a loose English
translation in Woodward, pp. 180-222.

The school at Deventer Erasmus calls "barbarous" in his *Compendium
vitae* (EE, I, 48, lines 34-35; Nichols, I, 7). He acknowledges in the same
place, however, that he was exposed to humanistic studies there. Alexander
Hegius (1433-1498), who studied Latin and Greek under Rudolf Agricola
(1444-1485) in 1474, was headmaster of St. Lebwin's School from 1483
until his death. Together with Zinthius he published a Latin grammar in
verse for the use of his students. Erasmus says that he was exposed to
Hegius as a teacher, though not on a regular basis. (See also EE, I, 106,
lines 60-63; Nichols, I, 66.) In his letter to Botzheim (1523) he says that
he saw Rudolf Agricola at Deventer, though he never heard him as a
teacher (EE, I, 2, lines 24-27; Nichols, I, 20; see also EE, I, 105-6, lines 56-59;
Nichols, I, 66). Agricola was among the first northern humanists to establish
a name in Italy. He studied there intermittently from 1468 to 1479 and
brought back to the north with him a contagious enthusiasm for Latin and
Greek studies. (On him see Lewis Spitz, *The Religious Renaissance of the
German Humanists*, pp. 20-40.)

I challenged my comrades to enter the lists with me, little thinking that the printing press would some day betray such trifles to the world."⁹ Many of his "trifles" have been lost, but of those preserved in his letters and poems, his judgment about himself is well founded. His earliest compositions in both poetry and prose reveal a mastery of the formal elements of Latin style. Indeed, the earliest letters at Steyn, written to Servatius Roger, a young monk from Rotterdam with whom Erasmus established a friendship, reveal him to be the teacher of his peers in reading and writing classical Latin.¹⁰ Erasmus urges Servatius to shake off the torpor and cowardice that have hitherto possessed him with respect to study.¹¹

⁹Letter to John Botzheim, Erasmus' catalogue of his writings, compiled in January, 1523 (EE, I, 2, lines 29-34; Nichols, I, 20-21).

¹⁰These letters are printed by Allen (EE, I, 77-90) and translated by Nichols (I, 45-52, with omissions), though the order of the letters is differently assessed. On their proper order, see EE, I, App. III, pp. 584-86. The letters reveal Erasmus reaching out in lyrical enthusiasm to gain the friendship of Servatius. He cites the lyrical works of Vergil (principally, *Aeneid* IV), Ovid, and Horace often in these letters (see Charles Béné, *Erasme et Saint Augustin*, pp. 32-33). These are the same sources that one finds in the first 13 non-religious poems of Erasmus (see below, note 18), three of which were probably written for Servatius (C. Reedijk, *The Poems of Erasmus* [Leiden: Brill, 1956], Carm. 5-7, pp. 143-48). Psychologically, this exuberance seems to be related to a peace Erasmus found in the monastery, following a period of great dejection before he entered. (But see Reedijk, *The Poems of Erasmus*, Carm. 6, lines 20 ff., p. 146, and note; one of his earliest extant letters reflects this depression: EE, I, 74-75; Nichols, I, 83-84). Servatius' coolness toward Erasmus' overtures led to a crisis after which Erasmus was content to settle for a less intense relationship. It was after the ardor cooled that Erasmus began to relate to Servatius through exhortations to learning. Erasmus wrote one poem for Servatius during the later phase of their friendship (Reedijk, *The Poems of Erasmus*, Carm. 8, pp. 148-52).
Servatius became prior of Steyn in 1504 and in 1514 wrote to Erasmus asking him to return to the monastery. His letter is no longer extant, but Erasmus' reply justifying his freedom is (EE, I, 564-73; Nichols, II, 141-51). Theoretically, Servatius had the power to force Erasmus to return. Realizing this, Erasmus petitioned the pope in 1516 for a dispensation from the vows that would tie him to the monastery (EE, II, 291-312; Nichols, II, 339-69; see above, note 7). His request was granted (EE, II, 433-37; Nichols, II, 461-63, translates the first of these letters with some omissions, though the omissions are not acknowledged).

¹¹EE, I, 87, lines 49-58; Nichols, I, 49.

When Servatius does not respond to his satisfaction, Erasmus admonishes him [12] and then instructs him as follows:

> It will also conduce greatly to your object if you will write to me more frequently than you do; but do not write in your old way with borrowed sentences, or even what is worse, heaping up expressions, here out of Bernard and there out of Claudian and fitting them or rather unfitly sewing them on to your own, as a crow might do with a peacock's feathers. That is not composing a letter, but merely putting letters together. Neither should you fancy that we are so dull as not to discern what you have taken from your own spring, and what you have borrowed from another's. It would be better for you to write as best you can (and I would rather you did it without preparation), whatever comes into your head. You need not be ashamed of barbarisms, if any such should occur; you shall have from us correction, and not ridicule. How is a wound to be healed if it is not laid open? Shake off your torpor, cast off the coward and put on the man, and set your hand even at this late hour to the work! Only look what a long time has slipped through our fingers, as they say. Four years have gone by, while you still stick in the same rut, whereas if you had followed our advice at first, you would by this time have come out such a man as might not only equal us in literature but instruct us in return.[13]

The literature through which Erasmus would instruct his friends and help them to cast off the onus of barbarism he described in a letter to his friend, Cornelius of Gouda,[14] written in 1489:

> My authorities in poetry are Vergil, Horace, Ovid, Juvenal, Statius, Martial, Claudian, Persius, Lucan,

[12]EE, I, 88-89, lines 1-31; Nichols, I, 51 (lines 4-31 omitted).

[13]EE, I, 89-90, lines 32-56; Nichols, I, 51-52. Erasmus exhorts another companion, Sasboud, in a similar vein (EE, I, 90-91; Nichols, I, 54-55).

[14]Cornelius was an older contemporary of Erasmus, the uncle of Erasmus' friend William Herman. He lived at this time in a monastery near Leiden. For biographical details, see EE, I, 92-93. His influence on Erasmus will be discussed below.

> Tibullus and Propertius; in prose, Cicero, Quintilian, Sallust, Terence. Then, for the observation of elegances, there is no one in whom I have so much confidence as Lorenzo Valla, who is unrivalled both in the sharpness of his intelligence and the tenacity of his memory. Whatever has not been committed to writing by those I have named, I confess I dare not bring into use.[15]

He had apparently drunk deeply from these writers very early in his life. Beatus Rhenanus, in his preface to the posthumous edition of Origen's works in 1536, says that as a boy Erasmus knew the comedies of Terence by heart.[16] While all of these writers were models of Latin style, Erasmus' own interest as an author was poetry. Writing to John Botzheim in 1523 he said:

> I will first give an account of what I wrote in verse, to which kind of study I was as a boy more inclined, so that it was with some difficulty that I turned my attention to prose composition. I succeeded easily, if indeed I succeeded at all; and there was no kind of poetry I did not try. The pieces that have fortunately been lost or hidden, we will leave to rest, and as the proverb has it, let sleeping dogs lie.[17]

The earliest poems, written at Steyn between 1487 and 1489 (with the exception of the first, which was written in 1483), are worldly in content and inspiration. Very little religious feeling can be read out of them.[18] Only one, a poem on old age, seems to speak as though something personal were at

---

[15]EE, I, 99, lines 97-105; Nichols, I, 64.

[16]EE, I, 55, lines 84-85; Nichols, I, 23. In 1523, Erasmus edited the comedies of Terence.

[17]EE, I, 3, lines 15-21; Nichols, I, 21.

[18]The principal subjects of the poems are joy and sorrow, love, friendship, the mutability of temporal things, patience, and spring. Sources of the poems, as traced by Reedijk, are consistent with the subjects. In Carm. 1-11 Erasmus' authorities are Vergil (cited or alluded to 56 times), Horace (14 times), and Ovid (10 times). By contrast, there is one allusion to the Bible and one to the Christian poet Prudentius. These are the only sources cited out of the religious tradition. Other Latin sources are Cicero, Propertius, Tibullus, and Lucretius.

stake.[19] But sometime in 1489 a change occurred, for there is a marked contrast between Carm. 1-11 and Carm. 12-25.[20] While the pagan poets are still important, religious sources are very much more in evidence.[21] And the subjects are much more religious in nature.[22] To cite only one example of the shift, in poem 7, on the mutability of temporal things, Erasmus draws an analogy between youth and summer on the one hand and old age and winter on the other. Winter comes as the leaves die and the flowers disappear. But his conclusion is: "Let us enjoy life, lest in vain it pass from us through numbness and death; let us make use of these days of youth, sweet friend."[23] But this sentiment, which can only be taken as the feeling of the poet himself in this poem, is regarded as a view to be combatted in Carm. 24.[24]

This change in emphasis is due to the influence on Erasmus of Cornelius Gerard,[25] a young Augustinian canon

[19]Reedijk, *The Poems of Erasmus*, Carm. 4, pp. 142-43. Erasmus returned to this theme in his greatest poem in 1506 (Reedijk, Carm. 83, pp. 280-90). Roland Bainton has translated the essence of this later poem in *Erasmus of Christendom*, p. 79. Bainton even goes so far as to say that Erasmus' fear of death in the years at Steyn was analogous to the same experience for Luther (p. 17; see also p. 98, n. 4).

[20]Erasmus himself makes a distinction between his earlier poems, attributing a first group to the period when he was "almost still in the world" (EE, I, 118, lines 10-17; Nichols, I, 61).

[21]In Carm. 12-25 (excluding 14-15, the combined effort of Erasmus and Cornelius) Vergil is alluded to 76 times, Horace 18 times, and Ovid 12 times. But note the appearance of religious sources: Old Testament 13 times, New Testament 17 times, and Christian poets 51 times (among whom Prudentius is cited 14 times, Fortunatus 13 times, and Honorius 7 times). See Charles Béné, *Erasme et Saint Augustin*, p. 47.

[22]For example, Carm. 17 in praise of Gregory the Great (the monastery at Steyn was dedicated to St. Gregory), Carm. 18 on the four last things (death, judgment, hell and heaven), Carm. 19 in honor of the Virgin, Carm. 20 on the quaking of the earth at the death of Christ, Carm. 21 on the descent of Christ into the underworld and his return, Carm. 22 in praise of St. Anne, and Carm. 23-25 on the foolishness of man.

[23]Reedijk, *The Poems of Erasmus*, p. 148, lines 27-28. If Erasmus was preoccupied with death (see above, n. 19), he certainly did not resolve it at this time in any religious sense.

[24]See *ibid.*, p. 211, line 18 and note.

[25]Reedijk was the first to attribute the change to the influence of Cornelius (*ibid.*, pp. 48-52, 88, 172). But for the extent of Cornelius' influence,

at a nearby monastery with whom Erasmus maintained a close friendship until 1499. The relationship between the two men, unlike that between Erasmus and Servatius, was intellectual from the beginning, and each retained his critical stance over against the other. This is nowhere more evident than in their "debate" on the relative merits of Lorenzo Valla (1405-1457),[26] Erasmus' choice, and Jerome Balbus (1460-1535),[27] Cornelius' choice, as the best of modern authors in terms of their fidelity to the classical tradition. Erasmus began the debate, asserting that Valla in his *Elegantiae*, had rescued literature from the barbarians.[28] He expresses surprise at Cornelius' assertion that Jerome Balbus is the only contemporary writer who knows the ancients. Erasmus cites many others,[29] among whom Valla is the most eminent. Cornelius replies that he has read Valla, and he attributes to the latter some credit for his own proficiency in Latin. But half in jest he criticizes Valla as despised by all men, citing as an example Poggio Bracciolini (1380-1459), the Florentine humanist and chancellor.[30] Erasmus responds that Cornelius is only trying to draw him into battle by his

the view recently developed by Charles Béné (*Erasme et Saint Augustin*, pp. 37-57) goes beyond Reedijk and seems to me essentially correct.

[26]The impact of Valla on Erasmus was very important. Erasmus made an epitome of Valla's *Elegantiae,* a treatise on Latin grammar illustrating the usage of words, first published in 1471. Erasmus arranged the words in alphabetical order (LB, I, 1069-1126). He later wrote a much fuller paraphrase of it. This earlier draft was first published in 1529. Interestingly enough, Cornelius Gerard was partly responsible for this. He probably had retained the manuscript from his early association with Erasmus. In any case, Erasmus hastened to provide an "authorized" version, published in 1531. For a full history of the publication of Erasmus' work on Valla's *Elegantiae*, see EE, I, 108, note.

As we shall see below, Valla continued to be a decisive influence on Erasmus. His discovery of Valla's *Notes on the New Testament* in 1504, which he published in Paris in 1505, bore an important relation to his work on the New Testament.

[27]Balbus was born in Venice but taught in several European universities and served in several royal courts. (For biographical details, see EE, I, 105, note.)

[28]EE, I, 108, lines 100-6; Nichols, I, 67. See above, n. 26.

[29]EE, I, 105-7, lines 47-77; Nichols, II, 66-67.

[30]EE, I, 110-11, lines 23-42; Nichols, I, 69.

jesting criticism. But he does battle, pointing out that the best men do not set out to please the multitude. As for Poggio, he was not completely free from barbarism, and certainly he possessed an acrimonious spirit. Valla could have avoided criticism by keeping silence about barbarism, but he chose the more courageous path. Poggio would have done better to correct his faults than to criticize Valla. Had he done so his judgment of Valla would have been different.[31]

The letters between Erasmus and Cornelius contemporary with Carm. 12-25 show the same shift in relation to the letters between Erasmus and Servatius that we find in the two groups of poems.[32] The high moral and even pious tone of Cornelius' letters is striking. He urges Erasmus to keep jealous rivalry far from their friendship.[33] He exhorts Erasmus to serve God[34] and calls him to humility.[35] In one of the last in this group of letters Erasmus says: "I am resolved for the future, since you advise me so kindly, not to compose anything but what may savor either of the praises of saints or of sanctity itself."[36] The letters throughout this group suggest a movement in the direction of this conclusion. For example, while Erasmus had cited Vergil's *Aeneid*, Book IV (on Dido) frequently in his correspondence with Servatius, it drops out completely in this correspondence. There is only

[31]EE, I, 112-15; Nichols, I, 70-71, many omissions. In a second letter written during the same month, Erasmus says that he cannot understand Cornelius' preference for Jerome Balbus among the poets, for he differs from a learned poet as a painting differs from a work of art. The next letter of Erasmus on the subject indicates that Cornelius had visited him in the monastery and had spoken disparagingly of Valla. He says the shamelessness of Cornelius' language makes him shudder, since Valla was the most persuasive of men. Instead of criticizing Valla, Cornelius should learn Valla by heart. (EE, I, 119-20; Nichols, I, 72-73) Erasmus in a number of his writings exhorts his readers to learn certain works by heart.

[32]EE, I, 92-122 (letters 17-30); Nichols, I, 58-77 (but with too many omissions to establish the implications of the letters). There are eleven letters by Erasmus, four by Cornelius.

[33]EE, I, 96, lines 35-37; Nichols, I, 63.

[34]EE, I, 102, lines 74-75; Nichols, I, 60.

[35]EE, I, 96, lines 8-11.

[36]EE, I, 118, lines 8-10; Nichols, I, 61.

one citation from Vergil, and that is of a satirical nature.[3] Citations from Ovid's *Ars Amatoria (The Art of Love)* also drop out completely. Horace is cited only twice. In other words, the sentimental verses of these poets are eliminated. When they are cited at all, it is on the intellectual rather than on the feeling level. Cicero's *De Officiis (On Duty)*, the first work edited by Erasmus (1501), is cited twice. In short, a moral restraint begins to appear. Still further, Erasmus cites Jerome and Augustine together four times. He also cites the opposition between Jerome and Rufinus, indicating that he knew the work of Jerome. Cornelius evidently suggested to Erasmus that he read the letters of Jerome, for Erasmus says at one point in the correspondence: "I am obliged to you for inviting me to the perusal of those letters. I have not only read them long ago, but have written every one of them out with my own fingers. While we find in them a great many darts with which the reproaches of the barbarians may be refuted, that one alone may suffice, which is so carefully prepared and sharpened for us in the page where, after commenting on the husks of the prodigal son, he brings in the example of the captive woman."[38]

If there is a suggestion in the letters that Cornelius is instrumental in changing the direction of Erasmus' interests, there is much more than that in the poem on which they collaborated.[39] Both Allen and Reedijk believe that the poem in question was by Erasmus and that Cornelius' share was to cast it into the form of a dialogue.[40] But in a letter describing their collaboration, Cornelius says that he not only put it into the form of an apologetic dialogue, but also that he interspersed his own replies to the speeches of Erasmus

[37]EE, I, 116, line 27.

[38]EE, I, 103, lines 20-26; Nichols, I, 75. Béné comments that although Cornelius did not introduce Erasmus to Jerome, it was nonetheless in these letters that he first began to make use of what he had known earlier. He uses Jerome here, however, not in the interest of piety, but in a way characteristic of humanism: to refute the barbarians. (*Erasme et Saint Augustin*, p. 44)

[39]*Carmen Lamentabile* (Reedijk, *The Poems of Erasmus*, pp. 161-70). My analysis follows that of Charles Béné, *Erasme et Saint Augustin*, pp. 48-52.

[40]EE, I, 96, n. 6; Reedijk, *The Poems of Erasmus*, p. 161.

and changed some of Erasmus' words.[41] Still further, he inserts thirty-five hexameter verses at the end of the poem. In the form in which Erasmus evidently wrote it, the poem is a "mournful song." In his four parts, Erasmus describes the cruel envy which forces the poet to abandon his poetry, and he expresses his sadness at seeing ancient poetry abandoned. Then he latches onto the hope that in his friend he will see a new Vergil and a new Cicero. Cornelius' replies are quite different in kind. In his first song, he cites Paul in Galatians, St. Luke, St. Jerome, and St. Leo, all of whom expressed themselves in poetic language. In his second song he describes the power of poetry in the Old Testament: Gideon blowing his trumpet is victorious, and David soothes Saul with a song. In his third song Cornelius says that the muses should celebrate Israel and the birth of Christ. Then in the epilogue Cornelius puts into the mouth of Jerome the statement that it is commendable to read the poets and right to flog those who laugh at this. Indeed, Job, Wisdom, the Song of Songs and the Psalms of David have utilized poetry, but they have done so in order to ornament the temple of God. They have despoiled the Egyptians for the sake of the Lord.

Cornelius thus changed the nature of the poem profoundly. He defended and justified poetry through appeal to the Bible and to Jerome, the most cultivated of the fathers. In doing so, Cornelius taught Erasmus that classical poetry was a means and not an end, that its role was to ornament the temple of God and not to seduce Christians.

Expression of the Tension in Treatises of the Monastic Period

It was probably during this same year, 1489, that Erasmus in his *De contemptu mundi (The Contempt of the*

[41]EE, I, 95-96; Nichols, I, 63 (but lines 1-19 in EE omitted here). The phrase *rudi confabulatione* (EE, I, 96, line 18) proves Cornelius' intervention, for he would not—and does not in the same letter—refer to Erasmus' part in the poem in those terms. It is his own contributions that he calls "uncultured speech." The letters also bear out the judgment that the poem was a genuine collaboration. (See Béné, *Erasme et Saint Augustin,* pp. 49-50.)

World) first made use of the lessons of Cornelius.[42] The treatise is divided into two sections of almost equal length, chapters 1-7 on the miseries of the flesh and the world, and chapters 8-11 on the happiness and pleasures of the solitary life.[43] The strife, factions, and uncertainties connected with active life in the world are contrasted with the peace and tranquility of life away from Babylon. What emerges, however, is a humanism which the religious consciousness has only begun to penetrate. This becomes clear in Erasmus' discussion of death in chapter 6 and of pleasure in chapter 11, each the culmination of an argument.

Death, he begins chapter 6, spares no one. All around us we see funerals. If we think that we need not worry about it because of our youth, we should reflect on the fact that few live to be old, that no matter what our age we cannot be certain of seeing the evening of this day's light. The nearness of death renders worthless our fame and wealth. We should remember, as Rudolf Agricola has told us, that virtue alone is beyond death, and that good deeds will always endure. Erasmus concludes: "If riches, pleasure, fame and other things of the same kind were trustworthy and useful—which is far from being the case—even so to one dying they are a burden. But then at last, virtue begins to be profitable. If these worldly things are not withdrawn from us, we are withdrawn

[42]LB, V, 1239-1262. The work was first published in 1521. Most critics agree that chapter 12 was probably added at the time of publication; it contradicts what is said in chapters 1-11 (but see Bainton, *Erasmus of Christendom*, p. 16). There has been only one English translation, that of Thomas Paynell in 1533. This has recently been republished in a facsimile edition with an introduction by W. J. Hirten (*De Contemptu Mundi*, Scholars' Facsimiles and Reprints, 1967).

[43]It is by and large the pagan poets to whom he had appealed before (Vergil, Horace, Ovid, but above all, in this treatise, Juvenal) that he draws upon to describe the negative character of the world. And he turns more and more to Christian sources in his characterizations of the pleasures of the solitary life.

For example, in chapters 1-7 Erasmus quotes from classical poets 43 times and from Christian writings 10 times. In chapters 8-11 on the other hand, he quotes from classical poets 22 times and from Christian sources 18 times. Of the Christian sources, the writing of Jerome is discussed, while Augustine, Cyprian, Ambrose, Lactantius, Thomas Aquinas and Albert the Great are mentioned.

from them. But virtue never forsakes our company and never ceases to help us."[44]

In chapter 11, the culminating discussion of the pleasure of the solitary life, Erasmus characterizes his style of life as Epicurean. He argues that pleasures of the body are vain and fleeting; only pleasures of the mind are perpetual and hence good. Moreover, one cannot enjoy both kinds of pleasure at once. Certainly, then, even Epicurus would expel the pleasures of the body and choose the more outstanding pleasures of the soul. What are the pleasures of this life of the soul? They are the contemplation of eternal life which lifts us beyond the depression of our present existence, and the foretaste of eternal life which is experienced by many here and now.[45] In establishing this position, Erasmus ap-

[44]LB, V, 1246F-1248E. This discussion should be contrasted with that on "The Remembrance of Death" in *The Imitation of Christ* (I, 23), the classic statement of the piety of the Brethren of the Common Life. Erasmus' phrase, "no man can be certain of seeing the evening of this day's light," recalls a similar passage in the *Imitation*: "In the morning, doubt whether you will live till night; at night, do not think yourself certain to live till morning." But the conclusion of the *Imitation* is quite different from that of Erasmus. Instead of virtue, it is Christ to whom appeal is made: "Keep your heart free, and always lift it up to God, for you have here no city long abiding. Send your desires and your prayers always up to God, and pray with perseverance that your soul at the hour of death may blessedly depart out of this world and go to Christ."

[45]LB, V, 1257C-1259A. It is instructive to compare this argument with Erasmus' last colloquy, "Epicureus," written in 1533 (in C. R. Thompson, *The Colloquies of Erasmus* [Chicago: University of Chicago Press, 1965], pp. 535-51). Continuity between this and the *De contemptu mundi* lies in the identification of pleasure with the soul or mind rather than with the body (see p. 540). But in "Epicureus" the good of the soul is not contemplation of eternal life or the experiencing of eternal life here and now; it is rather a good conscience. A good man may not always have good fortune (in worldly terms), and an evil man may not always be punished for his evil. But the good man will have a good conscience and the evil man will never be able to escape his bad conscience. Hence only the good can experience pleasure and happiness. The greatest good is repentance, through which one is forgiven his sins by God and receives a good conscience. One could infer from a comparison of these texts that while Erasmus' religious conscience underwent no profound alteration, the depth and specificity of the feeling that lay behind it did change considerably.

There is no indication that Erasmus' reference to Epicureanism was influenced (at least in the *De contemptu mundi*) by Lorenzo Valla's treatise *On*

peals to the writings of Jerome as Cornelius had done in his "apology," saving him (also like Cornelius) until the end, and then drawing upon him for arguments buttressing his position (not as an example of piety). Pagan literature is for him, in Jerome's image, the captive woman (Deut. 21:11-12) made to serve the ends of others. Despite the fact that there are many passages in Jerome's letters where pagan literature is severely criticized, Erasmus passes over these, drawing from Jerome only arguments supporting a positive attitude toward the classics.

A definite movement is discernible here. Although still very much a humanist, Erasmus has begun to take seriously the Christian religious tradition, following the lead of Cornelius. The step taken in this treatise is tentative enough and far from where he finally emerged, but it marks a real stage in Erasmus' development.[46]

Pleasure. But both here and in his *Elegantiae* Valla had argued that Epicurean pleasure, unlike Stoic virtue, was compatible with Christianity. (See on this, Jerrold Seigel, *Rhetoric and Philosophy in Renaissance Humanism* [Princeton University Press, 1968] pp. 144-60.) Erasmus never, like Valla, used the notion to exalt virtue and Christian ethics. (For another early reference on this theme, see Erasmus' *Formulae* [ca. 1498], in Thompson, *The Colloquies of Erasmus*, p. 594.)

For a discussion of Erasmus' Epicureanism and its relation to that of other Renaissance humanists (notably Valla and Thomas More) see Marie Delcourt and Marcelle Derwa, "Trois aspects humanistes de l'epicurisme Chrétien," in *Colloquium Erasmianum* (Mons: Centre Universitaire de l'Etat, 1968), pp. 119-33; E. L. Surtz, S.J., *The Praise of Pleasure* (Cambridge: Harvard University Press, 1957).

[46]My conclusions differ markedly from some that have appeared in the past. Two French critics, for example, have argued that what Erasmus says in his treatise proves that he knew nothing about the essence of monasticism (J. B. Pineau, *Erasme* [Paris: Presses Universitaires de France, 1923], ch. 3; Emile Telle, *Erasme et le septième sacrement* [Geneva: Droz, 1954], pp. 15-22). Even more, it proves that Erasmus was not interested in religion but only in himself. (But then, is there any twenty-year-old who is not?) This conclusion seems to have two consequences. On the one hand, insofar as Erasmus said what he meant, he meant something unchristian. On the other hand, since he wrote as he did from within a religious order, he reveals his own "bad faith." The difficulty with this kind of analysis is that Erasmus' own self-consciousness is secondary to same external criterion by which he is measured (in this case Roman Catholic orthodoxy). More recent interpretations by French scholars have focused the question as I have done here and

Erasmus' *Oration at the Funeral of Berta de Heyen,*
written about the same time as *The Contempt of the World,*
confirms the analysis of the development of his mind suggested up to this point.[47] His theme is the life of a Christian
woman and the way in which her daughters (to whom the
oration is addressed) should understand the meaning of her
death. A casual reading would suggest that the expression of
an explicitly Christian piety is much deeper here than in
The Contempt of the World. There is a greater balance between the use of classical and Christian sources,[48] and Erasmus states explicitly that the praise of a Christian's life
should not be based upon the classical practice of comparing
an individual's deeds with those of his ancestors, but rather

have arrived at similar conclusions. See, for example, Charles Béné, *Erasme
et Saint Augustin,* pp. 52-56.

A recent German interpretation has, I believe, gone too far in the opposite direction, attributing more to Erasmus' self-consciousness as a religious
thinker than is warranted by the texts. E.-W. Kohls, *Die Theologie des Erasmus* (Basel: F. Reinhardt, 1966), 2 vols., argues that Erasmus uses examples
from Christian literature to define the intention of those he takes from classical sources and that the whole work is intended to serve a Christian pedagogical purpose (Vol. I, pp. 21-23). But it is not nearly as evident as Kohls
wishes to argue that Erasmus has Christianized his classical sources here. As
has already been demonstrated in my analysis, Erasmus' emphases became
much more markedly Christian in later writings. It seems to me that Kohls'
analysis of this treatise as well as of the *Antibarbari* (see I, 54-56, 67-68) suf-
fers from his having concluded a priori (for I do not believe it can be derived from an analysis of the texts themselves) that because Erasmus used
classical allusions in his mature writings to support Christian aims, he must
have also been doing so self-consciously in his earlier writings. This kind of
argumentation assumes that the only possibilities implicit in Erasmus' earlier
views were those that actually emerged later in his life (see I, 29-30). But
this is as nonhistorical as dogmatic writing which takes some external criterion as a reference point. Many directions were possible for Erasmus, and
it is incorrect to interpret him as if, given what did develop, nothing else
was ever possible.

[47]The text is to be found in LB, VIII, cols. 551-560. The oration has never
been translated into English, and there is no critical analysis of the oration
in Erasmus literature. But see Kohls, *Die Theologie des Erasmus,* I, 200-3.

[48]According to my count, there are 16 citations from Scripture (6 from the
Old Testament, 10 from the New Testament), in addition to one citation
from Jerome (Erasmus justifies his own oration by pointing out that Jerome
had written letters consoling daughters on the death of their mother). There
are 15 citations from classical sources.

I

18

upon the Christian standard of virtue.[49] The emphasis, however, is much more upon "virtue" than it is upon "Christian." Christ is mentioned only twice.[50] The virtue seems to be much more important than the Christian label. And a glance at the "virtues" enumerated by Erasmus bears this out. Berta conquered her flesh through the power of her spirit, refusing to succumb to the enticements of wealth and physical beauty even while young.[51] When given by her family in marriage she lived as spiritual a life with her husband as possible, managing her home without wrangling and caring for needy children as well as for her own.[52] When her husband died she refused to marry again, giving her life instead to the service of religion. She supported religious orders, visited the sick in hospitals, opened her home to others while keeping it free from gossip.[53] Finally, and most worthy of praise, she maintained equanimity in the face of death. Not only did she keep her composure upon the death of her favorite daughter while those around her were losing theirs—many of the ancients did as much—but she was also able to conquer her love for her daughter through her love for Christ and to give thanks to God—which no ancient could do.[54] Likewise, when her own death was imminent, she placed her whole trust upon the Lord, knowing that the reward was great for those who struggled vigorously to conquer the flesh through the spirit. For this reason, it would be foolish to mourn her. "Berta triumphs in the seats of heaven,

[49]LB, VIII, 554A-B.

[50]The first is only a rhetorical flourish (LB, VIII, 554C). The second is important, for Erasmus singles out the love of Christ as the one thing Berta had which no pagan could have had (LB, VIII, 558D). Erasmus does not, however, press this explicitly Christian affirmation to the end of the oration, but returns to the theme of virtue without mentioning Christ. See below in this paragraph.

[51]LB, VIII, 554C.

[52]LB, VIII, 555C-E.

[53]LB, VIII, 555F-557B.

[54]LB, VIII, 557C-558D. This is one passage in which Erasmus does use the pagan citations to serve a Christian pedagogical function. Kohls might have cited this with much more effect than *The Contempt of the World*, where the citations are not clearly oriented in this fashion (see above, n. 46).

among the splendid processions of the gods, crowned with starry wreaths."[55] She has gone home, while we remain in this vale of tears as in a foreign land.[56] We shall follow her, Erasmus concludes his oration, if only "we cling fast to *the footsteps of virtue* which she treaded, and if we have a zeal for patience equal to hers, and hasten to the innermost parts of mercy, and are equally tenacious of justice and faith."[57]

As in *The Contempt of the World,* so in this oration the world is a vale of tears from which the Christian should seek to escape to his true home.[58] The virtues enumerated, with the single exception of the mention of the love of Christ, are natural human virtues which abound in classical literature. And it is virtue rather than the love of Christ which sounds the final note of the oration. We should cling, not to the footsteps of Christ, but to the footsteps of virtue. And even if Erasmus regarded the two as the same, the way in which he states the matter suggests that in his own mind he had not yet found the synthesis between the two that will characterize his later writings.

If there is still any doubt that Erasmus' self-consciousness had not yet synthesized his religious feeling with the humanistic spirit of classical antiquity, the treatise *Against the Barbarians* should dispel it. He began work on it while still at Steyn, as his correspondence with Cornelius testifies.[59]

---

[55]LB, VIII, 559D. Note that the imagery is classical, even if the context of the allusion is Christian.

[56]LB, VIII, 559E-560A.

[57]LB, VIII, 560A, emphasis added.

[58]Erasmus asserts for the first time in this oration that a Christian life in the world is more virtuous than a Christian life in a monastery, inasmuch as the world presents more obstacles to the attainment of virtue than does the monastery (LB, VIII, 554C-D). I believe the statement in context is intended to heighten the praise of Berta. It precedes the enumeration of her virtues and adds to their marvelous quality, since her virtue was achieved in the world where the odds against such achievement are very great. I do not believe the statement can be taken as a self-conscious affirmation of "worldly monasticism" (cf. Kohls, *Die Theologie des Erasmus,* I, 32; II, 28, n. 7).

[59]EE, I, 135-36; Nichols, I, 84-85. This letter (#37) should be dated 1489 rather than 1494 as Allen dates it, and letter #30 (EE, I, 120-22; Nichols, I, 73-74, with omissions) should be dated 1494. For in letter 37 Erasmus describes the treatise he is writing as composed of two books, one which refutes

I
20

But it was only after he left Steyn, sometime between April
25, 1492 (when he was ordained) and 1494, in the service of
the Bishop of Cambrai that he recast its earlier form—an
oration in defense of literature placed in the mouth of Cornelius—into a dialogue[60] among several of Erasmus' friends at
Halsteren, the country estate of the Bishop of Cambrai.[61]

the barbarians, another in praise of letters. He says both will be orations
placed in Cornelius' mouth. This version, now completely lost, was replaced
by a new version in four books cast in dialogue form in 1494. See below,
n. 61.

[60]The description of the setting of the dialogue and the initial banter of the
participants recall Plato's *Phaedrus*. The length and character of speeches
suggest that Cicero's *De Oratore* was his actual model. (see EOO, I.1, pp.
20-21; Béné, *Erasme et Saint Augustin*, pp. 69-71) The presence of this strand
in the earliest version of the *Antibarbari* shows that the "Platonic" elements
in the *Enchiridion* predated Erasmus' visit to England. They were in fact already present in 1494.

[61]This new form of the work was to have been in four books. In the preface he wrote in 1520 upon the publication of Book I (the only one that sur-
vives), Erasmus said that Book I refuted the prejudices of the superstitious,
Book II brought forward all the arguments against eloquence, Book III refuted these, and Book IV discussed the reason why he loved the poets so
deeply as a youth (EE, IV, 279, lines 20-37). He completed only the first two
books, showing the first to Gaguin when he arrived in Paris in 1495 and the
first and second to Colet when he went to England in 1499. Drafts of Books
III and IV he left with Richard Pace during his stay in Italy. But all these
materials, except for Book I, were lost and could not be recovered despite
some diligence on Erasmus' part.

Discovery by Allen and publication by Hyma of a copy of Book I predat-
ing the published version of 1520 has been of great benefit in helping us to
analyze Erasmus' intellectual development. The copy discovered at Gouda
predates the revised 1520 version and is doubtless very close to the form in
which Erasmus wrote the dialogue in 1494 or 1495. It reveals that the major
additions had to do with his criticisms of monasticism, which are much
stronger in the version published by Erasmus. He also added to the introductory speeches in order to draw the participants in the dialogue in sharper
relief. And he added the names of Greek fathers to the Latins who were
already mentioned in the earlier version. Most importantly, citations of
Augustine's *On Christian Doctrine* were not added later, bearing out the testimony of others that Erasmus had discovered the work in the monastery of
Groenendael near Brussels around 1494. (See EE, I, p. 590.)

The *Antibarbari* has recently been critically edited in the first volume of
the complete works of Erasmus projected by The Royal Academy of Holland,
EOO, I.1, 1-138. The introduction, pp. 7-32, reviews critical scholarship on
the book. (Secondary material in this volume is in English.) No published
English translation of the treatise exists.

After a discussion of the reasons why literature might have fallen on bad days[62] and a comparison of the setting at Halsteren with that in the *Phaedrus*, Jacob Batt, secretary of the city of Bergen and principal speaker in the dialogue, describes three kinds of enemies of literature: the uncultured who want to destroy literature, the unskillfully learned who want it controlled within narrow limits, and those moderns who approve good literature but want to be considered its best practioners. The dialogue itself deals only with the first group. Batt says there are three kinds of considerations: reasoned arguments against the ignorant, refutation through appeal to authorities, and discussion of the relation of Christians in the past to literature. Batt follows this structure, devoting most attention to reasoned arguments against the ignorant.[63] But it is the much briefer second and third considerations which reveal Erasmus' effort to make religion serve his humanism. The second, an appeal to authorities, finds Erasmus citing Jerome, as we might expect, and in the same manner as in *De contemptu mundi:* to argue in favor of reading classical literature.[64] But his second authority is new: St. Augustine. During the time when he was recasting the

[62]EOO, I.1, 45-64. Among these Erasmus takes two very seriously. One is that Christianity has discouraged literature and brought about its decay. The latter parts of the extant dialogue are intended partly as a response to this kind of criticism. The second reason given (and the last in the dialogue, suggesting that Erasmus placed great weight on it) is that we entrust our children to fools to be educated. Here we find one of the themes to which Erasmus returns again and again in his works on education.

[63]EOO, I.1, 74-105. I count eighteen arguments, some of them developed at great length. They are "topics" in the rhetorical tradition, rather than points of logic. For some of the arguments deny points made by others. For example, he argues that learning makes men more humble, but then he continues by adding that even if learning makes men evil, a literate evil man is more tractable than one who is not because he understands his own vice (a very dubious argument!). Or again, Batt argues both that the heathens achieved what they did by a divine plan and that nothing is in itself evil. The point is that the arguments taken cumulatively are irrefutable, not that all of them are logically compatible with one another.

[64]EOO, I.1, 111-13. The single difference is that the discussion here is based on Epistle 70 (to Magnus) rather than on Epistle 22. The use Jerome made (in both letters) of the passage in Deut. (21:11-12) which Erasmus had cited earlier, reappears here also.

Antibarbari into dialogue form, Erasmus read and studied deeply Augustine's *On Christian Doctrine,* obtained from a nearby monastery.[65] Erasmus focuses his attention on two

[65]*On Christian Doctrine* (Bks I-III, 396; Bk IV, 427) is Augustine's "hermeneutics." An excellent study has recently been published (Béné, *Erasme et Saint Augustin*) on the use made of this treatise by Erasmus from its first appearance in the *Antibarbari* to its last in *Ecclesiastes* (1535).

Because of its importance for Erasmus' development and his interpretation of Scripture, it would be good for us to have the content of the treatise before us. In his prologue, Augustine counters those who object to aids in interpreting Scripture. He is writing for those who need instruction in interpretation and know that they do. Books I-III deal with what must be understood: Book I with things, Book II with unknown literal and figurative signs, and Book III with ambiguous literal and figurative signs. Book IV deals with teaching what has been learned.

What are the things we must learn from Scripture? Principally love: of God, ourselves, our neighbors, and things below us. Of these, only God is to be enjoyed; all other things are to be used in order that we might love God. Any lesson found in Scripture that builds love in this sense is good, even if the person reading has misunderstood the writer (I.36). The medieval view that all knowledge has God as its end is Augustinian in its point of departure. We could go so far as to say that Augustine provides here a medieval Christian hermeneutic over against the hermeneutic of classical antiquity.

In Book II Augustine outlines seven steps in understanding Scripture, beginning with the fear of God and concluding with the ascent to God through which peace and tranquility are achieved. Knowledge is the third step and hence only an intermediate stage in "understanding." But that is the stage to be discussed here. How can we come to know "unknown" signs? For unknown *literal* signs we should study languages (II.11-15): compare translations, perhaps emend the text (as a last resort), etc. With regard to unknown *figurative* signs we need a much broader knowledge still: of the nature of animals, stones, and plants, of numbers, of music. Some things should be avoided (astrology, magic); some things are to be used as needed (art and other forms of imitation, social conventions of dress, rank, etc.). Still other things, all established by God rather than by men, are of different value: the writing of history, the study of nature are valuable; the study of the stars is hardly so. Of special value are institutions pertaining to reason: dialectic and rhetoric (II.38.38). In sum, no one seeking God should "pursue those studies which are taught outside of the Church of Christ as though they might lead to the blessed life. Rather they should soberly and diligently weigh them." (II.39.58; see also II.40.60)

In Book III Augustine turns to ambiguous signs. For literal ambiguous signs recourse must once again be had to language (III.1-3). For ambiguous figurative signs, our first task is to discover a method for determining them. Augustine's rule is that when something appears in Scripture that does not literally pertain to virtuous behavior or truth, it must be understood figuratively (III.10), e.g., words describing the bitterness or anger of God, things done by the ancients which would be considered vices or crimes today. When an ambiguous figurative sign has been located, there are several ways of

points in Augustine's treatise. He quotes and discusses extensively the discussion in Book II on unknown figurative signs, in which Augustine deals with the usefulness of various forms of knowledge. What is most interesting is his complete omission of the immediately preceding discussion on unknown literal signs where Augustine emphasizes the necessity of knowing languages for the interpretation of the text.[66] Erasmus also quotes from Augustine's Prologue, citing with approval the criticism of those who would carp at Augustine for daring to teach the art of interpretation which should rather be sought from heaven.[67]

It is evident from Erasmus' reading of Jerome and Augustine[68] that he was not yet the philologist in the service

understanding it: interpret a thing obscure in one passage by the same thing in another passage where it is not obscure (III.26); interpret the passage in a way consistent with the truth as taught in other passages of Scripture (III.27); have recourse to reason (III.28), though this is dangerous. Augustine concludes this book by presenting the seven rules of Tyconius for clarifying obscurities (III.30-37).

Book IV, on how to teach what has been learned, takes up the question so much a part of the humanistic tradition with which Erasmus identified himself: What is the relation between eloquence and wisdom? Augustine argues that wisdom is more important than eloquence, for eloquence is no sure sign of speaking the truth. Nonetheless, he goes on to say, writers of Scripture were eloquent; Paul and the prophets could match the Greeks and Romans (an assertion Erasmus contests in his comments on Paul's language in Romans). However, it is true that writers of Scripture were often obscure. But they spoke with an authority we do not have; we have no excuse for being obscure and should always strive for clarity. Teaching comes before delighting and persuading, but if the teaching is good, persuasion should be the end. Augustine concludes his book with a discussion of the three forms of speaking—subdued, moderate, and grand—providing examples of each (and from writers of Scripture as well as classical authors). But finally, he concludes, he who cannot speak both eloquently and wisely does better to speak wisely without eloquence than to speak foolish eloquence (IV.28).

Augustine's treatise has been translated into English numerous times. I prefer the translation by D. B. Robertson, *On Christian Doctrine* (New York: The Liberal Arts Press, 1958).

[66]EOO, I.1, 114-18.

[67]*Ibid.*, 131-32.

[68]Erasmus often cites the two together. In his actual discussions of them, he devotes twice the space to Augustine that he gives to Jerome. But he speaks most affectionately of Jerome. It was Jerome's passion for culture and eloquence with which he identified. But when he sought arguments in behalf of these, he found more in Augustine than in Jerome. (See Charles Béné, *Erasme et Saint Augustin*, pp. 88-91; and below, chapter II, notes 32 and 51.)

of God but still the humanist seeking a justification from the religious tradition for reading pagan literature. He cites none of the letters of Jerome criticizing pagan literature and cautioning readers against it. Even more telling is his omission of Augustine's discussion of the necessity of knowing languages for interpretation. Moreover, in arguing simply that literature should be valued, he was far from the spirit of Augustine, whose principal point was that whatever was valuable was so for the sole end of leading one to the love of God. There is no evidence that this is an end envisioned by Erasmus in the *Antibarbari*.

What we learn from the *Antibarbari* in this connection is discernible also in Erasmus' *Oration on Peace and Discord* written for Cornelius in 1488.[69] Men differ from beasts, he argues, in that seeds of peace have been planted in human nature, visible in the closeness of human relationships and the ways in which reason supports this closeness (e.g., through mutual protection, friendship, family ties). But ambition, greed, and bad habits have made men worse than savage beasts in their behavior toward one another. (Here Erasmus cites at length Juvenal, *Satire* XV, to illustrate the point.) If we look at the mutual harmony of the parts of the body, at the movement of the heavenly orbs, at the gift of friendship, we will see how contrary to nature this is. It is also contrary to our experience, for discord makes life miserable in so many ways, while peace brings happiness. So necessary is peace for human happiness that all the virtues are as nothing without this virtue. In a final appeal Erasmus says that those who would realize the nature of man, those concerned about faith and duty, those who wish to live safely

---

[69]LB, VIII, 545-552. No critical edition of this work exists, and no English translation has ever been published. There is a good summary discussion of it in Roland Bainton, *Erasmus of Christendom*, pp. 23-24. However, as I shall show in the discussion of this treatise, Professor Bainton goes much too far when he concludes: "This tract was more than an academic exercise because peace was imperative for the realization of the program which Erasmus had come to envision as his vocation—to reform society and the Church through education." (p. 24) This is to attribute to Erasmus a self-consciousness which he achieved only much later. What we actually see in this oration is a humanism akin to that of the *De contemptu mundi* and the *Antibarbari*.

and peacefully, and those interested in salvation should pursue peace.

One need only contrast this with the *Querela pacis* on the same theme, but written in 1517, to see the transformation which Erasmus' thought underwent.[70] Here, once again, he begins with the assertion that unlike the animals men have been given reason. But then he goes on to add: Christians have been given Christ, something even more excellent. The entire treatise then becomes a discussion of why Christians, who are supposed to be followers of Christ, the Prince of Peace, fight against one another and in doing so deny the essence of their religion. Here Erasmus' interest is clearly that Christians should be better than the heathens. Of the three things that invite us to peace—nature, reason, Christ— it is above all Christ to whom Erasmus makes his appeal. The youth of twenty at Steyn was far from the Christian humanist of 1517. The kind of appeal he later made to the Christian tradition had not yet entered his mind while he was in the monastery.

The Paris Years, 1495-1499: Softening the Tension

Erasmus had high hopes of traveling to Italy in the company of the Bishop of Cambrai, who anticipated receiving a cardinal's hat. When these hopes were disappointed, Erasmus asked and received the bishop's permission to go to Paris in order to study theology at the university.[71] The bishop sent him to the College of Montaigu headed by Jean Standonck.[72] Standonck had received his training as a youth

---

[70]On this treatise, see below, chapter II, note 124.

[71]On Erasmus' Paris years (1495-1499) see especially the introductory material by Allen in the letters for these years (EE, I, 144-238; Nichols, I, 194-99, many omissions). See also Augustin Renaudet, *Préréforme et humanisme à Paris (1494-1517)*, pp. 260-89; and Eugene Rice, "Erasmus and the Religious Tradition, 1495-1499," *Journal of the History of Ideas*, XI:IV (Oct., 1950), 387-411. Rice's article, which is very insightful, interprets the Paris years in terms of what Erasmus subtracted from the religious tradition. I move in the opposite direction: how Erasmus added a religious consciousness to his humanism and what that consciousness was.

[72]On Standonck (1450-1504), see Renaudet, *Préréforme et humanisme*, pp. 174-83; and *Humanisme et Renaissance* (Geneva: Droz, 1958), pp. 114-61.

from the Brethren of the Common Life in Gouda, and his aspiration from the time he became principal of Montaigu in 1485—to improve the quality of the clergy by training young men in moral qualities that would make them worthy leaders of the Church—reflects their influence. A severe discipline became one of the principal means of effecting moral growth. In a well-known passage written twenty years after his experience there, Erasmus characterized the discipline of Montaigu and Standonck:

> That college was then ruled by Jean Standonck, a man whose intentions were beyond reproach but whom you would have found entirely lacking in judgment. Because he remembered his own youth, which had been spent in bitter poverty, he took special account of impoverished students. For that he deserves much credit. And had he relieved the poverty of young men enough to provide a decent support for honest studies, while making sure they did not have too soft a life, he would have merited praise. But this he tried to do by means of bedding so hard, diet so coarse and scanty, sleepless nights and labors so burdensome, that within a year he had succeeded in killing many very capable, gifted, promising students; and others, some of whom I knew, he reduced to blindness, nervous breakdowns, or leprosy. Not a single student, in fact, was out of danger.[73]

Erasmus entered the school in September, 1495 and remained there until Easter, 1496, when the discipline imposed during Lent so adversely affected his health that he returned to Steyn and for a time considered remaining there.[74] During his academic year at Montaigu he studied the scholastic theology of the schools and attended Standonck's lectures on the *Sentences* of Peter Lombard. But his attention during this period was far from absorbed by this regimen. Shortly after he arrived in Paris, he was introduced to Robert Gaguin, the leading humanist in France at the

---

[73]C. R. Thompson, *The Colloquies of Erasmus*, pp. 351-52.

[74]EE, I, 50, lines 107-8 (letter to Botzheim); Nichols, I, 10.

time.[75] Indeed, his first published work was a complimentary letter, included in Gaguin's history of France, published September 30, 1495.[76] It was in Gaguin's home that he met Faustus Andrelinus, the Italian humanist, with whom he became a close friend. A few months later, in January, 1496, Erasmus published a number of his own poems.[77] While in Holland between April and September, 1496, recovering from the illness contracted at Montaigu, Erasmus collected some of the poems of his friend, William Herman, and upon his return to Paris promptly published them.[78]

When Erasmus returned to Paris in September, 1496, he was on his own, living as he now did apart from Montaigu and with only meager support from the Bishop of Cambrai. He supported himself by teaching rhetoric to young noblemen, and it was during this period (1496-1498) that he composed his treatise on letter writing[79] and his outlines of the later treatises, *Copia of Words and Ideas* and *On the Right*

[75]See on Gaguin, EE, I, 145-46.

[76]EE, I, 148-52. In his *Ciceronianus*, written some thirty years later, Erasmus in retrospect reversed his judgment: "Robert Gaguin not so very long ago was very popular, more, however, on account of his speeches than his writings. Yes, but in his own age. Now he would hardly be counted a Latin scholar." *(The Imitation of Cicero,* tr. Izora Scott [New York: Columbia University Press, 1910], p. 100) On this treatise, see below, chapter II, note 93.

[77]A description of the book (of which only two copies survive), together with the prefatory letter, are in EE, I, 154-58. For the poems see Reedijk, *The Poems of Erasmus,* #33-39, pp. 224-43.

[78]The *Sylva Odarum* was published on January 20, 1497. It contains eighteen poems by Herman dealing with his early life and one poem by Erasmus (Reedijk, *The Poems of Erasmus,* #40, pp. 243-45). Each poem is preceded by a brief argument, probably added by Erasmus at the time of publication. For other details concerning its publication, together with the prefatory letter of Erasmus, see EE, I, 160-64; Nichols, I, 119-20 has translated about half the letter.

[79]A pirated edition was first published in Cambridge, in 1521; Erasmus reissued an authorized edition in Basel, 1522. It contains, as an example of suasoria and dissuasoria, the *Encomium matrimonii*. On the latter, see below, pp. 34-35.

The definitive critical edition of the *De conscribendis epistolis* has recently appeared (EOO, I.2, 153-579; introduction in French by Jean-Claude Margolin, pp. 157-203). In addition to Margolin's introduction, see J. W. Binns, "The Letters of Erasmus," in T. A. Dorey, ed., *Erasmus* (London: Routledge & Kegan Paul, 1970), pp. 69-76.

Method of Instruction.[80] He became a close friend of his English pupils, Thomas Grey and William Mountjoy, under whose sponsorship he made his first momentous visit to England in the summer of 1499.

What can we say of Erasmus' intellectual development during the Paris years? What is most obvious is his gravitation toward humanistic circles. Despite the fact that he had gone to Paris to study theology, he made contact immediately with the small circle of humanists in the city. His first three publications were all related to them: his letter in Gaguin's history, his poetry addressed to Gaguin and Faustus Andrelinus, and Herman's poems for which Gaguin wrote a prefatory letter. And of course, his work as a teacher was squarely in the humanistic tradition of rhetoric. Moreover, there are some exuberant assertions which seem to support the kind of uncritical affirmation of pagan literature we have already encountered.[81] But at the same time, the moral restraint we detected in his letters to Cornelius is taken even further now and becomes a preference for Christian poets and writers. In a letter published at the end of his edition of the poems of William Herman, Erasmus writes:

> ... with more recent poets, who are also Christian, I am sometimes angry because they prefer as models Catullus, Tibullus, Propertius, Ovid, rather than St. Ambrose, Paulinus of Nola, Prudentius, Juvencus, Moses, David, Solomon, as if they were not Christian poets.
>
> But I should restrain myself from saying too much, especially regarding the poets I love most, since they will reproach me for this. With my dear Gaguin, I believe that one can treat religious subjects brilliantly in vernacular works, provided only that the speech is pure. I would even admit that one could use materials taken from the Egyptians; but not all of Egypt should be transferred.[82]

[80]On these, see below, pp. 83-86.

[81]In August, 1497, he wrote: "You want to know, sweetest Christian what we are about here. We dream. What dream, you ask. We dream of what we love—letters, than which nothing in life is more agreeable to us...." (EE, I, 181, lines 1-3; Nichols, I, 132)

[82]EE, I, 163, lines 85-96. This last sentence recalls Augustine's image in *On*

And later in the same year, he wrote to his English student, Thomas Grey:

> . . . choose for your reading all the best authors, and shun those that are lascivious or indecent, especially at your present age, which is naturally weak, and more prone to vice than disposed to the reception of what is right. But what purpose does it answer to read such books to the ruin of your character, when there is no lack of others which advance you much more in learning without any taint of indecency? Of those you will read, among the first, Virgil, Lucan, Cicero, Lactantius, Jerome, Sallust, and Livy.[83]

There is here a much more self-conscious insertion of—not to say preference for—Christian authors as models to be followed, combined with a discrimination among classical authors according to moral criteria.[84] However, this recogni-

Christian Doctrine of despoiling the Egyptians (II.xl.60). Béné contends that this is the first time Erasmus expounds Augustine without distorting him and that it was the influence of Gaguin which turned him more decisively in an Augustinian direction *(Erasme et Saint Augustin*, p. 100). But this passage is the only evidence for such an assertion. In light of the extent of the change in Erasmus during these years, Gaguin's influence was not determinative of any particular direction.

[83]EE, I, 189, lines 35-42; Nichols, I, 140.

[84]In a letter to a friend, otherwise unidentified, Erasmus commends the plays of Terence for their purity, propriety, and elegance of diction. Then he raises a criticism: "They pronounce it wicked for Christians to be readers of Terence's plays. Why, I ask. Because, they say, there is nothing in them but licentiousness and young men's low amours, by which the reader's mind will necessarily be infected." But, he responds, they do not understand that his intention was to expose men's faults. What does the *Eunuch* teach us through Phaedria, completely overcome by love, except that love is painful, tormenting, unstable? He concludes: "Terence's comedies, if rightly read, not only do not tend to overthrow morals, but are of the greatest use in correcting them." (EE, I, 124-25, lines 38-80; Nichols, I, 157-58, lines 56-75 omitted) Allen gives no very good reasons for dating this letter from Steyn in 1489. Given what we have seen here of Erasmus' intellectual development, this letter, if it has been properly placed by Allen, is the only writing prior to the Paris years in which Erasmus raises a discriminating question about a classical author and seeks to justify his reading on moral grounds. This sentiment belongs much more plausibly to the Paris period, where we find similar expressions for the first time. I would therefore agree with Nichols in this case and place the letter in Paris in 1498 or 1499.

tion is only tentative and not nearly as self-conscious as it will become later. One need only compare the earlier draft of the *De Ratione studii (On the Right Method of Instruction)*, written in 1497, with the published version of 1511.[85] In the former he discusses only secular classical literature. There is nothing on the Bible, the Christian fathers, or the Christian poets. But in the published version he recommends the reading of the Greek and Latin fathers, the Platonic philosophers, and the Christian poets. Moreover, he warns the reader not to be seduced by secular literature, and to exclude immoral texts.

To what can we attribute this more seriously religious humanistic stance of Erasmus in Paris, as tentative as it is? Two suggestions emerge from the letters of these years. The first is his attitude toward scholasticism. He went to Paris in order to study scholastic theology and maintained his resolution to complete a doctorate in theology even after he left Montaigu.[86] But he had nothing to do with the circles of thought related to scholastic philosophy and theology. Like Gaguin, who counselled against reading pagan philosophers, Erasmus ignored the revival of Platonism and the publication of the works of Aristotle in Paris during the 1490's by Lefèvre d'Etaples.[87] Even more significantly, in a letter to his student, Thomas Grey, he made clear his attitude toward scholasticism. I have lately become a Scotist, says Erasmus, who was always an ancient theologian *(vetus theologus).* The description which follows is in the best tradition of Erasmian irony and satire.[88] The Scotists are likened to Epimenides (who is also said to have published theological books).

[85]See below, chapter II, note 130.

[86]He probably obtained a bachelor's degree in 1498, but he never completed his doctorate. He was awarded a doctorate at Turin in 1506, during his sojourn in Italy. On this, see below, pp. 62-64.

[87]See Renaudet, *Préréforme* . . . , pp. 277-78 (but Gaguin had read the philosophers, see p. 272) , 280-85.

[88]EE, I, 190-93; Nichols, I, 141-44. Fortunately, in this case Nichols has translated the letter without omissions. The analogy between the Scotists and Epimenides is found also in the early *Formulae.* See Thompson, *The Colloquies of Erasmus,* p. 582.

One day, out for a long walk, "making many discoveries about *instances* and *quiddities* and *formalities,* he was overcome with sleep." He slept for forty-seven years, dreaming all the while of the subtlest of subtleties. After this time he awoke and began to behave as if nothing had changed in the meantime. So also the Scotists. Then Erasmus continues:

> What if you saw Erasmus sit gaping among those blessed Scotists, while Gryllard is lecturing from his lofty chair? If you observed his contracted brow, his staring eyes, his anxious face, you would say he was another man. They assert that the mysteries of this science cannot be comprehended by one who has any commerce at all with the Muses or with the Graces. If you have touched good letters, you must unlearn what you have learnt; if you have drunk of Helicon, you must get rid of the draught. I do my best to speak nothing in true Latin, nothing elegant or witty, and I seem to make some progress. There is hope that they will acknowledge Erasmus some time or other. But what, you will say, is the upshot of all this? It is that you are not henceforth to expect anything from Erasmus that would savor of his ancient studies or character. Remembering among whom I live, with whom I daily sit, you must look out for another comrade.[89]

Erasmus concludes that he is not directing his invective against theology itself (which he has always revered), but only against some psuedo-theologians of our time whose brains are rotten, whose language is barbarous, whose intellects are dull, and whose hearts are as black as ink!

It is safe to say that the theology in which Erasmus engages will not be scholastic theology. His complaint against it seems to be that it deals with problems as if they are unrelated to needs people have; nothing changes in forty-seven years. Genuine theology, however, will deal with persons, not with subtle ideas; it will deal with the here and now, not with problems manufactured in the minds of a few philosophers. When Erasmus says that he is an "ancient theologian," this does not mean that he has become self-conscious

[89]EE, I, 192, lines 74-86; Nichols, I, 144.

I
—
32

in placing the patristic tradition over against medieval scholastic theology. But it does mean that he recognizes in the past a kind of theology which is more congenial to him than the school tradition he is being forced to learn.

Second, in relation to the earlier letters of Erasmus, one is struck by his attitude toward himself when he becomes ill. This happened to him twice in Paris, once in Montaigu, and again later in 1498. In the earlier instance, he promised to write a poem for Saint Genevieve should he recover[90] and, as we have seen, considered remaining at Steyn where he returned to recover his health. In the later instance, he expressed a world-weariness and a desire to retire in peace to die.[91] In both instances, once the sickness had passed, so did the morbid sentiments that had accompanied it. But the striking thing is the kind of primitive religious consciousness on which Erasmus depended when alone and apparently lost in and to the world. It gives more than rhetorical substance to the "pleasure" of meditation on eternal life so highly extolled in *De contemptu mundi*. Erasmus never gave up the view that there is a radical difference between soul and body, life in the world and life for God. Its religious expression was to deepen significantly. What we see here is the awakening of a religious feeling that had long been present to the level of explicit awareness and acknowledgment.[92]

[90]Erasmus attributes his recovery to the saint in a letter to his father superior, Nicolas Werner (EE, I, 164-65; Nichols, I, 125-26). He did not actually write the poem (where the story is told in full) until 1532 (Reedijk, *The Poems of Erasmus*, pp. 150-55).

[91]On the occasion of his sickness in 1498 he wrote to his father superior, Nicolas Werner: "I have been almost killed by a slight fever, but one that recurs daily. I have now no liking for the world, and despise all those hopes of mine; I desire that life of holy rest, in which I may have leisure for myself and God alone, may meditate on the Holy Scriptures, and wash out with tears my former errors." (EE, I, 201-2; Nichols, I, 159; see also EE, I, 202; Nichols, I, 159)

[92]There were also other ways in which this religious consciousness was present. Erasmus preached in Paris and later expressed regret that his sermons had been lost (EE, I, 37, lines 14-16). Still further, he was in contact with missionaries from Windesheim who came to the Paris region for the purpose of reforming the monasteries there (see EE, I, 166-68; Nichols, I, 309-11; EE, I, 199-201; Nichols, I, 311-12). On one of these trips his friend

The kind of oscillation we see here suggests that Erasmus' religious consciousness and his humanism must both move toward one another if there is to be any meaningful fusion. It is part of the complexity of Erasmus that neither ever capitulated completely to the other; nor did the terms of their fusion remain always the same. But the tendency that emerges in Paris did continue, that is, the development of a religious consciousness that could function in the world and that, in the interest of doing so, maintained a healthy regard for human nature. He recognized his own limitations in relation to monasticism when he said in reflecting upon his illness of 1498: "My constitution, even when at its best, cannot bear vigils or fastings or any discomforts. I fall ill from time to time even here where I live so luxuriously; what should I do among the hardships of conventual life!"[93] His student, Christian Northoff, he cautioned to "avoid nocturnal lucubrations and studies at unseasonable times. They exhaust the mind and seriously affect the health. The dawn, beloved of the Muses, is the fit time for study. After dinner, either play or walk or take part in cheerful conversation . . . . Take as much food as is required, not for your pleasure, but for your health."[94]

This idea that one must have a due regard for what best serves human nature makes its appearance during these years nowhere more clearly than in the suasoria on marriage included in his treatise on letter writing. In it he argues that marriage has been sanctioned by God and Christ,[95] by lawgivers, and by nature. With regard to its natural character, the desire for marriage is innate within us, and it is folly to deny this. Like all natural things, men have a

---

Cornelius Gerard participated in the mission (see EE, I, 205-7; Nichols, I, 168, some omissions) .

[93]EE, I, 202, lines 9-12; Nichols, I, 160.

[94]EE, I, 173, lines 55-60; Nichols, I, 110. The entire letter reads like an outline of ideas that appear in publication years later in the *De pueris instituendis* (see above note 8, and below, chapter II, note 130) . Nichols unfortunately omits much of the letter.

[95]EOO, I.2, 401-4. In saying this the tone of Erasmus' appeal already sounds different from what we encountered in the *suasoria* on peace written at Steyn.

desire to mate. And since the end (procreation) for which marriage was intended has been sanctioned by God, marriage is holy as well. How, then, are we to justify the fact that Christ and the apostles did not marry? Christ did not marry because he was not subject to the law of nature; the apostles remained unmarried in order better to instruct the people. But what of monks? They are not divine, and they are not teachers in the sense in which the apostles were. How can their celibacy be justified? Erasmus justifies it on the ground that virginity will be our state in heaven and that a few examples on earth will thus be profitable. But he emphasized that they should be few[96] and in fact had said earlier that religious persons should be allowed to marry, the single life being barren and never commanded of Christians.[97]

Erasmus has thus begun to take the religious tradition seriously and, out of his own experiences as he reveals them to us during the Paris years, to bring the requirements of that tradition into relation to his dominant humanism. His humanism had begun to move toward religion, his religion toward his humanism. The process of their greater fusion is, I believe, the most interesting chapter in Erasmus' interesting life.

[96]EOO, I.2, 427.
[97]EOO, I.2, 403-4, 417-18.

II ERASMUS' INTELLECTUAL DEVELOPMENT: RELIGION AND HUMANISM— BOTH/AND: 1499-1516

Erasmus' First Visit to England, 1499-1500: The Influence of John Colet

In the late summer of 1499 Erasmus accompanied William Mountjoy to England. At Mountjoy's country estate in Greenwich he met Thomas More. Accompanying More on a walk one day, he soon found himself in the presence of the royal children—including the future Henry VIII—who were residing in the area. Erasmus was extremely embarrassed when More presented the future king with a literary present. Upon his return to his lodgings, he sat down and wrote in three days a poem for the prince.[1] This was not to be the last prank of this friend[2] who was so much like Erasmus in interests and temperament.[3] The friendship established on this

---

[1] Erasmus describes the incident in his letter to Botzheim, EE, I, 6, lines 4-28; Nichols, I, 201-2. The poem is Carm. 45 in Reedijk, *The Poems of Erasmus*, pp. 248-53. The preface to this poem, printed in the *Adagia* of 1500, is in EE, I, 239-41.

[2] Erasmus was to immortalize one in his colloquy "Exorcism or The Specter," in Thompson, *The Colloquies of Erasmus*, pp. 230-37.

[3] On Erasmus' visit to England in 1505-6, he and More translated Lucian and competed with one another in declaiming upon the same themes. See below, pp. 75-76.

brief trip to England was to last throughout the lifetime of both men.[4]

In October, Erasmus settled in Oxford, and as he had done in relation to Gaguin when he went to Paris, so upon his arrival in Oxford Erasmus introduced himself to John Colet (1467-1519).[5] Later Dean of St. Paul's (1504) and founder of St. Paul's School (1510) for which Erasmus wrote some of his educational treatises, Colet was at the time lecturing on Paul's epistles at the university.[6] In December, Erasmus left Oxford for London where he met Thomas Linacre (1460-1524) and William Grocyn (1446-1519), who had learned Greek in Italy; Grocyn had taught Greek to Thomas More at Oxford. Late in January, 1500, Erasmus left England and returned to Paris, but not before English customs had taken from him all the money he had received

---

[4]On the friendship between the two men the recent study by E. E. Reynolds, *Thomas More and Erasmus* (London: Burns and Oates, 1965) can be recommended. There is an excellent analysis of their relationship from beginning to end in Marie Delcourt, *Erasme* (Brussels: Editions Libris, 1944), chapter 3. For Erasmus' biography of More (written 1519) see EE, IV, 12-23; Nichols, III, 387-401; also tr. in Huizinga, *Erasmus and the Age of Reformation,* pp. 231-39.

[5]J. H. Lupton edited the works of Colet and translated most of them during the nineteenth century (*Opera Omnia.* London: Bell and Daldy, 1867-1876; reprinted, Gregg Press, 4 vols., 1965). His lectures on Romans and I Corinthians are among those translated. Lupton, in *A Life of John Colet* (1909; reprinted by Shoe String Press, 1961), added several other authentic writings by Colet not included in the earlier *Opera.*

Erasmus wrote a life of Colet after the latter's death (EE, IV, 514-27, lines 244-end; tr. J. C. Olin, *Christian Humanism and the Reformation,* pp. 176-91).

For a scholarly biography of Colet see, in addition to Lupton, F. Seebohm, *The Oxford Reformers: Colet Erasmus and More* (3rd ed.; London: Longmans, Green, & Co., 1896). On Colet's thought see E. W. Hunt, *Dean Colet and his Theology* (London: SPCK, 1956); and the following brief but telling studies: E. H. Harbison, *The Christian Scholar in the Age of the Reformation* (New York: Charles Scribner's Sons, 1956), pp. 55-67; and E. F. Rice, "John Colet and the Annihilation of the Natural," *Harvard Theological Review,* XLV:III (July, 1952), 141-63.

[6]Erasmus probably heard Colet lecture on Paul while at Oxford. Colet did not publish his lectures, however, a situation Erasmus regrets in a letter to him written several years after this initial visit to England (EE, I, 404, lines 15-18; Nichols, I, 375). On these lectures, see further, below, note 22.

from patrons while there—an incident he never forgot.[7]

The significance of Erasmus' first journey to England has turned on the interpretation of Erasmus' relation to John Colet. For shortly after Erasmus returned to Paris he began to study Greek; only one year later he wrote his *Enchiridion,* which is quite different from any of his earlier prose writings. Did John Colet, in the few months during which Erasmus knew him at Oxford, fundamentally change the direction of Erasmus' life?[8]

[7]See EE, I, 16, lines 19-27; Nichols, I, 227; EE, I, 343, lines 51-56; Nichols, I, 295; and EE, I, 538, lines 11-14; Nichols, II, 117. These recollections were written in 1523, 1501, and 1513 respectively.

[8]I believe the answer to this question is yes, as the discussion below will try to show. Colet made clear to Erasmus how his humanism could move toward fusion with his religious consciousness: through the exposition of sacred literature (not through editing the text of Scripture itself; that came to Erasmus only later, as we shall see). The following recent biographers have understood the matter this way: Charles Béné *(Erasme et Saint Augustin,* pp. 104-12, 189-94); E. H. Harbison *(The Christian Scholar in the Age of the Reformation,* p. 73); J. Huizinga *(Erasmus,* p. 33); M. Phillips *(Erasmus and the Northern Renaissance,* pp. 40-45).

Those who have denied the decisive influence of Colet seem to me to err in having lighted on the wrong point. The first to do so was Frederic Seebohm *(The Oxford Reformers,* 3rd ed., 1887, pp. 106-10), who argued that Colet turned Erasmus away from scholastic theology. But, as we have already seen, Erasmus never accepted scholastic theology, nor did he ever self-consciously reject it. Renaudet also has argued that Erasmus' English trip was decisive for his break with scholasticism and monasticism. But in addition to what has already been said, I might add that his attempt to link Colet's thought and, through Colet, Erasmus with medieval dissenters (Wyclif, the Lollards) is historically unrecognizable (see Renaudet, *Préréforme,* pp. 387-88; *Etudes Erasmiennes,* xvi, 196; *Erasme et Italie,* pp. 29-30; *Courants religieux et humanisme,* p. 21).

Still others have argued that it was the Neoplatonism of the English humanists that influenced Erasmus (Ivan Pusino, "Der Einfluss Picos auf Erasmus," *Zeitschrift für Kirchengeschichte,* XLVI [1927], pp. 75-96; Kohls, *Die Theologie des Erasmus,* II, 77, n. 171; Bainton, *Erasmus of Christendom,* pp. 59-60). There is more evidence for this position than for that of Seebohm or Renaudet. For while, as we have seen, Erasmus' knowledge of Platonism antedates his visit to England by many years and he was already much inclined to think in terms of a body-soul dualism, it is also true that Platonism played an important role in the *Enchiridion* (Plato himself is cited over thirty times), which the depth of his exposure to the Platonic tradition while in England helps to explain. But although this is true, it was not, I believe, the most important thing to be said about the influence of his English visit.

Kohls, in addition (II, 50, n. 105), plays down the influence of Colet on

The only source from which we can gain more than a speculative notion about the matter is the correspondence of Erasmus related to his English visit. What can we learn from it? First, Colet acknowledges in his response to Erasmus' introductory letter that while in Paris he had already heard of Erasmus through his letter in Gaguin's history, which "served me, when I read it, as a sort of sample and taste of an accomplished man with a knowledge both of literature and of a multitude of other things."[9] There is no suggestion, here or elsewhere, what the "multitude of other things" was. Colet is specific only about the fact that Erasmus was a man of letters. And this image of him is maintained throughout his English visit. Shortly after he arrived, as we have seen, he composed a poem for the future Henry VIII.[10] He was praised for this by John Sixtin, who urged him to further

the ground that he finds in Erasmus' earlier writings ideas that have in the past been attributed to Colet's influence. I have already suggested that Kohls imports later views of Erasmus into his early thought. But even if it is the case that the ideas appear earlier, it is still true, as I shall argue below, that Colet decisively influenced the way in which Erasmus would use those ideas.

In rejecting some of the views cited above, Albert Hyma has been led to deny and influence by Colet on Erasmus ("Erasmus and the Oxford Reformers, 1493-1503," reprinted in *The Youth of Erasmus,* pp. 343-65) . He seeks to lodge all decisive influence on the young Erasmus in the Brethren of the Common Life. But textual analysis discredits such reductionism.

[9]EE, I, 242, lines 5-7; Nichols, I, 205. Erasmus' introductory letter to Colet is lost. It is interesting that Colet goes on to say: "But that which recommends you to me most is this, that the Reverend Father with whom you are staying, the Prior of the House and Church of Jesus Christ, affirmed to me yesterday, that in his judgment you were a singularly good man. Therefore, so far as learning and general knowledge and sincere goodness prevail with one, who rather seeks and wishes for these qualities than makes any profession of them, you, Erasmus, both are and ought to be most highly recommended to me." When Erasmus, years later, wrote his "biography" of Colet, it was precisely for the combination of these two qualities, piety and learning, that he praised Colet.

[10]In a letter written from Oxford to John Sixtin, however, Erasmus intimates that he had passed beyond poetry. "We did wake [the Muses] not long ago from a more than ten years' sleep, and angry indeed they were, when they were compelled to chant the praises of the royal children. They chanted unwillingly and half-asleep some sort of ditty, so drowsy that it may well dispose anyone to slumber. I disliked it so much myself that I was glad to let them fall asleep again." (EE, I, 265, lines 148-52; Nichols, I, 211) He is of course exaggerating his distance from the poetic muse.

accomplishments as a bard.[11] And despite his disclaimers, in a letter written to this same John Sixtin only a few days later, Erasmus described himself as a poet.[12] Moreover, the occasion for this designation was Erasmus' role in a dinner conversation at the home of John Colet. Colet had thrown out the suggestion that God had first punished Cain because of the latter's pride in breaking the soil, whereas he had blessed Abel, who was content to live on what grew of itself, for his humility. This interpretation was hotly contested. Erasmus relates that a theologian present did his best to undermine Colet's interpretation through syllogistic reasoning, while he did the same with rhetorical arguments. The discussion at length became too serious for Erasmus, and he broke the heavy atmosphere with the lively story of a poet. Cain, he relates, dissatisfied with the meager harvest he obtained from tilling the soil, especially after having heard his parents discuss the situation in Paradise, attempted to persuade the guardian angel to relinquish a few of the grains of Paradise. He argued that God would not notice the aberration—and in any case had not forbidden it as he had the apples—and further, that God in making him a guardian of Paradise kept him out of heaven, while at the same time he did not have a share in the bounties of the earth which men would one day turn into Paradise. Through such arguments he persuaded the angel through promises of sharing in the bounties of the earth, to steal for him a few celestial grains. Naturally they grew as no grains of earth had ever grown, and in a few summers the crop had become so large that it could not escape the notice of the higher powers. God was greatly displeased and sent an army of ants, weasels, toads, etc., to destroy it. The guardian who had favored men was removed and as punishment clothed in a human body. Cain tried to appease God by a burnt offering of fruits, but when

[11]EE, I, 260; Nichols, I, 209-10 (the poem accompanying Sixtin's letter is omitted by Nichols). See Erasmus' reply, referred to in the note above, where he plays down his own accomplishments as a poet and praises Sixtin's ability (EE, I, 261-65; Nichols, I, 210-12 with many omissions).

[12]EE, I, 268, lines 16-17; Nichols, I, 215; also EE, I, 269, lines 32-35; Nichols, I, 216.

the smoke would not rise to heaven he was assured of God's anger and despaired. Erasmus had indeed fulfilled the role of a humanistic man of letters. He had retold the story of Prometheus![13]

But deeper currents were also at work. Erasmus had engaged in a serious discussion with Colet in Colet's garden on the question of Christ's agony in the garden, and especially over the meaning of the phrase: "My Father, if it be possible, let this cup pass from me; nevertheless, not as I will, but as thou wilt." (Matt. 26:39) Colet maintained that Christ's agony was over the Jews and the guilt he knew they would incur as a result of murdering him. Erasmus, on the other hand, argued that Christ's agony was his own suffering as a man facing what he knew lay ahead. As the discussion seemed to deadlock at this point, Colet suggested that they break it off and think about the matter further. As he reflected on their respective interpretations, Erasmus became more than ever convinced that he had been correct, and he wrote Colet a letter setting forth his interpretation once again.[14] He attempts to answer Colet's objections, which he restates: Why does Christ try to avoid death? What is the will which he submits to the will of his Father? If he does not want to die he loved us less; if he never refused to die, why try to avoid what he wanted? Erasmus responds that a man can have a horror of death who nevertheless does not refuse it. Indeed, he dies in spite of the horror because it will be efficacious for others; he makes the will of his Father his own will. Let us grant that at the moment of his death the heart of no martyr ever burned more ardently or joyously. But in the garden there was agony. And this is as it should be. Christ was not there in order to give us an example of courage, but rather of patience and obedience. Indeed, his life was throughout exemplary of these virtues. Erasmus concludes his letter by offering this to Colet as the first example of his apprenticeship in this kind of discussion. In his reply Colet does not

[13]EE, I, 268-71; Nichols, I, 215-19 (fortunately, the letter is translated in full). In the *Antibarbari* Erasmus says that we should imitate Prometheus in exerting our industry to become learned (EOO, I.1, 134, lines 10-13).

[14]EE, I, 249-53.

discuss Erasmus' major points but contents himself with falling back on the authority of Jerome whose interpretation agrees with his own.[15] To this Erasmus wrote another lengthy reply,[16] making two points that will be characteristic of him in all his later work on the Bible. He argues first that in the text itself there is not a shred of evidence to support Colet's interpretation. Nothing in the passage allows us to refer it to the Jews rather than to Christ himself. And in order to get at the meaning as clearly as possible Erasmus paraphrased the verse, at the same time restating what the verse would have had to say if it had had reference to the Jews. He argues second that Jerome is the only father who holds Colet's opinion; others hold the opinion of Erasmus. Moreover, even Jerome agreed with Erasmus in other passages of his writings. Why maintain the authority of one father in one passage so tenaciously? What we should do when the fathers disagree is not fall back on their authority but attempt to overcome their limitations and interpret for ourselves.[17]

In this discussion Colet and Erasmus followed the method Colet was following in his lectures on Paul. Contrary to the medieval scholastic tradition, Colet followed the text of Paul and sought to make clear Paul's meaning in his historical context. In Colet's hands, Paul came alive in a way he had not lived for many centuries.[18] This was the method Erasmus was to follow and which was to mark off Renaissance from Scholastic theology. In describing the difference between Abelard and Erasmus in this regard, Richard McKeon writes:

> The medieval theologian had tried to organize a
> body of doctrine, point by point, based on a body

[15]EE, I, 253-54.

[16]EE, I, 254-60. Erasmus later published this debate with Colet in an expanded form in his *Lucubratiunculae*, 1503, under the title *Disputatiuncula de tedio, pavore, tristicia Iesu*. The latter may be found in LB, V, 1265-94.

[17]EE, I, 257, lines 99-100, 120-28; 255, lines 20-40; 256, lines 63-69.

[18]See P. A. Duhamel, "The Oxford Lectures of John Colet," *Journal of the History of Ideas*, XIV (1953), 493-510; and chapter 3, R. P. Adams, *The Better Part of Valor* (Seattle: University of Washington Press, 1962).

of texts derived from Scriptures and Church Fathers; the new theologian returned to the text of the Scripture itself and its direct interpretation. The new emphasis, therefore, was upon the document and the writer, rather than upon the doctrine and the tradition.[19]

This agreement with Colet in method is more important than Colet's particular interpretations of Paul, which disagreed at many points with those of Erasmus published later, just as the two disagreed in their discussion of Jesus' agony in the garden.

Colet did more than simply discuss with Erasmus the interpretation of Scripture. He invited Erasmus to lecture on Moses or Isaiah just as he was lecturing on Paul's epistles. Erasmus' response to Colet's suggestion is very important as a statement of where he is at this point in his intellectual pilgrimage. He writes:

> You exhort me, nay, you almost demand reproachfully that, just as you are expounding St. Paul, so I should attempt to warm up the cooling students of this University during these winter months (as you put it) by expounding the ancient Moses, or the eloquent Isaiah. But I, who have learned to know myself, am well aware how scant is my equipment, and how little claim I may make for the learning which would be necessary for undertaking such a thing; neither do I feel that I have the strength of mind to sustain the ill will of so many men strongly defending their own point of view. . . . How can I have the effrontery to teach what I have not learned? How shall I warm up others when I am myself shivering?[20]

What does Erasmus mean when he says he is not equipped to carry out this task? Surely that he does not know the bibli-

---

[19]Richard McKeon, "Renaissance and Method in Philosophy," *Studies in the History of Ideas* (New York: Columbia University Press, 1935), III, 92-93; pp. 71-95 are devoted to Erasmus. (See further below, n. 67.)

[20]EE, I, 248, lines 76-89. For the full letter see EE, I, 245-49; Nichols, I, 220-23, lines 22-48 omitted. There is a full translation of the letter in J. J. Mangan, *Life, Character and Influence of Erasmus* (New York: Macmillan, 1927), I, 114-17.

cal languages. Colet had not been deterred by the fact that he did not know Greek. He used the Vulgate as an authoritative version in his lectures on Paul. Nor did he, until the appearance of Erasmus' Greek New Testament, understand the need for such knowledge.[21] But Erasmus knew the equipment necessary for scholarship. He heartily approved Colet's method of interpreting St. Paul, praising him for restoring the old theology over against the subtleties of scholasticism in which religious meaning was drowned in abstractions.[22] He even goes on to conclude:

> I did not come hither to teach poetry or rhetoric, which ceased to be agreeable to me after they had ceased to be indispensable. That sort of teaching I refuse, because it bears only a slight relation to my plan of life; your sort of teaching I must decline as beyond my capacity. In the case of the former you blame me undeservedly, dear Colet, since I have never proposed to myself the cultivation of what they call secular literature as a profession; to the latter task you exhort me vainly, since I know my exceeding inability for such an undertaking.[23]

Erasmus had never before said that secular literature bore "only a slight relation to my plan of life." This is one of those changes in direction which seems consonant with his development up to this point, but the decision that his plan of life was something different came to him here. He implies, though he does not say, that his plan of life now involves preparing himself for that to which Colet has summoned him but for which he is not yet prepared. There is a further hint that this is so in the last letter he wrote in England (from London). Describing his impressions of the country he says:

> But how do you like our England, you will say. Believe me, my Robert, when I answer that I never liked anything so much before. I find the climate both pleasant and wholesome; and I have met with

[21]EE, II, 257, lines 13-15; Nichols, II, 287.

[22]EE, I, 246-48, lines 19-73 (on English translations, see above, n. 20).

[23]EE, I, 248, lines 95-101; Mangan, I, 116.

> so much kindness and *so much learning, not hack-neyed and trivial, but deep, accurate, ancient, Latin and Greek,* that but for the curiosity of seeing it, I do not now so much care for Italy.[24]

Erasmus had caught a vision in England: from all his learned friends (especially More, Grocyn, and Linacre), a sense of the importance of Greek; from Colet a new kind of interpretation of religious literature that was both more faithful to the original sources and more conducive to piety. The correlation of these two insights was the real beginning of Erasmus' sense of vocation as a Christian scholar.

The Study of Greek and the Discovery of Origen

Is there any evidence that Erasmus in fact did put these two insights together? In a letter written to Colet in 1504, Erasmus says:

> Three years ago I wrote something on St. Paul's Epistle to the Romans and finished with a single effort some four volumes, which I would have continued if I had not been hindered, my principal hindrance being my constant want of Greek. Consequently, for about three years I have been entirely taken up with the study of that language, and I think that I have not altogether thrown away my labor. I also began to look at Hebrew, but frightened by the strangeness of the idiom, and in consideration of my age and of the insufficiency of the human mind to master a multitude of subjects, I gave it up.[25]

Thus, at Colet's instigation, Erasmus *did* try his hand at the exegesis of Scripture, either in England or shortly after he returned to Paris ("about three years ago"). But realizing that in order to pursue his studies adequately, he would need to know the language in which Paul wrote, he broke off his work in order to learn Greek.[26] That this is in fact

---

[24]EE, I, 273, lines 15-21; Nichols, I, 226; emphasis added.

[25]EE, I, 404-5, lines 31-38; Nichols, I, 375-76.

[26]My interpretation agrees with P. S. Allen, *Erasmus: Lectures and Wayfaring Sketches* (Oxford: Clarendon Press, 1934), p. 42; and E. H. Harbison,

what happened is verified by comments that begin to appear in the letters from Paris immediately after his return in 1500.

He makes his first reference to the fact that he is studying Greek in a letter to James Batt in March:

> My Greek studies are almost too much for my courage. I have not the means of purchasing books, or the help of a teacher. And while I am in all this trouble, I have scarcely the wherewithal to sustain life; so much is our learning worth to us.[27]

The following month, he writes again to Batt: "I have been applying my whole mind to the study of Greek; and as soon as I receive any money I shall first buy Greek authors, and afterwards some clothes."[28]

Progress came rapidly. The inclusion of some Greek proverbs in the first edition of the *Adagia*[29] was doubtless due to these efforts. By September, he can write to Batt: "I do wish, my dear Batt, that you knew Greek . . . because I find Latin literature incomplete without it. . . ."[30] And during the same month he wrote to another friend: "I am so enamored of this author [Homer], that even when I cannot understand him, I am refreshed and fed by the very sight of his words."[31] Erasmus wrote this as he was leaving Paris for

The Christian Scholar in the Age of the Reformation, p. 78. For a different interpretation, see W. Schwarz, *Principles and Problems of Biblical Translation* (Cambridge: Cambridge University Press, 1955), pp. 120-21.

[27] EE, I, 285, lines 22-26; Nichols, I, 233. Much of Erasmus' correspondence during this period is taken up with efforts to get money from patrons.

[28] EE, I, 288, lines 62-64; Nichols, I, 236.

[29] It was published in July, 1500. For the preface, see EE, I, 289-97; Nichols, I, 243-44 translates little more than the end of the letter. It contains 818 proverbs—664 from Latin authors, 154 from Greek. See the discussion of this edition in M. M. Phillips, *The Adages of Erasmus* (Cambridge: University Press, 1964), pp. 41-61. See also below, n. 33; and pp. 67-71.

[30] EE, I, 301, lines 66-67; Nichols, I, 261. Batt did not comply, for nine months later Erasmus wrote to James Tutor: "I am reading Greek, but by myself, for Batt has not time to spare, and is fonder of Latin." (EE, I, 363, lines 23-24; Nichols, I, 328) In the same letter, he refers to an effort to proselytize his friend William Herman, apparently with equally little success (EE, I, 363, lines 38-44; Nichols, I, 329).

[31] EE, I, 305-6, lines 2-4; Nichols, I, 270.

Orleans to escape the plague. As he was anticipating his return to Paris in December, he wrote to Batt:

> It is not only most convenient, but it is necessary for me to move back to Paris, both in order to proceed in those Greek studies which I have begun, and to finish the works I have in hand. . . . A little money must be scraped together from somewhere, with which I may get clothes, buy the whole works of Jerome (upon whom I am preparing commentaries),[32] as well as Plato, procure Greek books and hire the services of a Greek teacher. . . . It is incredible how my heart burns to bring all my poor lucubrations to completion, and at the same time to attain some moderate capacity in Greek. *I should then devote myself entirely to the study of sacred literature, as for some time I have longed to do.*[33]

Three months later still (March, 1501), Erasmus has acquired a Greek teacher, about whom he speaks rather unkindly.[34] Preoccupied now with his Greek, he justifies the

---

[32]In his attitude toward Jerome, we see Erasmus identifying himself as enthusiastically with the Christian tradition as he had done earlier with the classical Latin tradition. In a letter contemporary with this one, he wrote: "I have long ardently wished to illustrate with a commentary the epistles of St. Jerome, and in daring to conceive so great a design, which no one has hitherto attempted, my heart is inflamed and directed by some divine power. I am moved by the piety of that holy man, of all Christians beyond controversy the most learned and most eloquent; whose writings, though they deserve to be read and learned everywhere and by all, are read by few, admired by fewer still, and understood by scarcely any . . . . What a style, what a mastery of language, in which he has not only left all Christian authors far behind him, but seems to vie with Cicero himself. For my own part, I may be led astray by my partiality for that holy man, but when I compare the speech of Jerome with that of Cicero, I seem to miss something in the prince of eloquence himself." (EE, I, 332, lines 16-23, 38-43; Nichols, I, 289)

[33]EE, I, 320-21, lines 15-18, 38-41, 44-48; Nichols, I, 283; emphasis added. This makes it quite clear, if further proof were needed, what Erasmus' purpose was in learning Greek. It was not primarily in order to make the *Adagia* more complete. He had been working on that before he went to England; moreover, he would have waited longer to publish it had this been a primary purpose (see EE, I, 406, lines 82-86; Nichols, I, 378). It was rather to become a literary man in the cause of Christianity.

[34]". . . seeing the necessity of completing my Greek studies, I determined to employ for several months a Greek teacher; and a thorough Greek he is, always hungry, and charging an exorbitant price for his lessons." (EE, I,

labor it is costing him at his age (thirty-two) , speaking even more confidently of the treasures to be had through Greek:

> I have by a lucky chance got some Greek works, which I am stealthily transcribing night and day. It may be asked why I am so pleased with the example of Cato the Censor as to be learning Greek at my age. I answer, Reverend Father, that if I had had this mind when a boy, or rather if the times had been more favorable to me, I should have been the happiest man in the world. As it is, I am determined that it is better to learn late than to be without the knowledge which it is of the utmost importance to possess. We had a taste of this learning a long time ago [as a school boy], but it was only with the tip of the tongue, as they say; and having lately dipped deeper into it, we see, as we have often read in the most weighty authors, that Latin erudition, however ample, is crippled and imperfect without Greek. We have in Latin at best some small streams and turbid pools, while they have the clearest springs and rivers flowing with gold. I see it is the merest madness to touch with the little finger that principal part of theology, which treats of the divine mysteries, without being furnished with the apparatus of Greek. . . .[35]

Shortly forced to abandon Paris and his teacher, he nonetheless continues to make progress. By July his profi-

353, lines 65-68; Nichols, I, 314) . On his teacher, Hermonymus of Sparta, see the Letter to Botzheim, EE, I, 7, lines 22-24, and n. 22.

[35]EE, I, 352, lines 9-23; Nichols, I, 313. Erasmus then goes on, in a passage unfortunately omitted by Nichols (lines 26-41) to demonstrate how a knowledge of Greek would correct misinterpretations in the Vulgate. For example, Psalm 51:3 says in the Vulgate: "My sin is always confronting me;" but the Greek says, "my sin is always before me." The prophet here does not mean that the sin is always before his eyes, but rather that the memory of his sin never leaves his mind, and he expresses his regret for his sin as if it were actually present. Erasmus has already begun to put his Greek to work on the task for which he had set out to learn it.

It is also interesting to note that in the passage immediately following the one quoted, Erasmus calls attention to a pontifical decree he had referred to in the *Antibarbari*. But whereas he had cited it there in order to prove that Christians should read sacred literature, here he cites it to prove that theologians should have a knowledge of the biblical languages. His viewpoint has changed considerably. Compare EOO, I.1, 108-9 with EE, I, 353, lines 42-51; Nichols, I, 313-14. See below, n. 36 for an analogous example.

ciency has grown considerably. He remarks to James Tutor: "We have almost wholly deserted the Roman Muses for the Greek, and shall not rest till we have attained a moderate proficiency."[36] Little more than one year later he can announce that he has achieved his goal. "I am fully occupied with Greek, and it is not altogether lost labor, for I have advanced so far as to be able to write what I want in Greek tolerably well without preparation."[37] This indeed is a "moderate proficiency!"

As he leaves Paris and returns for a visit to Holland, a sense of "mission" in relation to his new-found Greek studies begins to breathe in his correspondence. He finds his former friends at Steyn and Haarlem boorish because they do not share his enthusiasm for Greek. In the same breath he speaks of the climate of Holland as particularly unpleasant on this visit.[38] It is as if the whole atmosphere had, in one moment, become intolerable. Moreover, he speaks of his studies with a distant vision, discounting the hardships and meager accomplishments of the present. Indeed, we hear him speak—like other men who have proven equally great—as one who knows that he is destined for greatness:

> I am not unaware that I have pursued a kind of study which some think strange, others endless, others unprofitable, others even impious; so they seem to the crowd of those who are professors of

[36]EE, I, 367, lines 30-32; Nichols, I, 332. One must take account of the "almost." For Erasmus had published an edition of Cicero's *De officiis* in April, 1501 (see the preface, EE, I, 355-57; Nichols, I, 318, where only a few lines are translated). But when he wrote this letter he was translating Euripides, Isocrates, and other Greek writers (EE, I, 365, lines 6-7; Nichols, I, 330), as he continued to do during this period (see EE, I, 390-93; Nichols, I, 356-57, but lines 1-91 omitted).

Note should be taken also of Erasmus' assertion here that he only wished to attain a moderate proficiency in Greek. In *On Christian Doctrine*, II.11-15, Augustine had said that we should learn languages and that we needed a moderate proficiency in them. Erasmus here shows awareness of a part of that text which he had failed to discuss in the *Antibarbari*. See above, n. 35, for an analogous example.

[37]EE, I, 381, lines 9-12; Nichols, I, 353.

[38]See above, n. 29; and EE, I, 366, lines 4-9; Nichols, I, 332; EE, I, 368, lines 59-64; Nichols, I, 333.

learning. But I am all the more encouraged, as I am sure of two facts, that the best things have never found favor with the crowd, and that this kind of study is most approved by the smallest number, but the most learned.[39] If Jerome was mad or unlearned, it is good to share the folly of such a man; it is good to be numbered in his unlearned flock, rather than in those other divine choirs. And even if we shall fail to reach the goal in this our course, it will not be discreditable to have at any rate striven to attain the very fairest objects. If men do not approve this purpose of mine, God, I think, will both approve and aid it; and some time hence men will approve, or at any rate posterity.[40]

At the end of July, 1501, Erasmus moved from Tournehem to St. Omer. It was here for the first time that he met Jean Vitrier, a Franciscan monk for whom he developed great admiration and whose life he was later to portray as exemplary for Christians.[41] Vitrier introduced him for the first time to Origen.[42] Since Erasmus' correspondence is sparse

[39]See also on this theme, *Enchiridion* (Holborn, pp. 90-91; Himelick, pp. 132-33).

[40]EE, I, 370, lines 29-42; Nichols, I, 335-36.

[41]EE, I, 372-73, lines 3-4; Nichols, I, 338 is the first mention of Vitrier. See EE, I, 372, n. on Gardianus for Allen's biographical note on Vitrier. Later, in the letter in which he wrote a biographical account of Colet, Erasmus wrote also about Vitrier; it is our only source for his life. (EE, IV, 507-14, lines 1-243; tr. John C. Olin, *Christian Humanism and the Reformation*, pp. 165-76)

[42]The first mention of Origen occurs in a letter contemporary with the meeting of Vitrier. "... encourage Adrian to supply me with a few books. I want him to send Augustine and Ambrose on St. Paul; and to beg Origen for a time from the people at St. Bertin, and be bound for me to return it; he shall not be disappointed. Moreover, I very much wish, if it can be done, to have the Homilies of Origen, which the Warden [Vitrier] has, sent with the rest. I should also be glad to welcome Lyra and any other writer upon St. Paul." (EE, I, 376, lines 6-11; Nichols, I, 343)

In his later life of Vitrier Erasmus says: "There was no writer on theology whose genius he more admired than Origen's. And on my objecting that I was surprised to see him take pleasure in the writings of a heretic, I was struck with the animation with which he replied that a mind from which there had issued so many works fraught with such learning and fervor could not but have been a dwelling place of the Holy Spirit." (EE, IV, 508, lines 24-29; Olin, p. 166) André Godin has shown that Erasmus' characteri-

during this period, there is little reference to Origen's impact upon him.[43] But writing to Colet three years later he remarks: "I have perused a good part of the works of Origen, under whose teaching I think I have made some progress. He seems to disclose some original springs and points out the principles of theological science."[44]

The 'Enchiridion,' 1501

What these principles of theological science were we can determine from the *Enchiridion militis Christiani (Handbook of a Christian Soldier)*, which Erasmus wrote at St.

zation of Vitrier (1521) correlates point for point with his characterization of Origen (1535, LB, VIII, 437-40), and that it was as a preacher that he revered them both. See "De Vitrier à Origène: Recherches sur la patristique érasmienne," *Colloquium Erasmianum* (Mons: Centre Universitaire de l'état, 1968), pp. 49-51. Was Erasmus projecting his image of one man onto the other? Godin has discovered twenty homilies of Vitrier, and he has concluded on the basis of an examination of them that Erasmus was not idealizing Vitrier after the fact. On the contrary, Vitrier's preaching verifies the exactness of Erasmus' characterization of him (p. 52).

[43]We have only one enigmatic reference in a letter of 1502: "Beg Adrian in my name to be patient about his books. For I intend to leave this place in a few days, but not before I have returned his volumes with many thanks. I am strangely pleased with myself for having undertaken this work; for I am confident that for the future I shall be glad to busy myself with all my heart in sacred literature." (EE, I, 378, lines 2-6; Nichols, I. 347)

[44]EE, I, 405, lines 38-41; Nichols, I, 376. Origen's *On First Principles* was published in 1481. The "revival" of Origen began in earnest when Pico published his nine hundred theses in 1486. Many of these related to Origen. He argued on a number of grounds that it was more reasonable to believe that Origen was saved than that he was damned. Pico's condemnation made traffic with Origen dangerous until the charges against him were lifted by Pope Alexander VI in 1493. In 1503 Aldus published some of the homilies of Origen on the Old Testament which had been translated by Jerome. A preface, written probably by Jerome Aleander, highly extolling Origen, accompanied the edition and gave rise to others. A complete edition of Origen was published in 1512. Erasmus prepared an edition which was published, however, only after he died. On the revival of Origen during the Renaissance see Edgar Wind, "The Revival of Origen," in Dorothy Miner, ed., *Studies in Art and Literature for Belle da Costa Greene* (Princeton: Princeton University Press, 1954), pp. 412-24; D. P. Walker, "Origene en France au debut du XVIe siècle," in *Courants religieux et humanisme*, pp. 101-19; Denys Gorce, "La patristique dans la réforme d'Erasme," in E. Iserloh and P. Manns, *Festgabe Joseph Lortz, Vol. I: Reformation Schicksal und Auftrag* (Baden Baden: Bruno Grimm, 1958), pp. 233-38.

Omer during this same period in 1501 when he discovered
the works of Origen; the book was worked up for publication at Louvain where it was first published in 1503.[45] The
Christian soldier, Erasmus says in his opening comments,
needs to be on guard. And for this purpose he needs weapons. What weapons are appropriate? There are two: prayer
and knowledge. On prayer he spends one page, on knowledge ten. The "knowledge" the Christian soldier needs constitutes the principles of theological science. These principles are not abstractions, the foundation for a new speculative metaphysic. They are sources of Christian living.[46] "No
temptation is so strong," Erasmus begins, "that the eager
study of sacred letters cannot easily check [it]."[47] For although "every doctrine of man is tinged by some darkness
of error, the teaching of Christ is wholly pure and clear and
sound."[48] How is Scripture to be read so that the purity of

[45]A critical text was published by Holborn, *Ausgewählte Werke*, 1933, pp.
1-136; reprinted in *Ausgewählte Schriften*, I, (1968), 56-375, together with a
German translation. The work has been rendered into English three times
in recent years. Matthew Spinka, ed., *Advocates of Reform* (Philadelphia:
Westminster Press, 1953), pp. 281-379 (some omissions); Raymond Himelick,
The Enchiridion of Erasmus (Bloomington: Indiana University Press, 1963);
John P. Dolan, ed., *The Essential Erasmus* (New York: Mentor-Omega Books,
1964), pp. 24-93. References in this book will be to the Holborn and Hime-
lick editions.

Most biographers deal with this treatise. Two good expositions in recent
literature in English are Roland Bainton, *Erasmus of Christendom* (New
York: Charles Scribner's Sons, 1969), pp. 65-71; M. M. Phillips, *Erasmus and
the Northern Renaissance* (London: English Universities Press, 1949), ch. 2.

The most complete analysis of the treatise is Alfons Auer, *Die vollkom-
mene Frömmigkeit des Christen nach dem Enchiridion militis Christiani des
Erasmus von Rotterdam* (Düsseldorf: Patmos, 1954). On the theology of the
Enchiridion see Ernst-Wilhelm Kohls, *Die Theologie des Erasmus* (Basel:
Friedrich Reinhardt, 1966), I, ch. 3. On the sources of the *Enchiridion*, see
Charles Béné, *Erasme et Saint Augustin ou influence de Saint Augustin sur
l'humanisme d'Erasme* (Geneve: Librairie Droz, 1969), pp. 127-86.

[46]"... I want to instruct you, not in scholastic quibbling, but in good living," he says later. (Holborn, p. 72; Himelick, p. 107)

[47]Holborn, p. 30; Himelick, p. 49.

[48]Holborn, p. 31; Himelick, p. 49. See also Holborn, p. 63; Himelick, p.
94: "Think of Christ, not as an empty word, but as nothing other than love,
candor, patience, purity—in brief, whatever he taught." But see below, chapter V, pp. 146-47 and notes 39-41.

the teaching of Christ is received by us? Through allegorical interpretation. "If you break through the husk and find the kernel, pondering one little line will have more savor and food value than the whole psalter when it is chanted through with reference only to the literal content. . . ."[49] How does one go about this kind of reflection? First, one may gain help from Christian writers who have interpreted Scripture in this manner. "From the interpretations of divine Scripture choose those which go as far as possible beyond literal meaning. After Paul, the best of the explicators of this sort are Origen, Ambrose, Jerome, and Augustine. . . ."[50]

Further on Erasmus adds: "In unveiling the hidden sense, however, one ought not to follow conjectures of his own mind but acquire a method and, so to speak, a kind of technique, something a certain Dionysius gives us in a book called *Concerning the Names of God* and St. Augustine in his work entitled *On Christian Doctrine*. After Christ, the Apostle Paul opened up certain allegorical fountains; and following him, Origen easily holds the leadership in this aspect of theology."[51] One's reading of Scripture may also

[49]Holborn, p. 34; Himelick, p. 54. See also Holborn, p. 70; Himelick, p. 105: ". . . if in the whole history of the creation you should look for nothing beyond the literal and the superficial, I do not see that you would be doing anything much more worth the effort than if you were to sing about the clay image made by Prometheus and how fire, stolen by a trick and laid on the image, put life into the mud. As a matter of fact, a poetic tale read allegorically may perhaps be more fruitful than an account from the sacred books where you content yourself with only the rind."

[50]Holborn, pp. 33-34; Himelick, p. 53.

[51]Holborn, p. 71; Himelick, p. 107. There is some evidence to indicate that Erasmus, in explicating his theology, followed the authors he names in these passages. According to Holborn's notes, for example, there are 170 citations of Paul's letters. Matthew is cited 70 times. The Old Testament is given a secondary place. Of the Christian fathers mentioned, Origen and Ambrose are cited twice each, Jerome four times, Augustine seven times. Holborn's editing, however, has been shown to be incomplete. Charles Béné *(Erasme et Saint Augustin,* pp. 127-86, tabulation, pp. 433-34) has demonstrated that there are more than twenty citations of *On Christian Doctrine.* And André Godin has pointed out that in the early chapters of the *Enchiridion* alone there are five definite allusions to the homilies of Origen that Holborn overlooks ("De Vitrier à Origène," p. 55, n. 8).

Can we specify the source of Erasmus' acceptance of the allegorical method? His elucidation of it recalls at least two of the points made by

profit from a knowledge of pagan literature, though one should not take up the moral habits of the pagans.

> ...for the early stages of this campaigning I would not disapprove of the new recruit's getting some practice in the works of pagan poets and philosophers; only let him take them up in moderation, in a way appropriate to his immaturity and, so to speak, in passing—without expending his life on

Augustine in *On Christian Doctrine;* namely, that every truth is to be appropriated for Christianity, regardless of its source, and that Scripture is to be interpreted in such a way that nothing unworthy of God is attributed to him. But these and other points are also to be found in Origen. In *On First Principles* IV.i-iii he argues that allegorical interpretation is necessary because many things taken literally, especially in the Old Testament, would be unworthy of God. Thus, while some of Scripture has a literal meaning, *all* of it has an allegorical meaning. Erasmus does not seem to be aware, in this first flush of discovery, that his allegorical method leans strongly toward a moral interpretation, while Origen's leans toward a mystical one. Erasmus does become conscious of this difference between himself and Origen later. In the *Ratio* (1518) he argues that all Scripture could not be interpreted allegorically [Holborn, p. 282], as he did again in 1530 in his interpretation of Psalm 33 [LB, V, 381C]. However, he added in the *Ecclesiastes* (1535) that all Scripture can be interpreted tropologically [LB, V, 1050A-B]. In the same treatise he reproves both Jerome and Origen for taking too much freedom with the literal sense [LB, V, 1028D] and believes, as he had said three years earlier, that the Platonic philosophy was the reason for Origen's having gotten into so much difficulty at this point [LB, V, 432]. Moreover, while it is unclear in Origen whether the higher interpretation denotes a better Christian, it is clear that there is no such "gnosticism" in Erasmus, potential or actual. Allegorical interpretation has for him only a functional significance; for Origen more seems to be involved.

The outcome of this discussion is, I believe, that Erasmus' use of the allegorical method is not reducible to what either Augustine or Origen or Jerome says about it. He does not say all that they say, and he takes from them notions congenial to the formation of his own viewpoint. As he becomes aware of some of the implications of ideas he takes for himself, he will modify them later (as I indicated above—see also below, chapter III). He was never the servant of his sources. On the contrary, it was the other way around.

On Erasmus' relation to all three of these fathers, see Denys Gorce, "La patristique dans la réforme d'Erasme," in *Festgabe Joseph Lortz*, I, 233-76. On Erasmus' relation to Jerome see E. H. Harbison, *The Christian Scholar in the Age of the Reformation;* W. Schwarz, *Principles and Problems of Biblical Translation.* On the priority of Augustine as an influence on Erasmus, see Charles Béné, *Erasme et Saint Augustin.* Apparently, André Godin is in the process of performing a similar service for Origen in relation to Erasmus (see "De Vitrier à Origène," *Colloquium Erasmianum*, p. 47).

them and rotting, as it were, on the crags of the Sirens. . . . I would by no means have you adopt the moral habits of the pagans as a result of studying their literature, but you may find much in such sources that is otherwise conducive to right living. And whatever good advice even a pagan author gives ought not to be scorned, seeing that Moses did not spurn the counsel of his father-in-law, Jethro [Ex. 18:13-27]. Literature shapes and invigorates the youthful character and prepares one marvelously well for understanding Holy Scripture, to pounce upon which with unscrubbed hands and feet is something akin to sacrilege.[52]

In order to be profitable, however, pagan writers, like Scripture itself, must be read allegorically. For "just as divine Scripture bears no great fruit if you persist in clinging only to the literal sense, so the poetry of Homer and Vergil is of no small benefit if you remember that this is all allegorical, a fact which no one who has but touched his lips to the wisdom of the ancients will deny. . . ."[53] But finally, nothing avails unless the reader comes to Scripture with a pure mind, ready to relate everything to Christ,[54] indeed knowing "that any truth you come upon at any place is Christ's."[55]

These then are the weapons of a Christian soldier. But no one can properly use instruments given to him for his

---

[52]Holborn, pp. 31-32; Himelick, pp. 50-51; see also Holborn, p. 35; Himelick, p. 55.

There is another reason also why one should supplement the study of Scripture with that of pagan literature: "It is impossible for the mystical sense not to be dull or trivial when it is not seasoned with skill in eloquence and a certain charm of language . . . ." (Holborn, p. 71; Himelick, p. 107).

[53]He goes on to add: "I should prefer, too, that you follow the Platonists among the philosophers, because in most of their ideas and in their very manner of speaking they come nearest to the beauty of the prophets and the gospels." (Holborn, p. 32; Himelick, p. 51. See also Holborn, p. 71; Himelick, p. 106).

The implication of this analogy is, of course, that Scripture is subject to the same canons of interpretation as any other literature. Erasmus henceforth accepted this implication in his work on sacred texts. He had already implied as much in his dedication of the first edition of the *Adagia* to Lord Mountjoy (see EE, I, 294-95, lines 172-97).

[54]Holborn, pp. 32, 33; Himelick, pp. 51-52.

[55]Holborn, p. 35; Himelick, p. 56.

good if he does not know who he is (and what his good is) . Who is man? He is a creature both bodily and spiritual.[56] "Plato puts two souls in one man; Paul, two men in the same man, so conjoined that neither may be divided from the other either in heaven or hell, but also so disparate that the death of one is the life of the other."[57] If this is the nature of man, then the task of the Christian is perfectly clear: "You should always try to advance from things visible, which are for the most part imperfect or of a neutral status, to things invisible,"[58] to "begin to reject the visible world in favor of the world unseen."[59] For although the body cannot live without the spirit, the spirit needs nothing from the body.[60] What does it mean to live by the spirit, to foresake the body? We can illustrate its meaning by reference to the mass:

> It is possible that you say mass every day but live selfishly, untouched by the misfortunes of your neighbors. As yet you are still in the fleshly stage of the sacrament. But if you take to heart what the mass really stands for when you receive it, that is, being one spirit with the spirit of Christ, one body with the body of Christ, a living member of the Church; if you love nothing except in Christ; if you think all your property belongs equally to all men; if the trials of other people grieve you as much as your own—in that case you are at last observing the sacraments with real profit, because you are doing it in a spiritual sense.[61]

It is the internalization of the Christian message rather than its formal observance which constitutes the touchstone of a true Christian, a follower of Christ.[62] "I am not impressed

---

[56]On the flesh/spirit dichotomy in Erasmus, see John Payne, "Toward the Hermeneutics of Erasmus," in J. Coppens, ed., *Scrinium Erasmianum* (Leiden: Brill, 1969) , II, 17-25. I agree with Payne that Kohls cannot succeed in deriving these categories primarily from Scripture (p. 17, n. 17) .

[57]Holborn, p. 48; Himelick, p. 73.

[58]Holborn, p. 67; Himelick, p. 101.

[59]Holborn, p. 69; Himelick, p. 104.

[60]Holborn, p. 72; Himelick, p. 108.

[61]Holborn, p. 73; Himelick, pp. 109-10.

[62]Erasmus' strong and persistent criticisms of monasticism and religious

by the fact that you never omit a watch, a fast, a period of silence, a prayer. . . . I will not believe that you are spiritual unless I see the fruits of the spirit."[63]

The Discovery of Valla's 'Notes on the New Testament,' 1504

In the *Enchiridion* Erasmus for the first time produces a synthesis between his Christianity and his humanism. The tension between the two is resolved in his own mind, for he has discovered a way in which the priority of his commitment as a Christian can be asserted without denying his love of classical literature and the ideal of learning which it inspired in him. But Erasmus was hardly aware at the time he wrote the *Enchiridion* where this synthesis would lead him vocationally. The course he envisioned in the *Enchiridion*[64] received a new impulse when, searching through the library of a Premonstratensian monastery near Louvain in the summer of 1504, he discovered Lorenzo Valla's *Notes on the New Testament,* which he carried to Paris and published in March, 1505. In his preface to these notes,[65] we find Erasmus speaking for the first time, not about the recovery of the old theology through a study of more ancient Greek and Latin authors, but rather about the recovery of the text of the

ceremonialism, which run throughout the book and particularly the sections under discussion, are based on this distinction—a critical one for him since it marked the difference between contemporary theology and "ancient theology," and between a true and false theologian.

[63]Holborn, p. 80; Himelick, p. 119. However, "visible forms of worship are not condemned, but God is not pleased by anything but the invisible state of righteousness. God is a spirit, and he is moved by spiritual sacrifices." Holborn, p. 85; Himelick, p. 126.

[64]The body of the work itself was an explication of what Erasmus regarded as the "old theology." At the end of the text he announces his progress in working on commentaries on Paul's epistles, and in this task aligns himself with the ancient theologians (Augustine, Ambrose, Origen). (Holborn, p. 135; Himelick, p. 199) His vision, then, whether writing his own theology or making available that of the ancients, was the interpretation of the "old theology."

[65]EE, I, 406-12; Nichols, I, 380-85 with omissions; translated in full in H. A. Oberman, *Forerunners of the Reformation* (New York: Holt, Rinehart and Winston, 1966), pp. 308-15.

Bible. He recognizes that this is a much more audacious undertaking than the interpretation of the fathers. For his entire letter is cast in the form of a defense of Valla, who went so far as to correct the New Testament. In his defense he uses arguments from his distant past; for example, extolling Valla's character in relation to Poggio, who was vile but is nonetheless venerated today. But something new and much more far-reaching in its significance appears here for the first time. Erasmus knows this and states the problem himself. "I suppose the most horrible clamor will come from those who could benefit most from the work, namely, the theologians. They will say that it is an intolerable insolence that the grammarian, having molested all other disciplines, does not restrain his impudent pen from Sacred Scripture."[66]

A knowledge of languages is important, not only for the restoration of the old theology, but even more for a restoration of the *source* of the old theology. "Indeed the whole task of translating Scripture is the task of the grammarian." And he continues:

> Nor do I assume that theology, the very queen of all disciplines, will think it beneath her dignity if her handmaiden, grammar, offers her help and the required service. For even if grammar is somewhat lower in dignity than other disciplines, there is no other more necessary. She busies herself with very small questions, without which no one progresses to the large. She argues about trifles which lead to serious matters. If they answer that theology is too important to be limited by grammatical rules and that this whole affair of exegeting depends on the inspiration of the Holy Spirit, then this is indeed a new honor for the theologian that he alone is allowed to speak like a barbarian![67]

[66]EE, I, 409, lines 111-15; Oberman, p. 311.

[67]EE, I, 410, lines 129-40; Oberman, p. 312. The force of this passage lies in the fact that Erasmus understood the degree of his departure from medieval scholastic theology in adopting this method. Richard McKeon highlights his self-consciousness of this method very well: "The task that Erasmus set for himself was the interpretation of a document to discover precisely what Paul said, or what the evangelists said, as indication ultimately of the philosophy of Christ. That Plato or Pythagoras or even Moses may

As Jerome wrote to Desiderius, a prophet is one thing, an exegete another: the prophet predicts, the exegete employs his erudition to translate what he himself understands. Erasmus, like Jerome, accepts the role of the exegete which falls within the purview of human talent and effort. If the theologian is to be identified with the prophet, then he will not be a theologian.[68]

But is there not a very great audacity in the grammarian's assertion that he will employ his erudition to alter Scripture? For does not every jot and tittle of Scripture hold a mystery? Erasmus responds unequivocally: "This very fact shows how much more wrong it is to corrupt Scripture and how careful the learned should be in correcting Scripture which has been adulterated through ignorance."[69] Moreover, "just as the reliability of our versions of the Old Testament should be established on the basis of the Hebrew manuscripts, so also the accuracy of the New Testament must be measured by the Greek textual witnesses [rather than by the Vulgate]."[70]

What of the contention that the ancient exegetes, who knew the languages, have provided an explanation for every passage already?

have said something similar is irrelevant to the problem; all the devices of the arts are exploited to determine the authenticity of the document, the accuracy of the text, the precision and sufficiency of the interpretation. Abailard, on the other hand, set as his task to discover truth by examining the various statements that had been made on a given problem.... The difference between the method of Erasmus and that of Abailard may therefore be stated as that between a use of the three arts oriented to an understanding of a passage (that is, the three arts arranged in accordance with the needs of grammar) and the use of the three arts oriented to a comparative estimation of a variety of arguments (that is, the three arts arranged under the dominance of dialectic)." ("Renaissance and Method in Philosophy," *Studies in the History of Ideas,* pp. 80-81) See also above, this chapter, n. 6.

[68]W. Schwarz, *Principles and Problems of Biblical Translation,* has developed this contrast between Jerome and Erasmus on the one side and Augustine and Luther on the other in a convincing manner.

[69]EE, I, 411, lines 158-61; Oberman, p. 313.

[70]EE, I, 411, lines 168-70; Oberman, p. 313. Erasmus supports this assertion by reference once again to the ruling of Clement V at the Council of Vienne (1311-1312) that teachers of the three languages should be trained. See above, n. 35.

> First, I would prefer to see the original with my
> own eyes rather than through someone else's, and
> further, the ancient exegetes, granted that they
> have said a great deal, left much for later interpre-
> ters to explain. Is it not true that in order to under-
> stand their interpretations, at least an average
> knowledge of languages is required? And finally,
> when you come upon old texts in various languages
> that are corrupt (as indeed they are), what will you
> do?[71]

Erasmus' attitude toward the authority of the fathers always
remained as stated here: They are to be taken seriously, but
they are no substitute for the original text.

The impression of this letter is unmistakable: Erasmus
has decided to become a *translator and editor* of the source
of theology itself, using his classical and Christian erudition
in its service. And this impression is verified by his subsequent behavior. Later during the same year (1505) Erasmus
made a second visit to England, and while there he worked
on his own Latin version of the New Testament, one which
differed significantly from the Vulgate and was destined to
appear in the second edition of his New Testament, 1519.[72]
At the time, however, he did not envision publication of a
Greek text of the New Testament.[73] Much in his own growing sense of himself and his vocation was to happen before
he finally reached that decision.

Erasmus in Italy, 1506-1509

Erasmus had long wanted to go to Italy, but circum-

---

[71]EE, I, 412, lines 185-91; Oberman, p. 314.

[72]See Allen's introduction to Erasmus' dedication of his edition of the New
Testament to Pope Leo X (EE, II, 181-83).

[73]For example, in 1507, while in Italy, Erasmus wrote to Aldus Manutius,
the Venetian printer: "I wonder what has so long prevented you from publishing the New Testament, a work, which if I guess aright, will be exceed-
ingly welcome even to the great majority of our class, I mean the class of
theologians." (EE, I, 437-38, lines 16-19; Nichols, I, 429) Apparently, Aldus
had planned an edition of the New Testament as early as 1499, though this
was not actually executed until three years after Aldus' death, or in 1518.
(See EE, I, 438, n. 17)

stances defeated his plans time and again.[74] Opportunity and desire finally met in 1506 when he was commissioned to accompany the two sons of the Italian physician of Henry VII to Italy where they were to complete their education.

Why did Erasmus want to go to Italy? We might suppose that the central place of Italy in the revival of classical literature and rhetorical excellence would be reason enough. And doubtless this lure played a part. But Erasmus' early expressions of sentiment for Italy state a much more concrete and limited aim: the acquisition of a doctorate in theology from the University of Bologna.[75] At the time when he actually made the journey, however, his stated aim was different. "We have come to Italy," he says, "principally for the sake

[74]In a late recollection (1535) Erasmus says he was thrice disappointed in his desire to go to Italy, once when he was seventeen, a second time at the age of twenty when he hoped to go from Holland, and a third time at the age of twenty-eight when he thought he might make the journey from Paris. He finally went, he says, when he was nearly forty. *(Responsio ad Petri Cursii defensionem,* LB, X, 1750E) His second disappointment doubtless refers to his association with the Bishop of Cambrai as the latter's secretary. The bishop was planning a trip to Italy in search of a cardinal's hat, but the journey was called off. To assuage Erasmus' disappointment he allowed the young man to go to Paris and enter the university as a candidate for a theological degree. Erasmus at this time was not twenty, however, but twenty-six.

Erasmus' earliest statement of his wish to travel to Italy occurs in a letter written from Paris in 1498 in which he explains why he cannot go that year (EE, I, 202, lines 13-20; Nichols, I, 160). During the next year, however, he speaks in one letter as if confident that he will make the trip to Bologna before the year is over (EE, I, 234, lines 25-29; Nichols, I, 194-95). Instead, he went to England and asserts that Mountjoy's bringing him to England prevented his traveling to Italy (EE, I, 273, lines 8-10; Nichols, I, 225). Once back in Paris in 1500, he speaks hopefully of making the journey (EE, I, 288, lines 61-62; Nichols, I, 236), but the opportunity continued to elude him.

[75]William Herman, writing to Servatius Roger after a visit by Erasmus to Steyn in February, 1499, says: "After Easter, Erasmus is to go to Bologna.... If things go on well, he will return in triumph with his degree." (EE, I, 228, lines 6-8; Nichols, I, 190) And Erasmus himself, writing to his friend James Batt from Paris one year later (April, 1500), asserts: "In the autumn, if possible, I shall go to Italy to take my Doctor's degree...." (EE, I, 288, line 61; Nichols, I, 236) Again, in 1501 he writes: "I have long felt the necessity of two things: to visit Italy, so that my little learning may derive an authority from the celebrity of the place, and to take the title of Doctor." (EE, I, 344, lines 105-7; Nichols, I, 296)

of Greek. . . ."[76] That is, he wanted to perfect the Greek studies on which he had striven so hard for several years past. Erasmus' assertions near the end of his life (1531) that "when I came to Italy, I knew more Greek and Latin than I do now" and that "I am not indebted to Italy for any letters that I have; I wish I owed her more" must be taken in the context of polemics against Italian critics who were calling into question both his erudition and his character.[77] That intentions expressed contemporary with the journey itself are more accurate is borne out by the events which marked Erasmus' stay in Italy.[78]

His party departed London in June and went to Paris, where Erasmus remained until August, supervising a revised edition of the *Adagia Collectanea*. In understanding one aspect of the significance of Erasmus' visit to Italy, it is important to take note of this revision. Twenty-three proverbs were added to the 818 of the first edition, making the total 841. The additions were largely from Greek authors; moreover, Greek equivalents were given for 143 additional proverbs. This was Erasmus' second effort to make use of Greek in his published writings, and it helped correct the slightness of the Greek in the 1500 edition of the *Adagia,* which he later (1535) looked back upon as an embarrassment.[79]

His first stop in Italy, September, 1506, was Turin, where he received the degree of doctorate in theology (dated September 4, 1506). Erasmus regarded it as important insofar as it conferred upon him an authority to speak about the-

---

[76]EE, I, 433, lines 2-3; Nichols, I, 420.

[77]The critic in this case was Alberto Pio. The passages quoted may be found in LB, IX, 1136, 1137, and are translated in Nichols, I, 446, 447.

[78]Erasmus' biographers paid little attention to his Italian journey before the end of the nineteenth century. E. H. R. Tatham was among the first to call attention to this lacuna ("Erasmus in Italy," *The English Historical Review*, X, [1895] pp. 642-62). Three years later Pierre de Nolhac published his *Erasme en Italie* (Paris: C. Klincksieck, 1898), an analysis of Erasmus' Italian journey based in part on previously unknown correspondence. In all essential respects, his remains the standard account; little has been added in the intervening years. More recent studies will be noted below in connection with specific points in my analysis.

[79]EE, XI, 183, lines 468-69.

ological matters,[80] even though, both in the passage asserting this and in another referring to the degree in his correspondence, he represents his friends as more eager for the degree to be conferred upon him than he was himself.[81] This is probably a false modesty, since Erasmus' desire for a doctorate in theology had by this time a long history and indeed was, as we have seen, his earliest stated reason for wanting to go to Italy. Nonetheless, at this point in his life, it was not his principal reason for the journey; otherwise he would have turned back. He did not do so but went instead to his intended destination, Bologna. From there, however, he was almost immediately driven by the approach of the papal army led by Julius II, seeking to take the city from the ruling Bentivogli. Erasmus took refuge in Florence, where he spent several weeks translating Lucian from Greek into Latin, occupying himself in this way, he said, so that he might not be without any occupation at all.[82] Erasmus seems not to have been at all mindful of the fact that at the time Leonardo da Vinci, Michelangelo, Raphael, Fra Bartolomeo, and Andrea del Sarto were at work in the city and that the secretary of the republic was Machiavelli.[83] The humanist scholar had his mind set on classical literature, especially Greek; anything outside that province failed to capture his attention or interest.

Erasmus arrived in Bologna in time to see Julius II ride triumphantly into the city at the head of his conquering army (November 11, 1506),[84] an event that was later to become the subject of a scathing satire from Erasmus' pen, *Julius Excluded from Heaven.*[85] He could not be too critical

[80]EE, I, 432, lines 4-6; Nichols, I, 418.

[81]EE, I, 432, lines 8-10; Nichols, I, 419.

[82]EE, I, 435, lines 33-37; Nichols, I, 421. These were published by Badius in Paris in November, 1506. See below, p. 75.

[83]See Nolhac, *Erasme en Italie,* p. 13.

[84]Erasmus' contemporary references to this event are oblique. He said only that "Pope Julius fights, conquers, triumphs, and in fact plays the part of Julius to perfection." (EE, I, 435, lines 38-39; Nichols, I, 421) But in his later writings he says at least twice explicitly that he witnessed Julius' triumphal entry (LB, VI, 455F; LB, IX, 361A).

[85]On this work, see below, pp. 78-79 and n. 119.

at the time (or at least, he could not be too open in his criticism), for he owed to Julius II a dispensation from the requirement of wearing his normal dress while in Bologna, a favor he requested because his habit resembled the dress of doctors treating victims of the plague.[86] This became the precedent for dispensations later granted him by Leo X assuring him freedom against possible recall to his monastery at Steyn.[87]

Erasmus remained in Bologna for thirteen months, from November, 1506, until December, 1507. While there he developed a close friendship with Paolo Bombasius, a professor of Greek in the University of Bologna at the time, in whose home he lived. How much Erasmus participated in the life of the university is not known. Doubtless, however, he profited much from his friend's knowledge of Greek to advance his own studies in that language. Much of his own work in Bologna was later lost, in particular, the editing of the later books of the *Antibarbari*[88] and declamations on the advantages and disadvantages of the monastic life. He also continued to work on his adages and on revisions of his two translations of Euripides published by Badius in Paris in 1506. It was this work in Greek which brought him into contact with the famous printer Aldus Manutius (1449-1515) and led to his remaining in Italy much longer than he had originally intended. In October, 1507, Erasmus wrote to Aldus, requesting that he reprint his translations of Euripides in the typography for which he had become famous.[89] Although justly famous since 1494, the Aldine Press had published nothing in 1506 or 1507 because of the tur-

---

[86]On two occasions in his later correspondence (1514, 1516) he describes the difficulty in which his ecclesiastical dress almost involved him (EE, I, 571, lines 171-91; Nichols, II, 148-49; EE, II, 304-5, lines 470-96; Nichols, II, 357-58).

[87]On the later dispensations see Allen's introduction and sources cited, EE, II, 291-93.

[88]See above, ch. I, n. 61.

[89]EE, I, 437-39; Nichols, I, 428-30. This letter is the earliest known specimen of Erasmus' own handwriting. A facsimile is reprinted in Nolhac, *Erasme en Italie.*

moil created by the wars in Italy. One might wonder whether Aldus would choose Erasmus, who was not that well known at the time, as the first author for his restored press to publish. He did accept Erasmus' offer, however,[90] and the slender volume was published in December, 1507. It was the only publication of the Aldine Press during that year.

Erasmus left Bologna and hastened to Venice,[91] where he was gladly received into Aldus' household and invited to join his "New Academy," a group of scholars both Italian and Greek who pledged themselves to speak only in Greek at meals and in regular gatherings called for the purpose. In the "statutes" of the New Academy, a fine was imposed upon any member who committed a solecism. After enough fines were collected, the statutes provided that Aldus should prepare a banquet for the members. Outsiders were welcome provided they spoke Greek or were willing to learn it and abide by the rules. Only ridicule of the group's purpose and failure to maintain the integrity of Greek were grounds for expulsion.[92] Erasmus did not profit from the New Academy as much as he might have. A northern European of delicate health, he required both more food and food more carefully chosen than Aldus provided, and to assure both he received Aldus' permission to eat alone in his room.[93]

[90]See Erasmus' second letter to Aldus from Bologna: EE, I, 440-42; Nichols, I, 432-35.

[91]On Erasmus' stay in Venice, see Deno John Geanakoplos, *Greek Scholars in Venice* (Cambridge: Harvard University Press, 1962), ch. 9.

[92]The statutes have been printed in Ambroise Firmin-Didot, *Alde Manuce et l'Hellénisme à Venise* (Paris: Firmin-Didot, 1875), pp. 435-40, who provides both the Greek text of the statutes and a French translation.

[93]Erasmus attributed his subsequent trouble with kidney stone to the bad wine he drank in Venice. In one of his later (1531) colloquies, *Opulentia sordida* (C. R. Thompson, *The Colloquies of Erasmus*, pp. 488-99), Erasmus satirizes in what many have regarded as a cruel way the experience of eating in the Aldine household. The colloquy was not meant, however, to reflect ingratitude toward an old friend; nor indeed did it reflect the considered opinion of Erasmus. Rather, it was in direct response to Julius Caesar Scaliger, an Italian resentful of Erasmus' attack against the imitation of Cicero *(Ciceronianus,* 1528), who accused Erasmus of immoderate eating habits during his stay in Venice. Erasmus' venom was intended for Scaliger, not for Aldus. See M. M. Phillips, *The Adages of Erasmus*, pp. 62-69.

The *Ciceronianus* has been translated into English and analyzed by Izora

Even so, Erasmus' contacts with members of the New Academy were regular and intense. He had come to Venice primarily to work on a new edition of the *Adagia*. The composition of that volume as it finally issued from the Aldine Press in September, 1508, was heavily indebted to the Greek scholars of the New Academy, as Erasmus himself testifies in a passage added in 1526 to one of his commentaries in the *Adagia* of 1508:

> At a time when I, a Dutchman, was supervising the publication of my book of proverbs in Italy, every one of the scholars who were there offered me, without being asked, copies of authors which had never been printed, and which they thought I might be able to use. Aldus himself kept nothing back among his treasures. It was the same with John Lascaris, Baptista Egnatius, Marcus Musurus, Frater Urbanus.[94] I experienced the kindness of some whom I did not know either by sight or by name. I brought nothing with me to Venice but the raw material of a future work, as yet confused and undigested, and culled only from well-known authors. It was great audacity on my part that set us both on, myself to write and Aldus to print. We broke the back of the work in nine months, more or less, and meanwhile I had had an encounter with a trouble I had not met before, the stone. Imagine how much of value I should have missed, if the scholars had not furnished me with manuscripts. Among these were the works of Plato in Greek, Plutarch's *Lives* and his *Moralia*, which

Scott, *The Imitation of Cicero* (New York: Columbia University Press, 1910). There have been three recent critical editions: Julian Gerard Michel, *Etude sur le Ciceronianus d'Erasme avec une edition critique* (Ph.D. thesis: University of Paris, 1951), which contains a French translation as well as a critical text; Angiolo Gambaro, *Il Ciceroniano* (Brescia: LaScuola, 1965); and Pierre Mesnard, EOO, I.2, 581-710.

On Scaliger, see Vernon Hall, "Life of Julius Caesar Scaliger," *Transactions of the American Philosophical Society*, New Series, XL, (1950), 85-170, esp. 96-114.

[94] John Lascaris (1445-1534) and Marcus Musurus (1470-1517) were Greek. (On them see Geanakoplos, *Greek Scholars in Venice*, ch. 5 [on Musurus] and *passim*); Baptista Egnatius (1473-1553) and Frater Urbanus (1440-1524) were Italians; all were members of the New Academy. Frater Urbanus was the first to publish a Greek grammar in Italian.

began publication just as my work was ending; the
Deipnosophistai of Atheneus, Aphthonius, Herm-
ogenes with the commentary, the *Rhetoric* of Aristotle with the notes of Gregory Nazianzen; Aris-
tides together with the notes, the little commentaries on Hesiod and Theocritus, the collection of
proverbs which goes under the name of Plutarch,
and the other called after Apostolius, which was
lent me by Jerome Aleander.[95] There were other
less important things, which have either escaped my
memory or need not be mentioned here. None of
these had hitherto been printed.[96]

The Aldine edition of the *Adagia* is no longer called *Adagia
Collectanea* but rather *Adagia Chiliades*. A glance at its composition reveals that it is in fact as well as in name a new
book and that Greek scholarship is largely responsible for
the difference. Instead of 818 adages (or 841 in the 1507 edition of the *Collectanea*) there are 3260. Of these, about four-
fifths are either new or substantially altered in form. And
2734 contain Greek passages of two to six lines or more in
length.[97] This was the edition in which the *Adagia* was given
the structure it was to retain, even though Erasmus continued to expand subsequent editions until the final edition
contained more than 4000 adages. The transformation from
the Paris edition of the *Collectanea* to the Aldine edition of
the *Chiliades* reveals the intensity and depth of Erasmus'
work with Greek scholars and manuscripts.

It is important to note as well that the Greek sources
with which Erasmus worked were largely manuscript
sources. Although Erasmus had worked with Latin manu-

---

[95]Aleander (1480-1542) worked closely with Erasmus in Venice; the two
even roomed together for a time. Later, when Aleander became a papal
legate and deeply involved in the turmoil with Luther, he and Erasmus developed great suspicion for one another. Until he learned better, Erasmus
attributed Scaliger's attack on him to Aleander, since it betrayed a knowledge of his stay in Venice with which only a person who was present could
have been familiar. On him, see EE, I, 502-3, introduction to Epistle 256.

[96]Phillips, *The Adages of Erasmus*, pp. 185-86. For a discussion of Erasmus' sources, see *ibid.*, pp. 86-95.

[97]See Phillips, *The Adages of Erasmus*, p. 75; Geanakoplos, *Greek Scholars
in Venice*, p. 272.

scripts in England and had published Valla's *Notes on the New Testament* from a manuscript copy, he had not previously edited manuscripts with a view to the publication of a more accurate text. He first engaged in this process in Venice. He gives expression to its difficulty in his commentary on the adage, *The Labors of Hercules:*

> And now, shall I mention another thing—the bad state of the books themselves, whether Latin or Greek MSS, so corrupt that when you want to quote a passage you hardly ever find one which does not show an obvious error, or make one suspect a hidden one? Here is another labor, to examine and correct the different MSS ... and a great many of them, so as to detect one which has a better reading, or by collating a number of them to make a guess at the true and authentic version. This must be done, if not all the time, at least whenever you quote, and quotations occur everywhere.[98]

And further below he adds:

> Now consider this with me; in other books there is often room for the mind to operate, there is the pleasure of discovery or creation, there is the possibility at any time, in any place, of completing a part of the work by sheer mental activity, and of hastening on your project by the quickness of your brain; here you are fettered to the treadmill, you cannot budge an inch, as they say, from your texts. You waste your eyesight on decaying volumes covered with mold, torn and mangled, eaten into everywhere by worms and beetles, and often almost illegible; in short, they are so bad that anyone who spends long over them may easily bring on himself decay and premature old age; they may even contain extraneous matter. How important that is I need hardly say—those who make trial of it find that out at once. Not to speak of that fact that if there is any pleasure in this kind of commentary it is for the reader alone, and nothing belongs to the writer except that hateful and monotonous busi-

II

[98]Phillips, *The Adages of Erasmus*, p. 197.

ness of collecting, scraping together, explaining, translating."[99]

This is a complaint Erasmus was to echo often as he worked on his critical edition of the New Testament. Venice was his apprenticeship for his later work in Basel.[100]

The list of manuscript sources cited by Erasmus as having been made available to him at the Aldine Press was almost exclusively manuscripts of Greek classical literature as opposed to patristic theological texts. In his letter of dedication to Lord Mountjoy, Erasmus says of the 1508 edition of the *Adagia:*

> The theological allegories, being proper to my profession, I propose to treat when I have the Greek volumes required for the purpose; and I shall do this the more readily, as I see that for many centuries this important subject has been neglected, while theologians are spending their entire pains upon subtle questions, which might be discussed without blame, if they did not exclude everything else.[101]

Italy allowed Erasmus to complete the training necessary for the tasks he was envisioning for himself, though it did not provide the ethos for that work.

The Aldine edition of the *Adagia Chiliades* did more

[99]*Ibid.*, p. 198. This passage anticipates Erasmus' satire on the follies of scholarly labor in *The Praise of Folly*, written one year after the adage quoted: "Let us go about, then, and compare the lot of the wise man with that of the fool. Fancy some pattern of wisdom to put up against him, a man who wore out his whole boyhood and youth in pursuing the learned disciplines. He wasted the pleasantest time of life in unintermitted watchings, cares, and studies; and through the remaining part of it he never tasted so much as a tittle of pleasure; always frugal, impecunious, sad, austere; unfair and strict toward himself, morose and unamiable to others; afflicted by pallor, leanness, invalidism, sore eyes, premature age and white hair; dying before his appointed day. By the way, what difference does it make when a man of that sort dies? He has never lived. There you have a clear picture of the wise man." (Hudson, ed., pp. 50-51)

[100]See Eileen Bloch, "Erasmus and the Froben Press: The Making of an Editor," *The Library Quarterly*, XXXV:II (April, 1965), p. 112; Raymond Marcel, "Les dettes d'Erasme envers l'Italie," in *Actes du Congres Erasme* (Amsterdam: North Holland Publishing Company, 1971), p. 166.

[101]EE, I, 445, lines 36-41; Nichols, I, 443.

than place the crown on Erasmus' Greek studies. It also made him a famous man. Previously known to limited circles among humanists in places Erasmus had personally visited, he now became a well-known figure to all men of learning and power in Europe. And this perhaps conferred upon him a greater authority than did the doctorate in theology which he obtained for the purpose. Erasmus was now a man to be listened to.

Even so, Erasmus had not received everything he was to take with him from Italy. Shortly after the *Adagia Chiliades* came off the press in Venice, Erasmus departed and made his way to Rome. He was in and out of the eternal city three times between February and July, 1509, when he left Italy, never to return. His reputation preceded him, and he was received as a royal guest when he arrived. Among the friends he made may be numbered Giovanni de Medici, later Pope Leo X (to whom he dedicated his edition of the New Testament), Cardinal Grimani (to whom he dedicated his first paraphrase, that on Romans), Cardinal Riario, and Tommaso Inghirami, librarian of the Vatican. Inghirami offered him the use of the Vatican archives, and Grimani, whose personal library numbered eight thousand volumes, suggested that Erasmus might live and work in his home. In a letter written to Cardinal Grimani six years after he left Italy, Erasmus describes his last meeting with the Cardinal, in which he was almost persuaded to remain in Rome, and says that he failed to return to the Cardinal's house before departing because he was afraid he might never leave had he done so. He even suggests that he may have made the wrong choice; he often longs for Italy.[102]

Nolhac says that if Erasmus had remained in Rome he would have exercised much more influence on the Catholic hierarchy than he did and that his enemies within the Church would not have dared to attack him, but that

---

[102]EE, II, 73-79; Nichols, II, 183-90. See also a letter written to Riario at the same time: EE, II, 68-73; Nichols, II, 191-94 (some omissions).

He expressed a similar longing even earlier, while domiciled in England (1512). See EE, I, 499-500, lines 4-9; Nichols, II, 60.

Erasmus sacrificed all this for his freedom.[103] Renaudet goes even further, stating that Erasmus' leaving Rome "was the greatest error of his life, and without doubt also his greatest misfortune. It was perhaps also a misfortune for western Christianity."[104] But it may also be that Erasmus sacrificed the peace he might have had in Italy for the fulfillment of his mission as a scholar, for which he was now fully prepared. In point of fact, he did obtain the protection of his Roman friends. It is true that much time in his later years was given over to polemics. But had he remained in Rome the climate there might have continued to draw him in the direction of classical (pagan) scholarship. In later years he was critical of the religious life of the city, suggesting that it was more reminiscent of classical Greece or Rome than of the apostles.[105] Perhaps, then, in maintaining his freedom Erasmus made possible the fulfillment of his career as a Christian scholar.

However that may be, Erasmus was drawn away from Italy by promises that were as unbelievable as they seemed real. Henry VII died on April 21, 1509. Upon the accession of Henry VIII, Erasmus received a letter from his patron, Lord Mountjoy, urging him to come to England and to receive the bounty of a king who appreciated and loved men of letters.[106] He left almost at once to spend the next five years in England.

Erasmus left Italy with much more than he had entered. On the formal side, he had obtained the authority of a doctorate of theology and the authority of the fame that accompanied the expanded edition of the *Adagia*. More substantively, he had acquired a much deeper knowledge of Greek

---

[103]*Erasme en Italie*, p. 90. Nolhac concludes: "Erasmus entered into his glory, but he ceased being happy." (p. 91)

[104]Augustin Renaudet, *Erasme et l'Italie* (Geneva: Droz, 1954), xi. See also, *ibid.*, p. 116, on the point made above by Nolhac.

[105]See his description of a sermon preached in the presence of Pope Julius II on the (ostensible) theme of the death of Christ. Erasmus says that the preacher spent more time praising Julius in the manner of a Roman orator than he did on the assigned theme. (EOO, I.2, 637-38; tr., Scott, *Ciceronianus*, pp. 62-63)

[106]EE, I, 449-52; Nichols, I, 457-60.

and of the art of editing manuscripts. Finally, he had acquired friends who in later years were to use their power to protect him and to make his controversial biblical work possible. In light of these conclusions, there is some justification for Renaudet's contention that both before (through Valla) and during his stay in Italy, Erasmus gained a critical philological perspective. But he goes too far in identifying this tool with Erasmus' Christian humanism. The tool itself was neutral, and as Erasmus observed at first hand while in Italy, it could be used for non-Christian purposes, Renaudet also errs in allying the critical philological method with a "religion of pure spirit," that is, a nondogmatic religion of morality and practical piety. Erasmus' religious consciousness, as we shall see, will not bear that degree of reductionism. Erasmus took from Italy what he wanted. And what he wanted were very specific tools and credentials. His humanism, even apart from its religious aspects (which Renaudet admits were northern in origin, not Italian), was different from any "Italian" label that might be placed upon it. Italy definitely contributed to Erasmus' humanism, even his Christian humanism, but his humanism cannot within legitimate limits bear the name of Italy.[107]

'The Praise of Folly,' 1509

Erasmus' first work after his return from Italy was *The Praise of Folly*.[108] He wrote it shortly after he had arrived in

---

[107]See *Erasme et l'Italie*, pp. x, xi, 119, 172-73, *passim; Etudes erasmiennes,* ch. 4, (summary statement, p. 176).

[108]Still the only critical edition of the text is that of J. B. Kan, *Moriae Enkomion* (Hague: Martinus Nijhoff, 1898), though Clarence H. Miller is preparing a new one.

There have been several recent translations into English. I prefer H. H. Hudson, *The Praise of Folly* (New York: Modern Library, 1941), whose analysis of the rhetorical structure of the work (pp. 129-42) is very helpful. But see also John P. Dolan, ed., *The Essential Erasmus*, pp. 94-173; and W. T. H. Jackson, ed., *Essential Works of Erasmus* (New York: Bantam Books, 1965), pp. 327-446, a reprint of the translation of Leonard Dean, 1946. See also C. H. Miller, "Current English Translations of 'The Praise of

England, while residing at the home of Thomas More[109] (to

Folly'; Some Corrections," *Philological Quarterly*, XLV:IV (October, 1966),
718-33.

There have been a number of book-length studies of the theme of folly
devoted to Erasmus and his contemporaries. In English, the best discussion
is Walter Kaiser, *Praisers of Folly: Erasmus, Rabelais, Shakespeare* (Cambridge: Harvard University Press, 1963), pp. 19-100. But see also Barbara
Swain, *Fools and Folly during the Middle Ages and the Renaissance* (New
York: Columbia University Press, 1932), esp. ch. 8. Shorter treatments also
very helpful are: Johan Huizinga, *Erasmus and the Age of Reformation*
(New York: Harper Torchbooks, 1957), ch. 9; M. M. Phillips, *Erasmus and
the Northern Renaissance*, ch. 3. The following recent works in German
should be especially noted: Barbara Könneker, *Wesen und Wandlung der
Narrenidee im Zeitalter des Humanismus: Brant, Murner, Erasmus* (Wies-
baden; Franz Steiner, 1966), ch. 5; Walter Nigg, *Der Christliche Narr*
(Zurich: Artemis, 1956), pp. 113-60; and Hans Schmitt, *Die Satire des
Erasmus von Rotterdam und ihre Australhung auf Rabelais, Alfonso de
Valdes, und Cristobal de Villalon* (Gelnhausen: F. W. Kalbfleish, 1965).

The *Praise of Folly* was prophetic of Erasmus' future in a sense different
from that discussed in my text: it was the occasion of his first public dispute.
His antagonist was a Louvain theologian and old friend, Martin Dorp. On
the literature of this debate, see below, this chapter, note 158. With publication of his New Testament in 1516, Erasmus was to become embroiled in
continuous controversy for the remainder of his life.

[109]In his dedicatory letter to More, Erasmus says that he wrote it while he
was returning from Italy (EE, I, 460, lines 1-11; Nichols, II, 2; the letter is
translated in English editions of the work; in the edition I follow, that of
H. H. Hudson, see p. 1). But this is a literary fiction. What is likely true is
that he conceived the idea and even jotted down some notes while en route.
But as he notes in two later letters, the work was written while he was living
in More's home. The first statement is his letter in 1515 to Martin Dorp, a
theologian at the University of Louvain, who had attacked Erasmus for publishing the treatise (on their controversy see the preceding note). Erasmus
wrote at one point in his reply: "But how did I come to do this thing? I was
staying for a while with my friend More after my return from Italy, and my
kidney pains were confining me to the house for a few days. My collection
of books was not yet delivered to me. And even if they had been brought,
the illness did not permit the strain of any serious study anyway. So I began
during my inactivity to play around with the idea of an encomium of Folly,
not, of course, with the intention of publishing anything, but rather to re-
lieve the discomfort of my illness with this sort of relaxation. I showed a
little bit of the work I had begun to some friends, just to share the fun with
someone and make it more amusing. Since they found great pleasure in it,
they insisted that I continue. I yielded, and in this task I spent seven days,
more or less, an expenditure of time which indeed seemed to exceed the
value of the theme." (EE, II, 94, lines 126-36; tr. in full in John C. Olin, ed.,
Christian Humanism and the Reformation, pp. 55-91, this passage, p. 61).
Still later, in the catalogue of his writings (letter to John Botzheim), Eras-

whom the work is dedicated), though it was not published until 1511. It is the book for which Erasmus is best known today, and all his biographers rightly pay close attention to it. Almost all interpreters recognize three parts to the work: a first section in which folly playfully and ironically mocks the foibles of man; a second section in which the playful mode is dropped and serious satire obtains; and a third section in which Christianity is foolishness—the foolishness which seeks the spiritual rather than the material and so from a worldly point of view is mad. Every critic has sought to interpret the *literary* meaning of this structure. But none of them has recognized the significance of the work in Erasmus' intellectual development. Analysis of the latter helps clarify the literary meaning in a way overlooked by other interpreters of the work, though what follows does not propose to be an exhaustive literary analysis.

First, it should be noted that the ironic satire in *The Praise of Folly* owes a good deal to Erasmus' Greek studies, especially to his affection for Lucian of Samosota (ca. 120-180), the most outstanding satiric critic of the hellenistic world.[110] During his stay in England in 1505 and 1506, Erasmus translated ten of Lucian's longer dialogues; his friend Thomas More translated another four. One of these, *The Tyrannicide,* was translated by both, and each wrote a declamation in reply to Lucian.[111] Erasmus left the translations and declamations with the printer, Josse Badius, on his way to Italy in 1506. While domiciled in Florence, awaiting the outcome of hostilities between the Pope and the Bentivogli in Bologna, Erasmus translated eighteen additional short dialogues and sent these to Badius in Paris. Badius published the twenty-eight translations of Erasmus together with the four by More and the declamations of the two men in No-

mus states once again that he wrote the work while residing at the home of Thomas More (EE, I, 19, line 6).

[110]Lucian's writings are most readily available in the Loeb Classical Library (7 vols.).

[111]See C. R. Thompson, *The Translations of Lucian by Erasmus and St. Thomas More* (Ithaca: Cornell University Press, 1940), pp. 29-44, for a summary and discussion of these declamations.

vember, 1506. [112] After his return to England in 1509, Erasmus once again turned to Lucian, translating eight additional treatises between 1509 and 1513. Seven of these were published in June, 1514, again by Badius.[113] One was lost and has only recently been recovered and published.[114] Of these thirty-six, only nine had been previously translated. Hence Erasmus did a great deal to make Lucian known.[115]

C. R. Thompson, the scholar who has given most attention to Erasmus' translations of Lucian, writes that

> One who possesses an ironic temper will derive the most pleasure from Lucian. Erasmus was such a man; hence his fondness for the writings of that author. He was the paramount Lucianist of the Renaissance. There were other Lucianists in his time, to be sure, but there was none greater, and none more generally praised and condemned for being such, than he. His *Moriae Encomium* was indisputably the best of the many Lucianic compositions of the age.[116]

It was doubtless through Lucian that Erasmus (as also Thomas More) came to understand the potential power of satiric irony in literature. Even so, he employed it to an end very different from Lucian, who was content simply to hold philosophic and religious ideas (among other things) up to ridicule. Erasmus wanted to ridicule them in the interest of transforming what was ridiculous (and perhaps evil) into something moral and more rational. Lucian might have written the first section of *The Praise of Folly,* but he would never have written the equivalent of the third section, in

[112]For the various prefatory letters to these translations, see EE, I, 416-17; Nichols, I, 391-92 (lines 19-28 omitted); EE, I, 422-24; Nichols, I, 406-9; EE, I, 424-26; Nichols, I, 371 (lines 1-29 and 41-61 omitted); EE, I, 429-30; Nichols, I, 409; EE, I, 430-31; Nichols, I, 415; EE, I, 434-35; Nichols, I, 420-21 (lines 3-23 omitted).

[113]For the prefatory letters to these, see EE, I, 512-13; Nichols, II, 65; EE, I, 561-62; Nichols, II, 133-34.

[114]C. R. Thompson, "Erasmus' Translation of Lucian's *Longaevi*," *Classical Philology*, XXXV:IV (October, 1940), 397-415.

[115]Thompson, *The Translations of Lucian*, p. 20.

[116]*Ibid.*, p. 1; see also, p. 45.

which folly is transformed by the humility of faith into a wisdom that includes reason but also transcends it. The praise of folly has as its end, not simply the display of the human condition, but also its reform.

This is nowhere more evident than in section 2, which in this respect is the point of connection between sections 1 and 3. In this section, for the first time in his writings, Erasmus engaged in *social* commentary for which he was from this time forward to become famous. The clue to the meaning of his section is *whom* he satirizes. In his transition from the first to the second section of the treatise, he writes: ". . . I suggest that for a time we shall look into the lives of men, and it will be apparent how much they owe to me and how many, the greatest along with the humble, follow me. *We shall not run over the lives of everybody, for that would take too long, but only the most notable;* from which it will be easy to form an opinion about the others."[117]

It is men in powerful places who are the targets of Erasmus' satiric barbs: merchants ("the most foolish and sordid of all"), learned men who instruct or write for others (grammarians or teachers of youth, rhetoricians, poets), lawyers, scientists, theologians, monks, kings and nobles, popes, cardinals, and bishops.[118] Criticism of those in power within the church bulks largest. The theologians, of course, Erasmus had criticized as early as his Paris years. But his criticisms take on much more significance when placed in the context of the responsibility of the learned and powerful for those below them in rank and power. What we have here, in other

---

[117]Hudson, ed., *The Praise of Folly*, p. 67, emphasis added.

[118]*Ibid.*, pp. 69-104. In two places in his later writings, Erasmus spoke of the social order as three concentric circles around Christ as its center. In the first circle was the ecclesiastical order, in the second the political order, and in the third the common people. Implicit in this notion of concentric circles is one we find clearly expressed in *The Praise of Folly* for the first time: that those who have greater power also have greater responsibility (to be like Christ). See, EE, III, 368-71, lines 231-371; tr. J. C. Olin, *Christian Humanism and the Reformation*, pp. 118-23; and in Holborn, pp. 202-4. Both these passages were written during the same year, the first in a letter prefaced to a new edition of the *Enchiridion*, the second in his treatise on theological method, *Ratio verae theologiae*.

words, is the first clear indication that Erasmus' program of scholarship had as its goal the reform of *society,* both political and (above all) religious. *The Praise of Folly* owed to Italy both evidence for corruption within the church (Erasmus had been dismayed by the actions of Julius II and by life in Rome among the religious) and the sense of confidence and authority necessary to call attention to it. From *The Praise of Folly* on, virtually everything Erasmus wrote had as its intention the reform of some aspect of society—the conduct of the schools, the behavior of rulers, the restoration of piety within the Christian church through reform of the church's leaders and structures. *The Praise of Folly* is inconceivable before 1509. Viewed in the context of a growing vision of his own life and its significance, it was a fusion of concerns he had long entertained literally bursting forth.

Striking confirmation of this interpretation is to be found in other works in which Erasmus was engaged between the time he wrote and published *The Praise of Folly* (1509-1511). One of these, *Julius Exclusus a coelis (Julius Excluded from Heaven),* represents the "warrior pope," Julius II, as prevented by St. Peter from entering heaven. The satiric irony of the treatise only makes the accusation (and the affront) all the stronger. Erasmus never explicitly owned authorship of the work, though he never explicitly denied authorship either.[119] The fact that (unlike *The Praise*

---

[119]For a recent survey of the evidence on the question of Erasmus' authorship of the work, see R. H. Bainton, "Erasmus and Luther and the Dialog Julius exclusus," in *Vierhundertfünfzig Jahre lutherische Reformation, 1517-1967. Festschrift für Franz Lau zum 60. Geburtstag* (Göttingen: Vandenhoeck and Ruprecht, 1967), pp. 17-26. There is an excellent discussion in Wallace K. Ferguson, *Erasmi Opuscula* (The Hague: Martinus Nijhoff, 1933), pp. 38-64, which also contains a text of the work (pp. 65-124), omitted from the Leiden edition of the *Opera Omnia.* The work has recently been translated into English by Paul Pascal, *The Julius Exclusus of Erasmus* (Bloomington: Indiana University Press, 1968), and is preceded by an introduction by J. K. Sowards. See also the latter's article, "The Two Lost Years of Erasmus: Summary, Review, and Speculation," *Studies in the Renaissance,* IX (1962), pp. 161-86, in which he speculates that one reason we have no correspondence from Erasmus' pen between 1509 and 1511 is that the correspondence was filled with the name of Julius and would be incriminating; hence, he had it destroyed.

of Folly) it satirized a particular individual—and one to whom Erasmus in the past had been indebted for favors received—explains his attitude.[120] But it is his work and shows him expressing a growing outrage at abuses of power and authority within the church.

Even more significant is Erasmus' revision of the *Adagia*, completed between 1509 and 1512[121] and published in 1515. In the 1508 (Aldine) edition, the first in which Erasmus added substantial commentaries of his own to the proverbs, all his commentaries had to do with learning and the problems associated with its acquisition and dissemination. The 1515 edition, by contrast, deals in a critical and satirical way (reminiscent of the second edition of *The Praise of Folly*) with the responsibilities and foibles of kings [122] and clergymen,[123] as well as with the foolishness of

---

[120]Erasmus, however, does mention Julius by name in the *Sileni Alcibiadis,* which was written during these years. But that commentary was not published until after the pope died. (See Phillips, *The Adages of Erasmus,* pp. 285-87). The pope's name begins to appear also in the correspondence after his death. Erasmus makes reference to him as a warrior pope in a letter written only three days after the consecration of his successor, Leo X (EE, I, 553, lines 82-84; Nichols, II, 123). This strengthens the case made by Sowards (see the preceding note) that before Julius died, Erasmus' letters had made similar references to the pope. Julius is also referred to critically by name in *On Copia of Words and Ideas* (tr., D. B. King and H. D. Rix [Milwaukee: Marquette University Press, 1963], pp. 63-64); this treatise was published in 1512, before the pope died.

[121]In the autumn of 1512, Erasmus wrote from London: "I have put in shape the work on Proverbs and so enriched it as to make it quite a different book, and, if I am not mistaken, a much better one, though it was not so very bad before." (EE, I, 517, lines 6-8; Nichols, II, 119). See also, Phillips, *The Adages of Erasmus,* p. 103.

[122]The adage, "Kings and Fools are Born, Not Made," (Phillips, *The Adages of Erasmus,* pp. 213-25) begins with the observation that although the most humble profession requires acquisition of the proper credentials, kingship, which is much more important to mankind, is hereditary. Since this state of affairs cannot be changed, the next best thing is to educate a prince. Erasmus then proceeds to state nine precepts that a teacher should impart to a king, all of them designed to teach the future king a sense of the *limitation* of his power.

This adage anticipates both his educational treatise *De ratione studii (On the Right Method of Instruction),* which will be discussed below, and his *Institutio principis Christiani (Education of a Christian Prince).* A critical edition of this latter treatise has recently appeared. Werner Welzig, *Erasmus*

war,[124] calling men of power to reform themselves and their offices. The *Sileni Alcibiadis (The Sileni of Alcibiades)*, one of his most famous commentaries in the *Adagia*, is character-

von Rotterdam Ausgewählte Schriften (Darmstadt: Wissenschaftlichs Buchgesellschaft, 1968), V, 111-357. It has been translated into English with a long and helpful introduction: Lester K. Born, *The Education of a Christian Prince* (New York: Columbia University Press, 1936; reprinted Octagon Books, 1965).

Some of his ideas on kingship, as on war and peace (see below, n. 124), are anticipated in the *Panegyricus* to Phillip of Burgundy in 1504 (LB, IV, 505-54; for the introductory epistle, composed while the work was in press, see EE, I, 395-97; Nichols, I, 363-65), as they are in his prefaces to his translations of Lucian (see above, n. 112). But now these tendencies came together in a self-conscious way.

[123]See the adages in Phillips, *Ignavis semper feriae sunt (For the lazy it is always a holiday)*, pp. 267-69, and the *Sileni Alcibiadis (The Sileni of Alcibiades)*, pp. 269-96, which will be discussed below.

[124]In 1511 or 1512 Erasmus wrote *Dulce bellum inexpertis (War is sweet to those who have not tried it)*. It was published in the 1515 edition of the *Adagia* (see Phillips, *The Adages of Erasmus*, pp. 308-53). A critical edition together with a French translation has recently appeared: Yvonne Remy and Rene Dunil-Marquebreucq, *Erasme: Dulce bellum inexpertis* (Brussels: Latomus, 1953).

In 1514 Erasmus wrote a long letter against war (EE, I, 551-54; Nichols, II, 120-25).

In 1517 he wrote *Querela Pacis (Complaint of Peace)*, his most famous work on the subject of war. A critical edition, together with a German translation has recently appeared: Werner Welzig, *Erasmus von Rotterdam: Ausgewählte Schriften*, V, 359-451. The treatise has been translated into English several times. Thomas Paynell's sixteenth-century translation was reprinted in a facsimile edition in 1946 (W. J. Hirten, ed., *The Complaint of Peace*, [New York: Scholars' Facsimiles and Reprints]). In 1950 the work appeared in a new translation (Jose Chapiro, ed., *Peace Protests!* [Boston: Beacon Press]); and again in 1964 (John P. Dolan, ed., *The Essential Erasmus* [New York: Mentor-Omega Books], pp. 174-204). The most complete analysis of the work is Elise Bagdat, *La 'Querela pacis' d'Erasme* (Paris: Presses Universitaires de France, 1924) which, in addition to analyzing sources, content, and influence of the work, translates it into French. See also Otto Herding, "*Querela Pacis*. Stil und Komposition," in *Actes du Congres d'Erasme*, pp. 69-87. In English, consult H. J. Hirten's introduction to the facsimile edition; R. H. Bainton, "The Querela Pacis of Erasmus, Classical and Christian Sources," *Archiv für Reformationsgeschichte*, XLII (1951), 32-48.

R. P. Adams, *The Better Part of Valor*, chs. 4-7, illuminates the political context in which these treatises on war were composed and shows that they belong to a humanist program for the reform of society. See especially ch. 6, his discussion of *Dulce bellum inexpertis*.

istic of Erasmus' criticisms. The Sileni, Erasmus comments, "were small images divided in half, and so constructed that they could be opened out and displayed; when closed they represented some ridiculous, ugly flute-player, but when opened they suddenly revealed the figure of a god, so that the amusing deception would show off the art of the carver." Thus, in a more generalized sense, the word is used "either with reference to a thing which in appearance seems ridiculous and contemptible, but on closer and deeper examination proves to be admirable, or else with reference to a person whose looks and dress do not correspond at all to what he conceals in his soul."[125] This sets the stage for Erasmus to expound straightforwardly what he had expressed ironically in *The Praise of Folly*. Socrates was a silenus. Externally, he was ugly, unfit for public affairs, and (so he said) knew nothing. But viewed from within, he rose above the pettiness of most men. There were other sileni, of whom the greatest was Christ. What power in weakness, what riches in poverty, what grandeur in humility did he not manifest. Within Christianity, many sileni have followed Christ, e.g., John the Baptist, the Apostles, and the great bishops of old. But the situation is reversed today.

> There are those who in name and appearance impose themselves as magistrates and guardians of the common weal, when in reality they are wolves and prey upon the state. There are those whom you would venerate as priests if you only looked at their tonsure, but if you look into the Silenus, you will find them more than laymen. Perhaps you will find some bishops too in the same case—if you watch that solemn consecration of theirs, if you contemplate them in their new robes, the mitre gleaming with jewels and gold, the crozier likewise encrusted with gems, the whole mystic panoply which clothes them from head to foot, you would take them to be divine beings, something more than human. But open the Silenus, and you find nothing but a soldier, a trader, or finally a despot, and you will de-

II

[125]Phillips, *The Adages of Erasmus*, p. 269.

cide that all those splendid insignia were pure comedy.[126]

In all his social criticism, Erasmus maintained the point of view established clearly in *The Praise of Folly* that the reform of society comes through the reform of its leaders rather than through a reform of its structures. His is much more a moral than a political critique. In this respect the judgment of J. H. Hexter is essentially correct:

> To the ancient and traditional social criticism and satire Erasmus imparted a high literary polish, and that is about all. His partial abandonment of the hierarchical framework on which that criticism had been hung, though probably not altogether conscious, is interesting; but it leaves his own efforts incoherent and invertebrate, lacking in the structural form which that framework provided for the writings of his predecessors. *The Praise of Folly, The Complaint of Peace,* and the long satirical adages are inadequate as social criticism because they point to the sickness of early sixteenth century Christendom but scarcely ever penetrate inward to discover the roots of the disease. Therefore their prescriptions, in the rare instances when anything so specific is suggested, are mere analgesics and plasters, not radical remedies.[127]

Hexter's judgment is, however, misleading. For while it is true that Erasmus lacked a detailed knowledge of politics and

---

[126]*Ibid.,* p. 277.

[127]J. H. Hexter, *More's Utopia: The Biography of an Idea* (New York: Harper Torchbooks, 1965), pp. 63-64. See also Fritz Caspari, "Erasmus on the Social Functions of Christian Humanism," *Journal of the History of Ideas,* VIII (1947), 78-106, who comes to a similar conclusion. Cf. C. R. Thompson, "Erasmus as Internationalist and Cosmopolitan," *Archiv für Reformationsgeschichte,* XLVI (1955), 191-95, for a statement more sympathetic to Erasmus on this issue. W. R. Scribner, *The Power of Wisdom: Social Thought of Erasmus, 1489-1518* (Master's Thesis: University of Sydney, Australia, 1967), fails to prove the counter-thesis that Erasmus' social commentary did involve a detailed knowledge of social institutions and actions necessary for their reform. At best he demonstrates a greater awareness of social complexity in Erasmus between *The Praise of Folly* and *The Education of a Christian Prince.* The evidence he cites only corroborates the thesis stated in the text, that Erasmus was a moral and religious rather than a political writer, and that his notion of reform followed the former rather than the latter stream.

government (a fact in itself not surprising), he did possess a much more detailed knowledge of the inner workings of religious institutions. And while he maintained with respect both to religion and politics that their reform hinged on the reform of leaders in each sphere, his judgments on theological method show that he did penetrate to the roots of the religious problem and that he made prescriptions for the remedy of the defects he discovered which were radical. All this becomes even more clear in the work of his Cambridge years, 1511-1514.

Preparation and Publication of the New Testament

The wealth promised Erasmus upon his return to England never materialized as he hoped it would.[128] As he said diplomatically on several occasions in his correspondence, he received more than he deserved but not as much as he needed. It was largely for this reason that in 1511 Erasmus accepted an offer from Bishop John Fisher to teach at Cambridge University. After a short visit to Paris in April, the purpose of which was to deposit the manuscript of *The Praise of Folly* with the printer Giles Gourmont (the work was published in June), he settled his affairs in London and made his way to Cambridge in August. There he remained until early in 1514, apart from visits to London as frequently as he could manage them.[129]

He was not long in Cambridge before we learn from his correspondence that he was busily engaged in completing his *De Copia verborum ac rerum (Copia of Words and Ideas)*.[130]

[128]In 1512 he wrote to a fellow countryman: "How often have I regretted that I did not embrace the fortune which you offered me three years ago at Louvain. At that time I was driven wild by exaggerated hopes and the mountains of gold I imagined in Britain. But fortune has lowered my crest; and now, if even a moderate provision be made for me there, I desire, like Ulysses, to see the smoke rising on my native land." (EE, I, 519, lines 11-15; Nichols, II, 84).

[129]A useful discussion of the various aspects of his life in Cambridge is H. C. Porter's "Introduction" in D. F. S. Thomson and H. C. Porter, eds., *Erasmus and Cambridge* (University of Toronto Press, 1963), pp. 3-103.

[130]In a letter from Cambridge to John Colet, dated October 29, 1511, Erasmus writes: "I am now entirely occupied with my *Copia*, so that it may

Erasmus made it ready for publication at the request of John Colet (to whom it is dedicated), who had used the fortune left him by his father to establish St. Paul's School for boys

be put as a sort of riddle—how can one be *in media Copia*, in the midst of abundance, and at the same time living in the greatest want? I only wish I could bring them both to an end together; for the *Copia* will soon be finished, if the Muses forward my studies better than Fortune has hitherto advanced my estate. This occupation has been in fact the reason why I have not answered your letter at greater length." (EE, I, 477, lines 1-5; Nichols, II, 34).

The work was published in 1512. In substantial part, it has recently been translated, *On Copia of Words and Ideas*, tr., D. B. King and H. D. Rix (Milwaukee: Marquette University Press, 1963). In addition to the introduction to the translation, see J. K. Sowards, "Erasmus and the Apologetic Textbook: A Study of the 'De duplici copia verborum ac rerum'," *Studies in Philology*, LV:II (April, 1958), 122-35.

Together with it, Erasmus issued an "authorized" version of the *De ratione studii (On the Right Method of Instruction)*, an earlier manuscript of which had fallen into the hands of an Englishman, William Thale, who surreptitiously published it in October, 1511 (see Allen's introduction to epistle 66: EE, I, 193). A loose translation into English has been made by W. H. Woodward, *Desiderius Erasmus Concerning the Aim and Method of Education*, pp. 162-78. A critical edition together with a more literal translation was produced as a doctoral dissertation: J. F. Larkin, *Erasmus' 'De ratione studii'; A Critical Edition and Translation with Introduction and Explanatory Notes* (University of Illinois, 1941). The definitive critical edition has recently been published, EOO, I.2, 79-151, with an introduction in French by J.-C. Margolin, pp. 83-109. The difference between the text published in 1511 and an outline for it written by Erasmus in 1497 (published by A. Hyma, "Erasmus and the Oxford Reformers," *Archiev voor Kerkgeschiedenis*, XXV, 129-43), has been discussed above, p. 31.

On the *De pueris instituendis*, on which he also worked during this period, see above, ch. I, n. 8. It is, as Margolin points out in his introduction to the critical edition, a summary of Erasmus' ideas on education (EOO, I.2, 9). For this reason it is probably the treatise which the student beginning a study of Erasmus' pedagogy should consult first. James D. Tracy has pointed out that passages added to this treatise around 1511 include those in which Erasmus criticizes Christian political and ecclesiastical leaders for their preoccupation with titles by which they should be addressed. It presents the sharper social criticism of "the ruling class" which appeared first in *The Praise of Folly*. See *Erasmus: Growth of a Mind*, pp. 290-92.

The most comprehensive discussion of Erasmus' theory of education is Woodward's introduction in *Erasmus Concerning the Aim and Method of Education*, pp. 1-160. See also T. W. Baldwin, *Shakspere's Small Latine and Lesse Greeke* (Urbana: University of Illinois Press, 1944), I, chs. 4-5, which demonstrates the seminal importance of Erasmus' educational treatises (especially the *De ratione studii*) for English educational practice during the sixteenth century and later.

in 1510. Erasmus regarded his *Copia* as an original contribution to education.[131] In it he enumerates a great variety of ways of expressing oneself in Latin (copia of words) and of developing persuasive arguments to support one's position (copia of ideas). In at least two places, he anticipates his later treatise against the Ciceronians, criticizing certain Italians he had met on his recent journey for following too slavishly the style of the ancients without regard to the requirements of a living language.[132] In the *De Ratione studii*, published together with the *Copia*, Erasmus argued that the best way of achieving these ends was to develop a sound knowledge of the rudiments of Latin and Greek and to have the student write themes based on his own interests. A good teacher, he argued, could by this method enable a student to be writing independent compositions of good quality within a short time. By way of example, Erasmus had begun as early as 1498 to provide examples of the kinds of subjects and compositions he had in mind. When some of this early material was published surreptitiously in 1518 he undertook an authorized version. The latter developed into formal colloquies on many subjects which began to appear in 1522 and were reissued with new additions until the final edition of

[131]He makes this assertion in the preface to the *De Copia* (EE, I, 511-12, lines 36-52; Nichols, II, 66), and again in a defense of the work against questions raised about it by William Budé (1468-1540), the learned French humanist and founder of the Collège de France (see Budé's letter, EE, II, 274, lines 69-84; Nichols, II, 301-2; and Erasmus' reply, EE, II, 364-65, lines 87-107; Nichols, II, 416).

[132]See *On Copia of Words and Ideas*, pp. 25, 31. James D. Tracy, *Erasmus: Growth of a Mind*, ch. 5, seems to me to go much beyond what the evidence allows when he claims that from the time of his Italian journey a greater simplicity of style is discernible in Erasmus, a movement toward sincerity rather than ornateness of speech. He cites instances from the 1508 edition of the *Adagia* which suggest a reaction against Italy and an affirmation of his Dutch origins. He does not go on to demonstrate from writings subsequent to the Italian journey a greater simplicity of style. To the extent that this aspect of Erasmus' mind has been analyzed, the evidence suggests that he was a master of Latin style and that he changed styles of writing according to the type of work he was composing. This had nothing to do with a chronological progression. See D. F. S. Thomson, "The Latinity of Erasmus," in T. A. Dorey, ed., *Erasmus*, pp. 118-24.

1533.[133] All three of these were important in England throughout the sixteenth century and later as school texts. T. W. Baldwin states that "he who wishes to understand the principles upon which the sixteenth-century grammar school was founded in England would be very unwise to begin anywhere else than with Erasmus."[134]

As important as his textbooks for Colet were, Erasmus pointed out even in the *Copia* itself that this was not the serious study he had set for himself and that he could not allow it to encroach too much upon his time.[135] What was the "serious study" he had in mind? Was it his Greek studies?

We have already taken note of his translations of a number of Lucian's dialogues. In the same vein should be mentioned translations of Plutarch, always one of his favorite classical authors.[136] He refers to translations he has made from Plutarch's *Moralia* in 1512, 1513, and 1514.[137] But these translations from Lucian and Plutarch were in every case presents to patrons whom Erasmus was constantly pressing for financial support. These, then, were not "serious

[133]All the colloquies, including the very early material, have recently been translated by Craig R. Thompson, *The Colloquies of Erasmus*, 1965. Professor Thompson's work definitely supplants earlier translations. For a general discussion of their content, see M. M. Phillips, *Erasmus and the Northern Renaissance*, pp. 102-22. For more specalized treatments consult Elsbeth Gutmann, *Die Colloquia Familiaria des Erasmus von Rotterdam* (Basel und Stuttgart: Helbing und Lichtenhahn, 1968); Martha Heep, *Die Colloquia Familiaria des Erasmus und Lucian* (Halle: Niemeyer, 1927); Leonard Hegland, *The Colloquies of Erasmus: A Study in the Humanistic Background of English Literature* (Master's Thesis: University of Illinois, 1951); Preserved Smith, *A Key to the Colloquies of Erasmus* (Cambridge: Harvard University Press, 1927).

[134]T. W. Baldwin, *Shakspere's Small Latine and Lesse Greeke*, p. 77.

[135]*On Copia of Words and Ideas*, pp. 11-12.

[136]In one of his letters from Cambridge he wrote: "It is indeed a tiny book, but to give it a compendious praise, it is Plutarch's, the work of an author never surpassed in learning or in charm by any produced by Greece, that fertile parent of great intellects. I know not indeed whether it has been given to any other to couple so rare a power of expression with the exactest knowledge." (EE, I, 548-49, lines 6-11; Nichols, II, 111).

[137]EE, I, 517, lines 22-24; EE, I, 528, lines 7-11; Nichols, II, 77; EE, I, 548-49; Nichols, II, 111-12.

For Erasmus' prefaces to these various translations, see EE, I, 520-21; EE, I, 529-30; EE, I, 548-49; Nichols, II, 111-12; EE, I, 573-74; Nichols, II, 113-14.

study" but work done for money or diversion or both. The same can be said of some of his translations from classical Christian authors, for example, his translation of the Office of Chrysostom[138] and of Basil's commentary on Isaiah.[139]

The meaning Erasmus intended for "serious study" begins to gain clarity in the only reference he makes while at Cambridge to his teaching position. He said: "Up to this time I have lectured on the Grammar of Chrysoloras, but only to a few pupils. Perhaps with a larger audience we shall begin that of Theodorus. Perhaps too we shall undertake a theological lecture, for that is now talked of."[140]

And in a letter written to Servatius Roger (his friend of earlier years at Steyn, now prior of the monastery) just after he departed Cambridge in 1514, Erasmus stated that "I spent several months at Cambridge teaching Greek and Divinity...."[141] Although Erasmus tells us what he was doing in Greek (and his translations for patrons provide additional evidence), he does not tell us what he did in theology.

---

[138]EE, I, 467, lines 1-3; Nichols, II, 21. On the work in question, see EE, I, 467, n. 1.

[139]He mentions in a letter to Colet (Sept. 13, 1511) that he is beginning his translation (EE, I, 467, lines 17-18; Nichols, II, 22). Later in the same month, he expresses doubt in a letter to John Fisher that the commentary is genuine (EE, I, 469-70; tr. in Jean Rouschausse, ed., *Erasmus and Fisher: Their Correspondence, 1511-1524* [Paris: Vrin, 1968], p. 41). In another letter to Colet one month later, he says he has almost given up the translation, not only because he suspects that the work is not genuine, but also because the patron for whom it was intended suspected him of having simply copied an earlier translation (EE, I, 477, lines 9-16; Nichols, II, 35).

[140]EE, I, 473, lines 8-15; Nichols, II, 29. Manuel Chrysoloras of Byzantium (d. 1415) taught Greek in Florence from 1396—the first to do so in Italy— and afterward at Pavia. Theodore Gaza (d. 1475) came to Italy in 1435 and taught Greek in Ferrara, Rome, and Naples. In *The Right Method of Instruction* Erasmus says that Gaza's grammar is the best. See Woodward, *Erasmus Concerning the Aim and Method of Education*, pp. 163, 170. In 1516 Thierry Martens published the first two books of Gaza's grammar in Greek with a Latin translation of Book I by Erasmus. In 1518 Martens again published the work, this time with a translation of both books by Erasmus. See Erasmus' preface to the 1516 edition, EE, II, 264-66.

[141]EE, I, 569, lines 134-36; Nichols, II, 146.

Letters written in November and December, 1511, suggest that his subject was Jerome.[142]

For almost one year after these references (until autumn, 1512), no mention is made of Jerome. We know that during this year—when Erasmus was more in London than in Cambridge—he was engrossed in additions to the *Adagia*. The striking thing about these additions, as we have seen, is the appearance for the first time in straightforward commentary of social and religious criticism aimed at the reform of state and church. In the course of these commentaries, Erasmus alludes to his work on the Christian classics, especially Jerome and the New Testament.[143] As soon as the *Adagia* was completed, he turned to these texts, as a letter written in the autumn of 1512 makes clear: "I have put in shape the work on Proverbs. . . . I shall finish the correction of the New Testament; I shall finish Jerome's Epistles. . . ."[144] For the remainder of 1512 and for all of 1513 Erasmus was engaged largely in emending the texts and in providing philological and theological commentary on Jerome and on the New Testament. He began with the New Testament, completing his work on the collation of texts by July, 1513; then he turned to Jerome.[145] The way in which he subsequently refers to his labor on these theological classics makes clear that this was indeed "serious study." In September, 1513, he writes: "The work of correcting and commenting upon Jerome interests my mind so warmly that I feel as if I was inspired by some god. I have already emended almost the whole by collating many ancient copies; and this puts me to an incredible expense."[146] No idea here of a scholar trying to make money, but one so eager to undertake his scholarship that he is willing to underwrite himself from very scarce resources. In July, 1514, after he had left England, Erasmus wrote to Servatius Roger:

[142]EE, I, 492, lines 4-7; Nichols, II, 47; EE, I, 495, lines 34-37; Nichols, II, 53.

[143]See *The Adages of Erasmus*, pp. 266-67, 275-76.

[144]EE, I, 517, lines 6, 13-14; Nichols, II, 119.

[145]EE, I, 527, lines 58-59; Nichols, II, 73.

[146]EE, I, 531, lines 13-17; Nichols, II, 87.

During the last two years, beside other employments, I have corrected the Epistles of Jerome, distinguishing with daggermarks the spurious additions, and illustrating the obscure passages with notes. I have also corrected the New Testament from the collation of ancient Greek manuscripts, and annotated more than a thousand places, not without profit to theologians. I have begun a commentary on the Epistles of St. Paul, which I shall finish when I have published what I have already mentioned.[147]

Erasmus had resolved to publish Jerome and the New Testament in the same spirit in which his newly revised edition of the *Adagia* was, at the time he wrote this letter, being reprinted: to reform church and society through education.

The way in which this came about was symbolic of the fusion then taking place in his own mind. In 1513 Erasmus had entrusted his manuscript of the *Adagia* to the bookseller Francis Berckman, with instructions to carry it to the Paris printer, Josse Badius. Instead, Berckman spirited the manuscript off to Basel where he gave it to the Froben press. Froben had reprinted the Aldine edition of the *Adagia* earlier during the same year (1513), from which fact Erasmus drew the conclusion that his new work would be published only after Froben had sold the earlier edition he had reprinted.[148] There is reason to believe that Erasmus was dissembling in this protest. He concludes it with the comment that he has another copy of the *Adagia*, even more complete than the one given to Berckman and therefore can take his revenge. Presumably this means that he could himself carry the manuscript to Badius in Paris. But when he left England in June, 1514, he traveled instead through the Low Countries and Germany, where he was received by learned soci-

---

[147]EE, I, 570, lines 152-58; Nichols, II, 147. Much earlier in his Cambridge correspondence Erasmus alludes to his intended work on St. Paul. He wrote to Colet in his first letter from Cambridge, August 24, 1511: "I shall venture perhaps even to attack your author, Paul. Only look at the boldness of your Erasmus." (EE, I, 466, lines 20-21; Nichols, II, 20). Between this remark and the letter to Servatius in 1514, however, there is not a word about his work on St. Paul.

[148]EE, I, 547, lines 152-61; Nichols, II, 109.

eties in various cities as the brightest star of the learned world.[149] His destination was (not Paris but) Basel. His introduction to the printer, John Froben, reads as if Erasmus had been as intent on meeting and working with him as he had been earlier on making the acquaintance of Aldus Manutius:

> I delivered to John Froben a letter from Erasmus, adding that he was my intimate friend, and had entrusted me with the business of publishing his Lucubrations, so that whatever I did would stand good as done by Erasmus himself. I added at last that I was so like him that whoever saw me saw Erasmus. He then broke into a laugh, as he detected the hoax. His father-in-law paid our bill at the inn, and transferred us with our horses and baggage, to his own residence.[150]

As soon as he arrived, the *Adagia* was put in type and appeared early in 1515.

Thus it seems that Erasmus used Berckman as a foil for meeting Froben and that he was more than happy to have the famous Basel printer produce his *Adagia*. But the New Testament was a different matter. Apparently he intended that for Aldus, for he had hardly arrived in Basel when he announced that he was about to leave for Italy.[151] However, he found the circle of learned men associated with the Froben press congenial enough to detain him through the fall and winter. Meanwhile, Aldus died in February, 1515, and Froben pledged to match any offer Erasmus might receive for his manuscript.[152] By August, 1515, Erasmus and Froben had reached an agreement, for Erasmus mentions

---

[149]See, for example, letters exchanged with the humanists James Wimpfeling of Strassburg and Ulrich Basius of Freiburg. Wimpfeling: EE, II, 7-9; Nichols, II, 158-59; EE, II, 17-24; Nichols, II, 159-60 (lines 8-176 and 195-261 omitted). Zasius: EE, II, 9-10; EE, II, 24-25; EE, II, 25-27; Nichols, II, 161-63 (lines 16-27 omitted); EE, II, 30-31; Nichols, II, 164 (lines 14-32 omitted); EE, II, 35-36.

[150]EE, II, 22, lines 187-94; Nichols, II, 160.

[151]EE, II, 5, lines 40-41; Nichols, II, 158.

[152]EE, II, 63, lines 36-37; Nichols, II, 196.

that his New Testament is being published in Basel.[153] Work began in September; the date of the New Testament is February, 1516, and that of the annotations, March 1, 1516.

This first edition was entitled *Novum Instrumentum*. It included a dedication to Pope Leo X,[154] a preface to the annotations,[155] the *Paraclesis* or exhortation to the reader, an *Apologia* for his Greek text and Latin translation, and an introduction to his methodology, *Methodus*. The entire work was about one thousand pages, and all of this was printed in six months! Erasmus corrected the Greek manuscript while the work was in progress and expanded the annotations from an original thirty folio pages to eighty, working at the press while the type was being set, much as he had done with the 1508 edition of the *Adagia* at the Aldine Press in Venice. In a letter written three months after publication of his work, he described the laborious process through which he had just gone:

> In this work, however, I did what in fact I usually do. I had intended to carry the thing through with a light hand, calling attention to some small details, and just to point out the passages, as it were, with my little finger. Well, when the work was on the verge of publication, I was urged to alter the received version either by correction or by interpretation. The accession of labor, which I thought would be very light, I found in effect to be extremely heavy. I was then persuaded to add some annotations of a more exhaustive kind. The result, as I need not tell you, was that everything had to be rearranged. There was this additional trouble; I thought that they had some emendated copies at Basel, and when I was disappointed in this expectation, I was forced to correct beforehand the manuscripts which the printers were to use. Another thing: two fairly good scholars had been engaged to correct the press, one a lawyer, the other a theologian, who had besides some knowledge of Hebrew; but they, being unpracticed in that employ-

---

[153]EE, II, 137, lines 10-12; Nichols, II, 216.

[154]EE, II, 181-87.

[155]EE, II, 164-72.

ment, could not complete what they had undertaken, and I was obliged to take upon myself the
revision of what they call the last proofs. The writing and printing of the book were going on at the
same time, a sheet being completed every day.
Meanwhile, I could not devote my whole time to
this business. Jerome was in the press at the same
time [it appeared in the summer of 1516], and
claimed a fair share of my attention. And I was
firmly resolved either to die at work, or to get clear
of that treadmill before Easter. Finally, the size of
the volume deceived me. The printer said that it
had grown from thirty to a little less than three
times thirty pages; it exceeded eighty-three pages if
I am not mistaken. Thus, consumed for the greater
part of my time in things of this kind which were
not my province and which had not been foreseen,
I was wearied and almost broken down when I
came to the annotations. But I accomplished what
I could, considering the limit of time and the state
of my health. Some things I purposely passed over,
and shut my eyes to many points upon which soon
after publication I held a different opinion. Ac-
cordingly I am preparing a second edition. . . .[156]

True to his word, Erasmus began immediately to work
on a second edition. For the second edition of 1519 the title
was changed to *Novum Testamentum,* which it retained
thereafter. Much new introductory material was added, including an "Argument" for each book and a much expanded
discussion of method, the *Ratio verae theologiae,* published
in 1518 and included in the 1519 edition. Many additions
were made to the annotations. In addition, Erasmus substi-
tuted for his more conservative translation of 1516 a more
radical translation (in the sense that it departed further
from the Vulgate) which he had prepared in England in
1505-6. This edition came to over three thousand pages. In
subsequent editions (1522, 1527, 1535) there were expan-
sions of the annotations and a few changes in the text, but

[156]EE, II, 253-54, lines 43-70; Nichols, II, 281-82, lines 62-66 omitted in
Nichols without acknowledgment, but included in my translation. See also
an earlier letter in which Erasmus described this edition as "hurried out
headlong rather than edited." (EE, II, 226, lines 1-2; Nichols, II, 251)

the form achieved in the 1519 edition remained substantially intact.[157]

Erasmus' edition of the New Testament was the crowning achievement of a man given to study and gradually becoming aware of this task as a life-goal. It would seem now that the goal had been reached. In reality, Erasmus had only arrived at the real starting point. In addition to the numerous editions of his New Testament and the later paraphrases (which will be discussed in subsequent chapters), he began to make available editions of the ancient Christian writers. Jerome, as we have seen, appeared almost simultaneously with the New Testament (June, 1516). Subsequently, he was responsible for editions of Cyprian (1520), Arnobius and Athanasius (1522), Hilary (1523), Irenaeus (1526, editio princeps), Ambrose (1527), Augustine (1528-29), Chrysostom (1530, Latin translation), Basil (1532, editio princeps of Greek edition), and Origen (1536, published

---

[157]There has been surprisingly little attention devoted to Erasmus' New Testament. Of the texts themselves, only the introductions have been critically edited (H. Holborn, *Erasmus Ausgewählte Werke*, pp. 137-74; reprinted together with a German translation in G. B. Winkler, *Ausgewählte Schriften*, III, 1-115). Only the *Paraclesis* has been translated into English (J. C. Olin, *Christian Humanism and the Reformation*, pp. 92-106). Pierre Mesnard, "La Paraclesis d'Erasme," *Bibliothèque d'Humanisme et Renaissance*, XIII:I (April, 1951), 26-42 provides a good introduction to the *Paraclesis* as well as a translation into French. See further, below, chapter III, n. 2.

On the publication of the New Testament by Erasmus, see the introductory material to the prefatory letters in Allen (EE, II, 164-66, 181-84); and A. Bludau, *Die Beiden Ersten Erasmus-Ausgaben des Neuen Testaments und Ihre Gegner*, pp. 1-33.

On the text of the New Testament (which I shall not deal with) see K. W. Clark, "Observations on the Erasmian Notes in Codex 2," *Texte und Untersuchungen*, LXXIII (1959), 749-56; F. Delitzsch, *Handschriftliche Funde, Vol. I: Die Erasmischen Entstellungen des Texte der Apokalypse* (Leipzig: Dörffling und Franke, 1861); Bo Reicke, "Erasmus und die Neutestamentliche Textgeschichte," *Theologische Zeitschrift*, XXII:IV (July-August, 1966), 254-65; and C. C. Taralli, "Erasmus' Manuscripts of the Gospels," *The Journal of Theological Studies*, Vol. XLIV (1943), 155-62.

On the annotations very little work has been done. See Marvin Anderson, "Erasmus the Exegete," *Concordia Theological Monthly*, XL:XI (December, 1969), 722-33; Bludau, pp. 48-58; two articles by C. A. L. Jarrott: "Erasmus' Biblical Humanism," *Studies in the Renaissance*, XVII (1970), pp. 119-52; and "Erasmus' 'In Principio Erat Sermo': Controversial Translation," *Studies in Philology*, LXI:I (January, 1964), 35-40.

posthumously) .[158] Unfortunately, much of his later life was also taken up with defenses of his work on the New Testament, most especially of his Latin translation.[159] They reflect

[158]Robert Peters, in an interesting study of the prefaces of Erasmus' editions of the fathers, suggests that the order in which Erasmus edited the fathers was related to the turmoil going on about him. For example, his edition of Cyprian in 1520 was suggested by the need for church unity, so pressing a concern at the time of *Exsurge Domine,* the papal bull against Luther. Moreover, in raising questions, as he did, about the authenticity of Cyprian's writings, Erasmus may have been implicitly questioning the Reformers who wanted to use the witness of the early church to undercut the authority of the medieval church. Again, his editions of Athanasius in 1522 and Hilary in 1523 may be related to their proven orthodoxy and Erasmus' concern to prove his own at a time when he was being pressured to write against Luther. Irenaeus he edited after he had written against Luther. In his preface, he portrays this father as one who takes us back to apostolic times. Erasmus was presenting a man of peace in a time of division. One could say the same for his attitude toward Chrysostom, edited the following year. Augustine he worked upon in earlier years, but he published an edition of his works only later. Why? Because he might have been seen as supplying Luther with more patristic ammunition. Likewise Origen, condemned as a heretic, was edited only toward the end of Erasmus' life. "Erasmus and the Fathers: Their Practical Value," *Church History,* XXXVI:III (September, 1967) , 254-61.

The actual evidence set forward to substantiate the points made in this article is hardly convincing and in some cases altogether nonexistent. The thesis becomes particularly weak in the discussions of Irenaeus and Chrysostom. But the article nonetheless has a suggestive power and invites reflection.

[159]The attacks began even before his New Testament appeared and continued throughout his life. And they came from all parts of Europe. The first attack came from Louvain in the person of Martin Dorp (1514) . Other Louvain theologians later entered into the fray: Jacob Latomus (1518) and Francis Titelmans (1529) . A fellow humanist, Lefèvre d'Etaples, attacked Erasmus (1516) in a quarrel that was at length patched over. He was not so fortunate with his other French enemies: Peter Sutor (1525) and Noel Beda (1529) . A bitter dispute broke out between Erasmus and an Englishman, Edward Lee (1520) , that was magnified out of all proportion to its significance. From Spain Erasmus was attacked by men who were associated with the Complutensian Polyglot Bible, published by Cardinal Ximenes in 1522 (it had been printed in 1514, before Erasmus' New Testament, but was not circulated immediately): Stunica (1519) and Carranza (1522) . The Italians were the last to join in the chorus of dissent: Albert Pio (1525) and Peter Cursius (1535) .

Allen has biographical accounts of all these men. The most complete account of Erasmus and his disputants is August Bludau, *Die Beiden Ersten Erasmus-Ausgaben des Neuen Testaments und ihre Gegner,* Part II (pp. 58-145) .

The controversy with Dorp, which was finally resolved, appears in Eras-

the fact that the scholar, as he reached the pinnacle of his success, graduated into a new world—a world of religious revolution. In it he continued to function in his own terms: those he had developed during the years of struggle toward maturity of vision and competence.

Conclusion

Before we shift our attention to Erasmus' mature thought as it appears in his work on the New Testament, let us recapitulate where we have journeyed with him in his intellectual pilgrimage.

Erasmus wrestled with great disparities in his intellectual heritage until he could pull them into a unity which was his own. Imbued with the tenets of the *Devotio Moderna* as a child, he abandoned its narrow vision of life for the broader intellectual currents of Latin literature, to which he was naturally drawn. When he entered the monastery at Steyn it was as a lover of pagan letters. Reminded of his religious commitment by Cornelius of Gouda, he began to acknowledge it consciously, but in such a way that he remained in his own mind a man of letters. The years in Paris, where

mus' correspondence and not, as in all the other cases, in published apologies or responses. For the correspondence see EE, II, 10-16; Nichols, II, 168-70 with omissions; EE, II, 90-114; tr., Olin, *Christian Humanism and the Reformation*, pp. 55-91; EE, II, 126-36. See also Thomas More's letter to Dorp in defense of Erasmus: E. F. Rogers, *St. Thomas More: Selected Letters*, pp. 9-64. For an account of the controversy with Dorp see Pierre Mesnard, "Humanisme et théologie dans la controverse entre Erasme et Dorpius," *Filosofia* XIV:IV (Nov., 1963), 885-900; and Henry de Vocht, *Monumenta Humanistica Lovaniensia* (Louvain, 1934), pp. 139 ff.

On Erasmus and Latomus see Béné, *Erasme et Saint Augustin*, pp. 289-333; and Jacques Etienne, *Spiritualisme érasmien et theologiens louvanistes* (Louvain, 1956), pp. 163-86.

On the dispute with Lefèvre d'Etaples see Margaret Mann, *Erasme et les debuts de la réforme française (1517-1536)* (Paris: Honoré Champion, 1934), chs. 2-3. Erasmus and his critics at the Sorbonne are dealt with by A. Renaudet, *Etudes erasmiennes*, ch. 6.

On the controversy with Edward Lee, see Allen's introduction to Ep. 1037 (EE, IV, 108-11). The fullest account is in Bludau (see above).

On the Spanish critics, see Marcel Bataillon, *Erasme et l'Espagne* (Paris, 1937), pp. 98-105; and Bludau.

On the Italians see Renaudet, *Erasme et l'Italie*, pp. 225-37.

he went to obtain a doctorate in theology, placing him as they did in the mainstream of the religious tradition, only heightened the tension between what he loved and where he was forced to live. Prepared by the tension of this juxtaposition for some resolution, he found it in the learned and pious aristocrats whom he met in England. The fusion then born in his mind was that of a theologian revitalizing the Christian life through the recovery of a more ancient and more adequate theology. Now his humanism would serve his religion, not the other way around. In the *Enchiridion,* for the first time, his humanism is integrated with his earliest religious consciousness. Christ is the center from which everything else is judged. Christ teaches us to love; we learn what love means from Scripture read allegorically. The moral precepts of pagan authors are valuable in stimulating this process of understanding Scripture, as is their eloquence. But they are no longer to be accepted uncritically, and their morality is below what a Christian's should be. After the *Enchiridion,* Erasmus seemed destined to produce commentaries on Scripture and the ancient theologians. This would indeed have utilized his knowledge of languages and literature. But an even more fruitful path was opened up for him when he discovered Lorenzo Valla's *Notes on the New Testament,* and the idea formed in his mind of translating Scripture itself. His journey to Italy contributed both a more exacting knowledge of Greek and of manscript study and a sense of confidence in his own powers—this latter aided by the expanded reputation he gained as a result of the *Adagia* published in Venice. The fusion of his Greek studies with the work of social criticism and reform appeared immediately after his Italian experience in *The Praise of Folly* and was followed in the next major revision of the *Adagia* as well as in the *Colloquies.* The reform toward which this criticism pointed was to be achieved through a new kind of education, one based on a return to the sources of Christian theology and piety. His decision to publish the New Testament in Greek, together with translation and annotations, was reached only gradually as all these purposes came together in his mind. It was no academic exercise; scholarship never was that for Erasmus. It was rather a propaedeutic to the reform of religion and society, and it was in this respect that he viewed his work as a contribution to the Christian church.

When John Colet wrote, upon seeing Erasmus' New Testament, "The name of Erasmus will never perish,"[160] he had in mind the work of the reformer which he had himself so greatly influenced. In speaking as he did, he was seeing Erasmus as Erasmus saw himself. Not *Folly,* but the renewal of Christian life through the recovery of the sources of that life was that for which he believed he would be remembered.

Let us turn now to what that recovery meant to him in religious terms.

[160]EE, II, 258, lines 47-48.

III THE CHRISTIAN HUMANIST AND THE BIBLE: METHODOLOGY

Erasmus, as we have just seen, did not become fully self-conscious of his ultimate role as a Christian scholar until perhaps 1512. But a tacit knowledge of that role was present much earlier.[1] He was writing commentaries on Scripture as early as 1500 or 1501. And he was beginning to criticize the Vulgate by comparing it with the Greek text as early as 1504. Moreover, Erasmus' practice of exegesis was even then accompanied by theoretical reflections on his practice: in the *Enchiridion* (1501) and in his preface to Valla's *Notes on the New Testament* (1505).

This dialectical juxtaposition of theory and practice remained characteristic of Erasmus throughout his life. Each is found in his work on the New Testament: in the various introductions on the one side and in the annotations and paraphrases on the other. His practice of exegesis continued through his revisions of his edition of the New Testament and his paraphrases, as well as in his interpretation of some

[1] I use tacit knowledge in the sense defined by Michael Polanyi: a knowledge we act on before we can describe it. Self-consciousness presupposes tacit knowing. For we always know more than we can tell. See *Personal Knowledge* (New York: Harper Torchbooks, 1964), Part II; and *The Tacit Dimension* (Garden City: Doubleday, 1966), Ch. 1.

of the Psalms. This practice led to some revisions which were expressed theoretically in the *Ecclesiastes* (1535), the last work he published before his death.[2]

The Primacy of the Moral in Interpretation

Focusing for the moment only upon Erasmus' theory of interpretation, we can say first that the dichotomy between

[2]I agree with John B. Payne (see article cited below in this note, p. 14, n. 6) against Rudolf Pfeiffer (review of Holborn, *Erasmus Ausgewählte Werke, Gnomon*, XII [1936], pp. 625-34) and E.-W. Kohls (*Die Theologie des Erasmus*, II, 131, n. 798) that Erasmus does have a "hermeneutic" and not simply a "biblical philology," and that this is fairly systematically stated in the *Ratio verae theologiae*. Indeed, the article by Pfeiffer delineates many of its aspects very well. The same cannot be said for the only book-length treatment of the subject: J. W. Aldridge, *The Hermeneutic of Erasmus* (Richmond: John Knox Press, 1966). Of all the discussions of Erasmus' method of interpretation, this one is least to be recommended. The writer shows very little historical understanding of Erasmus, and his judgments are usually misleading when they are not simply wrong (see John Payne's review of the book in *Journal of Ecumenical Studies*, V, [1968], pp. 176-78; and the note in Kohls, cited above).

Most of the studies of Erasmus' method of interpretation focus on the various introductions to his edition of the New Testament, especially on the *Ratio*. See Louis Bouyer, "Erasmus in Relation to the Medieval Biblical Tradition," in G. W. H. Lampe, ed., *The Cambridge History of the Bible* (Cambridge: Cambridge University Press, 1969), II, 492-505; J. Coppens, "Erasme exégète et théologien," *Ephemerides theologicae Lovanienses*, XLIV (1968), 191-204; Carl S. Meyer, "Erasmus on the Study of Scriptures," *Concordia Theological Monthly*, XL (1969), 734-46; A. Renaudet, *Etudes erasmiennes*, pp. 136-53; and W. Schwarz, *Principles and Problems of Biblical Translation*, pp. 144-62.

Several other studies cover all his works on method. Charles Béné, *Erasme et Saint Augustin*, pp. 127-86, 215-80, 372-425 and tabulations, 434-38, 443-46, seeks to prove the Augustinianism of Erasmus in all these works; Henri de Lubac, "Les Humanistes chrétiens du XV-XVIe siècle et l'herméneutique traditionnelle," *Archiv di filosofia*, 1963, pp. 175-77; and *Exégèse médievale*, II.II (1964), 427-53 describe the major emphases of each work, but only cursorily.

By far the most adequate treatment of Erasmus' hermeneutics is John Payne, "Toward the Hermeneutics of Erasmus," in J. Coppens, ed., *Scrinium Erasmianum* (Leiden: Brill, 1969), II, 13-49. I follow him in my description of the movement of Erasmus' thought on interpretation.

There has been one study of the *Ecclesiastes* (which, like the other works we are discussing, has not been translated): Robert Kleinhans, *Erasmus' Doctrine of Preaching: A Study of 'Ecclesiastes'* (Doctoral Thesis: Princeton Theological Seminary, 1968).

flesh and spirit that we saw in different forms in the *De contemptu mundi,* the letters from Paris, 1495-1499, and the *Enchiridion,* reflects a basic distinction that remains with Erasmus throughout his life. The relative emphasis between the two, however, changes. In the *Enchiridion* he emphasized allegory almost exclusively as a method of interpretation, for through allegory he found a means by which he could place the classical literature he loved in the service of religion; *both* classical works *and* Scripture could and should be interpreted allegorically. When he discovered Valla's *Notes on the New Testament* he was excited by the fact that Valla had applied the same canons of *grammatical and literary* criticism to Scripture as he had to other kinds of texts. In his preface to Valla's *Notes* he announced confidently—for the first time—that grammar was a necessary propaedeutic to theology. Thereafter, the grammatical interpretation became more important for him, and this change is reflected in his introductions to the New Testament, where the literal and spiritual interpretations stand in tension with one another. By the time he came to write the *Ecclesiastes* Erasmus had moved further still from the wild flights of fancy encouraged by allegory.

Beneath these changes, however, was a more fundamental criterion which Erasmus never abandoned and which, indeed, may account for the changes: the primacy of the moral meaning of scripture. Even in the *Enchiridion* the spiritual interpretation was much more tropological (moral) than allegorical (mystical);[3] that is, Erasmus focused his at-

---

[3]According to medieval interpreters, who developed ideas derived from Origen, Scripture has a fourfold meaning: literal, tropological or moral, allegorical, anagogical. In the words of Nicholas of Lyra, the literal tells us what happened, the allegorical what we must believe, the moral or tropological what we must do, and the anagogical what we may hope for.

On this method Erasmus commented in the *Ratio:* "... it is not enough to examine how eternal truth (on which men are divided) shines variously in different ways: according to the historical sense which is simple, the tropological which pertains to habits and common life, the allegorical which discusses secret things about the mystic head and body, the anagogical which touches upon the celestial hierarchy. But we must also consider in the case of each of them the steps, the differences, the method of discussion." Erasmus goes on to urge that interpreters follow the example of Origen who dis-

tention on redirecting the life of the believer through action rather than on knowledge, whether of the propositions of faith or of some higher truths given only to a few. "Let this be the first and most important goal for you, this your prayer, this one thing do," Erasmus writes in the *Methodus*, "that you may be changed, seized, hasten toward, transformed into the things you have learned."[4] Indeed, he encourages allegorical interpretation of classical as well as Christian texts precisely for the upbuilding of the moral life.[5] And in the *Ecclesiastes* he goes so far as to say that the believer can depart from the actual meaning of the passage when by doing so he can build up the moral life.[6] Moreover, although he turns from the allegorical interpretation to the extent of saying, in opposition to Origen, that every passage of Scripture does *not* have an allegorical meaning, he affirms at the same time that every passage *does* have a moral meaning.[7] The moral is not limited as the literal and allegorical methods are.

cussed passages of Scripture (e.g., the temptation of Abraham) in many ways and did not even hesitate to correct matters of historical fact. But in a passage added to the end of this paragraph in 1523 he says that we should imitate Origen or Ambrose "save only that each is excessive and frequently more injurious to the historical sense than is right." (Holborn, p. 284; see also *Methodus*, Holborn, pp. 157-58)

In the *Ecclesiastes*, Erasmus says that the early fathers made no distinction between the three kinds of spiritual meaning (allegory, tropology, anagogy). (LB, V, 1034D-E)

[4]Holborn, p. 251. See also the whole of the *Paraclesis* which speaks in this vein.

References to all the prefaces *(Methodus, Apologia, Paraclesis, Ratio verae theologiae)* will be to the Holborn edition.

[5]Holborn, p. 71; Himelick, p. 106. Henri de Lubac suggests that Erasmus employed allegory in order to divorce religion from its formal ceremonial observances *(Exégèse Médievale,* II.II, 444). But this comes to the same thing: the formal observance of religion does not necessarily make one a better person—which it is the aim of religion to do.

[6]LB, V, 1028C. See also Erasmus' exegesis of Psalm 4 (1525), LB, V, 274D: and Psalm 33 (1530), LB, V, 381C. In this judgment he is following St. Augustine, who wrote in *On Christian Doctrine* (I.xxxvi.40): "Whoever finds a lesson there [in Scripture] useful to the building of charity, even though he has not said what the author may be shown to have intended in that place, has not been deceived, nor is he lying in any way." (See also III.iii.6; III.xxvii.38)

[7]*Ecclesiastes*, LB, V, 1050A-B. James D. Tracy, *Erasmus: Growth of a Mind,*

III

This primacy of the moral is evident in the structure Erasmus gives to the most systematic treatise he wrote on his method of interpretation, the *Ratio verae theologiae* (1518). "God speaks to us truly and efficaciously in the sacred books to the extent that he spoke to Moses from the burning bush," writes Erasmus, "only if we come to the conversation with pure minds."[8] "Those most harmful of true plagues, I mean glory and fame, which innate ferocity follows naturally, should be far from us. So also should yielding to the determination to quarrel, or what is worse, to blind rashness."[9] On the other side of these, the wisdom of true theology (to paraphrase James 3:17) is purity, peacefulness, gentleness, mercy, and good fruits without uncertainty or insincerity.[10]

The Authority of Tradition

So then, the first and principal preparation of the true theologian—one who would interpret Scriptures—is moral purity. Other kinds of preparation follow this one. Of these the first requisite is a knowledge of languages: Latin, Greek, and Hebrew. The fact that theologians have often been deceived argues against the adequacy of translations—despite Augustine's contention that the Septuagint was sufficient in the case of the Old Testament. It is not necessary to have a perfect knowledge of these languages; few enough have eloquence even in Latin. A basic knowledge which enables one to refer back to the sources is adequate.[11]

ch. 8, fails to establish his thesis that Erasmus' use of allegory was related to his craving for peace. In particular, he asserts rather than demonstrates that Erasmus, after turning away from allegory as espoused in the *Enchiridion* and in his prefaces to the New Testament, turned back to it once again in his *Paraphrase of Mark* late in 1523. Apart from the fact that he does not clearly show that this paraphrase leaned much more heavily on allegory than those on Matthew and John which immediately preceded it, he fails even to mention the *Ecclesiastes* which points to the continued and consistent revision of the allegorical in favor of the moral meaning of Scripture.

[8] *Ratio* (Holborn, p. 179).

[9] *Ratio* (Holborn, p. 179).

[10] *Ratio* (Holborn, p. 181).

[11] *Ratio* (Holborn, pp. 181-84). Despite the stricture against Augustine, Erasmus is following *On Christian Doctrine* (II.11-15) in arguing that

After a knowledge of languages, we should, as Augustine also recommends in *On Christian Doctrine,* acquire a knowledge of dialectic, rhetoric, arithmetic, music, and nature; as well as of places, especially those mentioned in Scripture.[12] Likewise, if we learn the customs of the places to which the apostles wrote their letters, they come to life much more for us. However, the interpreter should not grow old in profane studies.[13]

Among Christian writers, the ancient fathers are much superior to the scholastic theologians:

> . . . let him compare these ancient theologians, Origen, Basil, Chrysostom, and Jerome with these more recent ones. He will see a certain golden river flowing in the former, certain shallow streams echoing back, and these neither very pure nor flowing from their own source. The ancients thunder out oracles of eternal truth; in the moderns you have little fabrications of men whose examples vanish through insomnia the more closely you examine them. The ancients move you in a straight course toward the door of evangelical truth; the moderns struggle among the prolixity of human questions or smash into the Scylla of pontifical power or into the Syrtes of scholastic dogma or into the Symplegades of divine and human law, unless you prefer to make this Charybdis. The ancients, on the basis of the solid foundation of Scripture, raise a strong edifice into the heavens; the moderns, by the foolish arguments of men or even by flatteries not less foolish than monstrous, are raised to infinity by a huge superstructure. The ancients will satisfactorily carry you into the happiest gardens, in which you will be both delighted and satisfied; while the moderns will tear you to pieces and torment you among thorny hedges. The ancients have all the fullness of majesty, the moderns no splendor at all, saying many sordid things and few worthy of the

knowledge of the three languages is necessary and that this knowledge need not be perfect.

[12]*Ratio* (Holborn, pp. 184 ff.).

[13]*Ratio* (Holborn, p. 192).

dignity of theology, so that I abstain from a comparison of morals.[14]

Of the ancient theologians mentioned here, Origen always remained a favorite of Erasmus as did Jerome. Origen he represents as "the most skillful in theological matters,"[15] one who "furnished material for almost all Greek writers," admirable in his zeal for editing and discussing sacred literature, and leaving behind material for thought that is of very great assistance to preachers.[16] And even though Erasmus reproved Origen for pressing allegory too far, he never lost his enthusiasm or love for the greatest fountain of patristic wisdom.[17] His enthusiasm for Jerome, as we have seen, followed him from the monastery at Steyn throughout his life.[18] Jerome was the first of the fathers edited by Erasmus, his works appearing the same year as the first edition of the New Testament. For this edition, Erasmus wrote a life of Jerome, his most substantial biography, in which the justification of Jerome's (and Erasmus') synthesis of classical and Christian learning is the central motif. It is for this, much more than for his interpretation of Scripture,[19] that Erasmus loved

[14]*Ratio* (Holborn, pp. 189-90; see *Methodus,* Holborn, pp. 154-55).

[15]EE, V, 7, lines 106-8 (Preface to the *Paraphrase of Matthew*).

[16]EE, VII, 102, lines 36-51 (Preface to Origen's *Commentary on Matthew*). In his exegesis of Psalm 38, Erasmus says Origen is the fountain from whom the genius of almost all the Greeks has been watered (LB, V, 432C). See also *Ecclesiastes,* LB, V, 857A, where Erasmus refers to Origen as the teacher of all the Greeks and praises his works as valuable for preachers.

[17]He voices this criticism in the *Ratio* (Holborn, p. 280) and later in the *Ecclesiastes* (LB, V, 1028D). But in one of the last things he ever wrote, Erasmus says: "Although I cannot help being distressed at so grave a loss [of the works of Origen], nevertheless my greatest sadness is over the loss of what he wrote on the New Testament, in which he had the help of Hebrew literature, and did not need to appeal at all times to dubious allegories in obscure matters. There is no point at which Origen does not flash, but he flashes nowhere more than when he treats the sermons and acts of Christ." (EE, IX, 338, lines 4-13; Preface to his edition of Origen's fragments on Matthew)

[18]On Erasmus' interest in Jerome see Allen's introduction to Ep. 396 (EE, II, 210-11).

[19]Jerome, like Origen, was finally criticized for his excessive allegorizing (*Ecclesiastes,* LB, V, 1028D), but as in the case of Origen, this did not affect Erasmus' love for him.

him.[20] Chrysostom he praises as skillful in commonplaces,[21] though his references to Basil and Chrysostom are never as specific or as lengthy as his comments on Origen and Jerome. He commends Chrysostom in the *Ecclesiastes* for his emphasis on the tropological interpretation of Scripture,[22] and he commends both Basil and Chrysostom as special helps to preachers.[23] One name, omitted in the quotation above, but mentioned in many others and more glaring for its absence, is St. Augustine. It is true to say that Erasmus never loved Augustine as he did Origen and Jerome. In a letter to John Eck in 1518, he asserts that he learned more from one page of Origen than from ten of Augustine,[24] though he goes on to add that he nonetheless thinks so much of Augustine that he is editing his works as he had done the works of Jerome. This entire letter is for the most part a defense of his preference for Jerome over Augustine. In one interesting passage, he contrasts Jerome, born of Christian parents near learned Rome, with Augustine, born of pagans in barbarous Africa. Jerome was brought up on Scripture; Augustine did not read Paul until he was over thirty. Jerome studied Scripture for thirty-five years; Augustine began to teach it when he had not yet even learned it. Jerome knew the three languages necessary for biblical study; Augustine knew only Latin.[25] Near the end of the letter he comments that as a youth he preferred Augustine to Jerome and then changed his mind.[26] If this is to be taken at face value, it must be interpreted to

[20]Erasmus' *Hieronymi Stridonensis vita* was omitted from LB. It has been critically edited by W. K. Ferguson, *Erasmi Opuscula* (The Hague: Martinus Nijhoff, 1933), pp. 125-90. The biography has never been translated into English. A useful study of Erasmus as a biographer has recently been published, though the writer fails to substantiate the theses developed through detailed consideration of Erasmus' work as a biographer. Only two pages are devoted to his life of Jerome. (Peter G. Bietenholz, *History and Biography in the Work of Erasmus of Rotterdam* [Geneva: Droz, 1966], pp. 51-98)

[21]*Ratio* (Holborn, p. 296).

[22]LB, V, 1036D-E.

[23]LB, V, 856E-F.

[24]EE, III, 337, lines 252-54.

[25]EE, III, 335-36, lines 199-219.

[26]EE, III, 337, lines 263-65.

mean that Erasmus knew Augustine through the piety of the Brethren of the Common Life in which he was educated as a youth. For when he comes into focus for us through his writings, his preference is solidly for Jerome. It may very well be that the process through which Erasmus had to go in order to reappropriate the religious tradition of his youth accounts much more adequately for his lack of enthusiasm for Augustine than the fact that the Protestant Reformers made Augustine their own. Erasmus' opinions were well established before the Reformers ever came on the scene. All of this having been said, Erasmus learned a great deal from Augustine. In fact, his discussion of the interpretation of Scripture draws more from Augustine's *On Christian Doctrine* than from any other single source.

Of the "moderns" severely criticized in the passage quoted, not all are included. We have already had occasion to see Erasmus' love for and debt to Lorenzo Valla. He was familiar also with Nicholas of Lyra, one of the most outstanding commentators on Scripture during the Middle Ages, of whom he is generally critical.[27] Thomas Aquinas he always respected. In a striking passage in his annotation to Romans 1:5, Erasmus wrote:

> It is remarkable to note how Thomas Aquinas agonizes over this passage, a man whose greatness has stood the test of time. For there is no recent theologian, at least in my opinion, who can outdo him in carefulness, in the sanity of his wisdom, and in the breadth of his learning; moreover, he had a skill in language and had studied widely in literature, and he was worthy of such knowledge, for he skillfully put to use all the resources that were available to him in his day.[28]

[27]Lyra is compared unfavorably with Valla in 1505 (EE, I, 410, lines 115-31). Erasmus' critical strictures continued throughout his life including, as we shall see, his work on Romans.

[28]LB, VI, 554E. In his Life of Colet Erasmus represents Colet as reproving him for praising Thomas (EE, IV, 520, lines 424-44; tr. Olin, *Christian Humanism and the Reformation*, p. 183). Erasmus evidently was not impressed; he maintained a high respect for Thomas as we can see in this annotation. For an account of Erasmus' knowledge of and attitude toward the scholastics, see C. Dolfen, *Die Stellung des Erasmus von Rotterdam zur Scholas-*

It is really the Scotists, those under whom he first studied scholastic theology and of whom he was already severely critical in 1496, who are the principal targets of this attack.

One important consideration in Erasmus' preference for the ancient fathers over the scholastics is the heterodoxy of the former. Beda criticized Erasmus for following the fathers who were heterodox rather than the scholastics who taught only the faith of the Church. The controversy over the revival of Origen had to do precisely with his heterodoxy.[29] The same was true of the other fathers. Erasmus often remarked that they disagreed among themselves, that there were many versions of eternal truth. The function of this contention in his hopes for reform was to undermine religious formalism, whether of practice or belief. At one point in the *Ratio* he remarks: "Dogma certainly does not seem to me at all necessary for piety."[30] Erasmus found support for this judgment in the fathers, who did not agree on practices or dogmas, but who did agree on the inculcation of the Christian life.

But even in relation to the ancients whom he loved, Erasmus always maintained a critical attitude.[31] And this went far beyond his changing attitude toward allegory. Already in his preface to Valla's *Notes* he had said that it was better to look for oneself at the original sources than to view them through the commentaries of others, adding also that the ancient commentators had left much to be explained. In the *Methodus* and the *Ratio verae theologiae* he goes much further. Not only did they ignore certain things, they were also sometimes deceived; they were not always alert, they were misled by having to argue against heretics;

tischen Methode (Osnabrück: Druck von Meinders und Elstermann, 1936); see also E. L. Surtz, " 'Oxford Reformers' and Scholasticism," *Studies in Philology* XLVII:IV (October, 1950), 547-56.

[29]See D. P. Walker, "Origène en France," *Courants religieux et humanisme,* pp. 101-19, *passim.*

[30]Holborn, pp. 205-6.

[31]In the Preface to the *Annotations* in 1516, after listing the fathers he had consulted, Erasmus added that sometimes he had agreed with them, sometimes not (EE, II, 167, lines 34-38; see also lines 57-61).

they were sometimes obscure. Moreover, things have been added to their writings by impostors which we must guard against accepting as the opinions of the fathers themselves.[32] In sum, the fathers were closer to the truth of Christianity than more modern theologians, and they deserve to be taken seriously. But they are not that truth themselves, only interpreters of it. We should therefore stand on their shoulders and in doing so (through reference to the sources themselves) see even more than they saw.

The Various Senses of Scripture

These then are the tools for interpretation: a pious mind; a knowledge of the three languages; acquaintance with the wisdom of the ancients, including rhetoric, dialectic, music, arithmetic, and nature; close attention to the ancient Christian fathers. But finally our point of reference is the source itself. How are we to use our tools in understanding the text of Scripture?

In the first place, Erasmus says that Scripture has many senses.[33] Even the fourfold sense does not exhaust the nuances of Scripture, but distinctions must be made within it according to the steps by which a given interpretation is arrived at and the methods of argumentation.

The literal sense for Erasmus means both the grammatical and the historical meaning. For the grammatical meaning our recourse is to the original languages. We cannot rely on the Vulgate, for the text is corrupt.[34] The function of the annotations, Erasmus explains in his prefatory letter to that aspect of his work on the New Testament, is to protect the integrity of the text, so that the reader does not stumble because of past ignorance or carelessness. Hence the text has

---

[32]*Methodus* (Holborn, pp. 160-61); *Ratio* (Holborn, pp. 295-96). See also *Ecclesiastes* (LB, V, 1027A, 1028A).

[33]Erasmus affirmed this view as early as 1499 in his exchange of letters with John Colet on the proper interpretation of Christ's agony in the garden. He wrote: "...the holy books are so rich that various meanings can be elicited from them and none of these should be rejected if only it is probable and not contrary to piety...." (EE, I, 255, lines 15-17)

[34]*Methodus* (Holborn, p. 152); *Ratio* (Holborn, 182).

been emended; solecisms have been removed. The Vulgate has been compared with Hebrew and Septuagint sources.[35] Still further, the literal meaning has been clarified through a variety of examples and by different kinds of distinctions.[36] Attention to the historical context—that is, not only to what is said, but also by whom, to whom, in what words, at what time, on what occasion, and with what antecedents and consequences—further clarifies the literal meaning of a text.[37] Indeed, these methods take us as far with the literal meaning as it is possible to go.

The most significant additions Erasmus made in his expansion of the *Methodus* into the *Ratio verae theologiae* were lengthy discussions of the philosophy of Christ and of the allegorical method of interpreting Scripture.[38] In the latter, which concerns us here, he drew heavily from Augustine's *On Christian Doctrine*.[39] Allegorical interpretation has three, perhaps four, functions:

> Now by means of tropes and allegories and similes or parables, Scripture is hidden or indirect, sometimes to the point of obscurity of a mystery, whether this is aimed at Christ, whom Scripture announces through the word of the prophets . . . or whether he wished to exercise our laziness by this difficulty so that afterwards there would be more gratitude for results acquired by great effort; or whether by this plan he wished that his mysteries and secrets be hidden from the profane and impious and in such a way that in the meantime hope of understanding might not be blocked for pious searchers; or whether this kind of speech was especially pleasing because, while it is especially efficacious for persuading it is revealed equally to the learned and the unlearned. . . .[40]

[35]EE, II, 167, lines 42-52, 61-62, 66-69; see also *Apologia* (Holborn, pp. 170-71).

[36]EE, II, 167, lines 52-56.

[37]*Ratio* (Holborn, p. 196).

[38]*Ratio* (Holborn, pp. 202-59; 259-91).

[39]See the tabulation in Béné, *Erasme et Saint Augustin*, pp. 435-36. See above, ch. I, n. 65, for a summary of Augustine's *On Christian Doctrine*.

[40]*Ratio* (Holborn, pp. 259-60). On the last point mentioned, see the

Allegory thus moves beyond the grammatical and historical interpretations in two important respects: it applies everything to Christ, and it presupposes a pious mind as a condition for penetrating the mysteries.[41]

There are passages in Scripture which are obviously meant to be taken allegorically.[42] For example, when Christ says in the Gospel of John (2:19) that in three days he will raise up a temple, the disciples knew that this was not meant literally. Paul knew that a true Jew was not one who had been circumcised but one who was free from desires and passions.[43] Moreover, there are tropes which pertain neither to grammar nor to rhetoric, but rather to idioms of a particular language. For example, the Greeks say *eupathein* to mean he is moved by kindness, but the Latins do not.[44] Again, there are hyperboles in Scripture, as when the Psalmist, describing a tempestuous sea, says the water rises to the heavens and descends into hell.[45] Still further, there are ambiguities in Scripture. Augustine suggests that if these can be made clear by solecisms, then that is permitted. But where, asks Erasmus, does Augustine follow his own example?[46] A much better rule—and one also suggested by Augustine—is to discern what trope is being used (e.g., metaphor,

---

Paraclesis: "Only a very few can be learned, but all can be Christian, all can be devout, and—I shall boldly add—all can be theologians." (Holborn, p. 145; tr. Olin, *Christian Humanism and the Reformation* p. 100)

[41] This follows naturally from the preceding section of the *Ratio* in which Erasmus had argued that Christ is the center of Scripture and the goal toward which we aim. For he is the only one in whom there was a perfect harmony between what he taught and how he lived (Holborn, pp. 209-10). This is the justification for applying everything to Christ, since that brings it immediately back to the believer and the question how he shall live. Christ, however, spoke in figures, as did his apostles. The purpose of allegorical interpretation is to help us understand these figures so that we can understand the heart of Scripture in the interest of becoming like Christ.

[42] As will be evident from the following discussion, "allegory" is used in a very broad sense by Erasmus.

[43] *Ratio* (Holborn, pp. 264, 265).

[44] *Ratio* (Holborn, p. 266).

[45] *Ratio* (Holborn, p. 268). See LB, VI, 618D-E.

[46] *Ratio* (Holborn, p. 272).

irony); this is a great help in resolving ambiguities.[47] Another is to collate an obscure passage with the same thing in a clear passage.[48]

Allegorical interpretation is also necessary for passages in Scripture which, if taken literally, would be absurd. This applies to many passages in the Old Testament. To take only one example, in the creation story it is said that God created light on the first day but the sun and moon only much later. This clearly cannot be taken literally and be true. These same kinds of absurdities appear in the New Testament, even though not as frequently. When Christ says that his followers must eat his body and drink his blood, he cannot be understood to be speaking literally.[49] It can be taken as a general rule in passages like these that anything is figurative if it seems to command a crime. If the passage is morally upbuilding when read literally, then allegorical interpretation is not necessary.

Allegorical interpretation, however, can be taken too far. And we should adopt the general rule that unless the passage requires allegory, we should not force it. "The reader should be warned that in this matter Origen, Ambrose, Hilary frequently sin, and there are others who freely imitate Origen and remove the grammatical sense out of a zeal for forcing allegory, when there is no need to do so."[50] In passing this judgment, Erasmus recognizes that allegorical interpretation, like the grammatical and historical, is limited in its ability to aid the believer in understanding Scripture. Indeed, Erasmus went so far in his treatise against Luther as to declare that "there are some secret places in the Holy Scripture into which God has not wished us to penetrate more deeply and if we try to do so, then the deeper we go, the darker and darker it becomes, by which means we are led to acknowledge the unsearchable majesty of the divine wisdom,

---

[47]*Ratio* (Holborn, pp. 197, 259, 263, 271-72).

[48]*Methodus* (Holborn, p. 159); *Ratio* (Holborn, p. 292).

[49]*Ratio* (Holborn, pp. 277-78; see also pp. 274-76).

[50]*Ratio* (Holborn, p. 280; passage added, 1523).

and the weakness of the human mind."[51] The Scriptures, in the final analysis, are divine, not human.[52] Human modes of interpretation can help us to understand, but as Augustine had said in *On Christian Doctrine,* knowledge is not synonymous with wisdom, only a stage on the way toward it. Erasmus seems very much inclined from this point in his life forward to accept the judgment of Jerome which he had quoted in his Preface to Valla's *Notes:* "Let them explain Jerome's intention when he wrote to Desiderius: 'It is one thing,' he said, 'to be a prophet, but to be an exegete is something else. In the case of the prophet the Spirit predicts things that are to come; the exegete, on the other hand, employs his erudition and command of vocabulary to translate what he himself understands.' "[53] Here we find the final tension and perhaps the limits of Erasmus' synthesis of humanism and Christianity. For him, somehow "studies are transmuted into morals"; [54] there is a necessary connection between understanding and transformation.[55] In the last analysis, this necessary connection is the piety and good faith of the believer.

[51]E. G. Rupp, *et al.,* eds., *Luther and Erasmus: Free Will and Salvation* (Philadelphia: Westminster Press, 1969), p. 38.

[52]See *Apologia* (Holborn, p. 168).

[53]EE, I, 410, lines 140-45; tr. Oberman, *Forerunners of the Reformation,* p. 312.

[54]*Paraclesis* (Holborn, p. 148; tr. Olin, *Christian Humanism and the Reformation,* p. 105).

[55]"The first step, however, is to know what he taught; the next is to carry it into effect." *Paraclesis* (Holborn, p. 145; Olin, p. 101)

III

IV THE CHRISTIAN HUMANIST AND THE BIBLE: THE METHODOLOGY AT WORK IN THE ANNOTATIONS AND PARAPHRASE OF ROMANS

The Annotations

In his preface to the first edition of the annotations, Erasmus says that in them he has tried to clarify the text and, when possible, with fewer words rather than with many;[1] that he has used the fathers, though in some cases he has dissented from them.[2] These are in reality two principal features of the annotations: textual criticism and consideration of the opinions of the fathers. Let us see how Erasmus carries out each task, beginning with the second.

An analysis of the changes (in every case additions) made in each edition of the annotations on Romans reveals

---

[1]EE, II, 166, lines 4-8; 171, lines 198-99.

[2]He names Origen, Cyril, Chrysostom, Hilary, Jerome, Ambrose, Augustine, Theophylactus, Basil, Beda. But the last three names were added in the 1522 edition (EE, II, 167, lines 33-34).

In another preface written for the 1527 edition, he says that he has discovered many passages in Chrysostom and Athanasius which agree with his interpretations (he was then in the process of completing a Latin translation of the works of Chrysostom). He deplores the fact that translators of these men (as also of Theophylactus) used the Vulgate text, since it often did not coincide with the Greek, resulting in a situation in which a commentator was not commenting on the verse given in Latin! (EE, VI, 466-67)

some interesting data regarding Erasmus' use of the fathers. The 1516 edition is striking for its dependence upon Latin writers (with two exceptions). Jerome leads the field; he is cited in twenty-eight different discussions.[3] Origen is second (twenty-five citations). Ambrosiaster[4] (twenty-one citations) and Augustine (fifteen citations) follow. Theophylactus, a Greek writer whom Erasmus calls Vulgarius both in this and in the 1519 edition, is cited eleven times.[5] Only three medieval thinkers are mentioned: Bernard of Clairvaux (once), Thomas Aquinas (six times), and Nicholas of Lyra (five times). Of these, only Thomas reappears in subsequent editions.[6] Erasmus drew on two humanist thinkers of his own period: Lorenzo Valla (twelve times) and Lefèvre d'Etaples (six times). Lefèvre fails to appear in subsequent editions,[7] and Valla is cited only twice more.

[3]In my tabulation, a writer was counted only once in the discussion of each point, even if cited more than once in a particular discussion.

It is natural that Jerome should have dominated the field in this first edition, since Erasmus published Jerome's works during the same year.

[4]The work Erasmus cites as by "Ambrosiaster" is by an unknown author, though it is included in the works of St. Ambrose. Erasmus, who published a complete edition of the works of Ambrose in 1527, was the first to cast doubt on the Ambrosian authorship of these commentaries on Paul's epistles. However, he makes no reference to their non-Ambrosian authorship in his annotations, either before or after 1527. He consistently refers to the commentary on Romans as by Ambrose. See on "Ambrosiaster," Alexander Souter, *A Study of Ambrosiaster* (Cambridge: Cambridge University Press, 1905; Texts and Studies, Vol. VII); and Souter, *The Earliest Latin Commentaries on the Epistles of St. Paul* (Oxford: Clarendon Press, 1927), ch. 2.

[5]Vulgarius is a misreading of "Bulgarian." Theophylactus, the exegete in question, became Archbishop of Bulgaria in 1078. Vulgarius appears both on the title page and in the text of the 1516 edition, but only in the text of the 1519 edition. In the 1522 edition Theophylactus replaces Vulgarius in every case where the latter had appeared earlier.

Incidentally, I have retained the Latin form, Theophylactus, in preference to the usual anglicized form, Theophylact, for purely aesthetic reasons. It sounds better!

[6]Some reference from Thomas is added in every edition except that of 1522, for a total of sixteen references.

[7]Perhaps because of the quarrel between the two humanists that erupted in 1517. Since Erasmus' references to Lefèvre in 1516 were critical (though only mildly so), he would not want to open the wound which had been so delicately healed.

In the 1519 edition, in which many notes are added, Erasmus' authorities change somewhat. Jerome is no longer first but fifth (thirteen citations). Origen now heads the list (seventy-eight citations), followed by Ambrosiaster (fifty-nine citations), Augustine and Theophylactus cited as Vulgarius (thirty-five citations each), and Cyprian (three citations).[8] Augustine is cited more and more in later chapters of Romans as the debates on predestination and original sin take shape. Aquinas is cited seven times. Apart from these, Erasmus made only occasional use of other writers.[9] The number of citations from Origen, Theophylactus, Ambrosiaster, and Augustine suggest that Erasmus was working in 1519 with these four authors constantly before him.

In the 1522 edition there are fewer changes than in any other. There are six additional citations of Augustine and Theophylactus, four of Ambrosiaster, three of Origen, and one of Cyprian.

In the 1527 edition there are two striking changes. The first is the large number of additional notes. The second is the fact that virtually all these additional citations come from Greek authors. This edition is as heavily dominated by Greek commentators as the 1516 edition was by Latin commentators. Additions from most writers who were frequently cited earlier are few: Origen, five times; Ambrosiaster, six times; Augustine, four times; Hilary, three times;[10] Tertullian[11] and Jerome, two times. But there are thirty additional

---

[8]The three references to Cyprian in this edition are striking since there are only two additional references to him in all the other editions. The references here are doubtless accounted for by the fact that Erasmus was working on his edition of Cyprian at the time he was making these revisions. His edition of the works of Cyprian was published in 1520.

[9]Athanasius is cited twice, Didymus once, Hesychius twice, Hilary twice, Valla once.

[10]Erasmus published an edition of Hilary's works in 1523. He is cited three times in each of the last two editions of the annotations, though only twice in the first three editions.

[11]This is the only edition of the annotations in which Tertullian appears, despite the high regard in which Erasmus held him. "Among the ancient interpreters of Scripture, Origen the Greek and Tertullian the Latin writer seem especially outstanding . . . ." (EE, VII, 102, lines 16-17) This is per-

citations of Theophylactus. And a new Greek name appears for the first time:[12] Chrysostom, cited seventy-six times.[13] Erasmus seems to have discovered the dependence of Theophylactus upon the works of Chrysostom at this time. For in twenty-five of the seventy-six citations of Chrysostom he begins with a phrase like: "Chrysostom and Theophylactus interpret the passage in this way." And he notes several times that Theophylactus is dependent upon Chrysostom's homilies.

In the 1535 edition, it is as if the work of a lifetime had come together.[14] Now, instead of either Latin or Greek interpreters, both are cited, and with almost equal frequency. Chrysostom heads the list of additional citations (forty-nine), followed by Theophylactus (thirty-four) and Origen (twenty-four). Among Latin interpreters, Ambrosiaster is cited twenty-three times and Augustine and Jerome, eleven each.[15] Erasmus shows himself here the master of patristic literature on Paul.

Turning from the number of citations to the function of the fathers in Erasmus' discussions, we can delineate four ways in which he uses the fathers. First, he reports opinions of the fathers which agree with his own analyses; second, he cites them in defense of his own interpretations; third, he points out differences among them in order to justify his departures from commonly held views; finally, he criticizes

---

haps accounted for by the fact that Tertullian did not write commentaries on Scripture.

[12]Chrysostom is cited in the preface to the annotations in 1516 but not in the text. Reference is made to him in a special preface to the 1527 edition in which his name first appears. See above, n. 2.

[13]Erasmus began publishing translations of the works of Chrysostom in 1525. In 1530 he published a complete Latin edition of his works. Chrysostom figures prominently in both the 1527 and the 1535 editions of the annotations.

[14]Béné shows something of the same movement described here in relation to Erasmus' use of Augustine's *On Christian Doctrine*. See his final conclusion, *Erasme et Saint Augustin*, pp. 447, 448.

[15]Other Latin writers cited are: Hilary (three times), Aquinas (two times), and Cyprian and Valla (once each). The Greek writer Theodore Gaza is cited once.

errors he discovers in their works. Let us look at each of these briefly.

Quite often, Erasmus simply reports opinions which concur with his own analyses. Sometimes he states his own opinion under the authority of one of the fathers, as when he begins a note: "He speaks about 'obedience to the faith,' as Chrysostom observes, because. . . ." Or: "Origen points out the correct sequence of this whole Pauline argument. . . ." Or: "Augustine, in his book *On Christian Doctrine* IV.7, indicates the framework of this passage. . . ."[16] But more frequently, he will state his own opinion and then add references to the fathers which concur with his own.[17] In some cases when he does this, his own opinion was originally stated without additional authority, and the authorities were added in subsequent editions.[18] In a few of these instances, there is evidence of greater discrimination with regard to the views of the fathers with each later edition. For example, in a note on Romans 5:6, he states his own opinion in the 1516 edition, adds the authority of Ambrosiaster, Origen, and Theophylactus in the 1519 edition, and then in the 1535 edition acknowledges that the views of Ambrosiaster and Origen were not as straightforward as he had interpreted them to be earlier.[19] Erasmus is very scrupulous in his use of sources. Only in one instance in Romans does he seem to twist the meaning of another writer in order to make him concur with a point he wishes to establish.[20]

[16]LB, VI, 558D; 568E; 583D.

[17]LB, VI, 579C; 581E; 582D-E; 600F.

[18]LB, VI, 579C; 593F.

[19]LB, VI, 583F-584C.

[20]In his long note on Romans 5:12, Erasmus interprets Theophylactus as supporting his position. He translates from Theophylactus' commentary on Romans as follows: "For by this fall even those who had eaten nothing from the tree became mortal by their own crime, just as though they themselves were subject to sin, because he had sinned." (LB, VI, 588C-D) But Theophylactus' Greek is correctly translated in another way: "For when he had fallen, even those who did not eat from the tree became mortal due to him, just as though they themselves had sinned, inasmuch as he sinned." (PG, Vol. 124, col. 404C) In other words, whereas Erasmus wants to say that we follow Adam's sin by imitation and says Theophylactus supports this view,

Sometimes Erasmus uses the authority of the fathers for the purpose of heading off criticism. For example, after stating his opinion, he concludes with phrases like the following: "This is the way in which Chrysostom, Theophylactus, and the Greek scholia all interpret . . . in case you reject it as something which I have dreamed up." Or: "If you do not trust my judgment, this punctuation is to be found in the manuscript of Paul which we have often mentioned." Or: "We are not the first to advance this interpretation [of original sin], for this whole passage is explicated in the same way by the man, whoever he was [Pelagius], whose scholia on all the Epistles of Paul have come down to us under the name of Jerome." Or finally: "If anyone is offended that I have removed *praescientia* [foreknowledge] from this passage, he should know that that is the interpretation of Theophylactus, the Greek interpreter, and also of a recent interpreter. . . ."[21]

In the examples just mentioned, Erasmus finds defense for his own views in concurring opinions of the fathers. In other cases, however, he justifies his own deviations from accepted views by appealing to the *heterodoxy* of the fathers. The most striking example in Romans comes in the long note (the longest in the annotations on Romans) on Romans 5:12: "Therefore as sin came into the world through one man and death through sin, and so death spread to all men because all men sinned." Erasmus argues that most of the fathers have admitted at least two interpretations: either that sin came through our physical descent from Adam, or that sin came through our imitation of Adam. At one point in his annotation he writes: "I grant that the Church has the authority to interpret Scripture, but the teachers of the Church, no matter how famous they may be, hesitate over many passages of Scripture, cannot agree on many of them, and actually interpret some of them falsely. Not one of them contends that this passage cannot be understood in a differ-

the latter actually holds the position against which Erasmus is arguing: that in Adam's sin all of us became sinners.

[21]LB, VI, 580E; 584E; 586B; 587B; 606E.

ent sense—except for Saint Augustine, after he became embroiled in the conflict with the Pelagians."[22]

But almost as frequently as he finds support in the fathers, Erasmus also criticizes them. Sometimes he takes them on as a class. He will not, he says, engage in controversy as the fathers did: simply in order to score points against an opponent.[23] The ancient commentators were amazingly gullible, especially in their willingness to accept books as authentic which were obviously spurious.[24] The Greek interpreters often erred in emending passages of Scripture too freely which have little relevance to apostolic doctrine.[25] The Latin interpreters were equally given to quibbles; many of them have often labored mightily over a passage which is perfectly clear.[26] And of course the scholastics are censured for their quibbling which has little relation to Christian piety.[27] At other times, Erasmus levels criticisms against the distortions of particular fathers, and there is hardly one among his favorites who does not receive his due of criticism. In Romans we find explicit strictures against Origen,[28] Hilary,[29] Ambrosiaster,[30] Jerome,[31] Augustine,[32] Thomas Aquinas,[33] Nicholas of Lyra,[34] and Lorenzo Valla.[35]

[22]LB, VI, 589B; see also 601E-F.

[23]LB, VI, 591C.

[24]LB, VI, 653D.

[25]LB, VI, 649E-F.

[26]LB, VI, 618D.

[27]LB, VI, 558D. Throughout chapter 1, Erasmus refers negatively to "the philosophers." He doubtless has the scholastics in mind, particularly the Scotists. See LB, VI, 563D; 563E; 564D-E.

[28]LB, VI, 606F; 635E-F; 653D.

[29]LB, VI, 594D.

[30]LB, VI, 641B-C.

[31]LB, VI, 557A; 630C.

[32]LB, VI, 585B; 638B-E. In this latter passage Erasmus uses the error of Augustine as a justification for returning to the Greek sources.

[33]In LB, VI, 554E-555A, Erasmus extols Thomas as the best among the medieval theologians, excusing his limitations by saying that he lived in barbarous times. But this does not prevent him later from criticizing Thomas on errors of grammar (LB, VI, 614C) and history (LB, VI, 641B).

[34]LB, VI, 655, 656.

[35]LB, VI, 594D.

When we shift attention from Erasmus' use of the fathers to his use of the received text of the Bible (the Vulgate), the question of authority is considerably intensified. For now the authenticity of the source of Christianity itself is being questioned. And there is no doubt that Erasmus questioned it insofar as the Vulgate was regarded as the infallible and perfect Scriptural text. One of his most interesting criticisms is an annotation which, except for the 1522 edition, he augmented each time he published the New Testament. In it we can see a radical attitude become tempered with the passage of time. He writes in the 1516 edition: "... Some people think that this Translator [of the Vulgate] never made a mistake and that he wrote under the inspiration of the Holy Spirit. I challenge them then to make some sense out of [his translation of] this passage, if they can." Then, in 1519 he adds an even more radically critical note: "In fact, the flatness of his translation is here so great, and its incompleteness so evident, as to be a sufficient indication of how far we should trust him in other passages." In 1527 he has begun to modify his earlier boldness: "I refer to the awkwardness of his language, not to the content. We do not have to believe that the Holy Spirit inspired him throughout the whole translation." Evidently, Erasmus had come to believe in 1527 that perhaps the translator of the Vulgate *was* inspired by the Holy Spirit. Apparently writing under this assumption in 1535 he seeks to excuse his mistakes: "In my opinion, the best excuse that we can make for the Translator is that in his day the common people were accustomed to imitate the Greeks in their way of speaking; and his translation was aimed at them, not at educated men."[36]

But the question of interpretation is not answered by criticizing the Vulgate or excusing its mistakes. How is the text to be understood? The movement of understanding is from letter to spirit. Annotating the phrase, "set apart for the Gospel" in Romans 1:1, Erasmus comments: "Thus he

---

[36]LB, VI, 571E-572C. See also 601B-C (added 1527); 612F-613B (added 1535); 619F-620D (added 1535); 628E-F (added 1519); 644C (added 1519).

began to be 'Paul' in the Gospel, as he had been also under Judaism, but with a different connotation. Under Judaism it had been a title of arrogance; but now he was wonderfully separated from Moses [and joined] to Christ; he had gone from the letter to the spirit, from trusting in words to grace."[37] This theme recurs throughout the book. In Chapter 4 Erasmus uses it to describe the paternity of Abraham: "... he [Paul] creates two Abrahams, one who was justified through faith before circumcision, and who was the spiritual father of the Gentiles; and one who was justified through faith while circumcised, and who with his double name is the father of the Jews who believe."[38] Thereafter, the theme is applied to all who believe. "For at the moment when we perceive in our minds that we are dead along with Christ, the desires of our flesh are suppressed and vanish."[39] "Thus we should understand that to offer a living sacrifice holy and acceptable to God is the same thing as not conforming to this world (for this world is ignorant of the will of God and still clings to idolatrous rituals or the ceremonies of Moses, and still lives by the whim of its passions), but instead being transformed in a renewal of mind, so that we deny the will of the flesh and are able to discover the will of God."[40] Clearly, the end of interpretation is the transformation of the believer from fleshly to spiritual existence.

One does not arrive at the goal, however, by a leap, but by a process which begins with the letter itself. Indeed, large questions of theology are often decided by small points of grammar.[41] Consequently, a first task is to discover Paul's opinions and intentions, how he reached a particular point,

[37]LB, VI, 554C.

[38]LB, VI, 580C-D.

[39]LB, VI, 594E; see also 628D-E; 628E-629B.

[40]LB, VI, 629E-F.

[41]In 5:12 (LB, VI, 584F-585B), Erasmus shows that 'destine' and 'predestine' are verbs with the same meaning. Deciding this point of grammar enables us to say that Christ was predestined. Again in 5:12 (585D-F), Erasmus concludes that the Greek of the passage in question cannot be taken to mean that all men sinned physically in Adam, and therefore must be taken to mean that we sin with Adam through imitation of Adam's sin. See also 601B-C.

and the conclusion toward which his words tend.[42] Erasmus employs all the tools of grammar to this end. A few questions can be decided on the more narrow grounds of correct grammar and syntax. Erasmus does not hesitate to correct solecisms,[43] to decide some questions on the basis of what the grammar will permit,[44] and to correct commonly held views of the meaning of a word.[45] He calls attention to idioms that make a difference when translated from one language into another.[46] Erasmus also applies the tools of language in a broader, heuristic sense, clarifying the meaning of a word through the suggestion of alternatives,[47] or elucidating the word through phrases,[48] examples or illustrations,[49] and analogies.[50]

Erasmus does not limit himself, as he says he will in his preface to the annotations, to grammatical explication. We find in his annotations the whole range of his views of bibli-

[42]LB, VI, 591C-D.

[43]LB, VI, 619F-620D.

[44]On Romans 5:7 (LB, VI, 584D), he writes: "'Righteous' and 'good' in this passage do not mean some person, but a thing, namely righteousness and goodness themselves; they are of the neuter gender, not masculine...." See also 580C-D; 582D-F; 600C-D; 601D-E; 612F; 631F-632C; 643D.

[45]LB, VI, 581E: "The word *vulva* does not mean the female sexual organs, as the uneducated people take it, but the womb in which the fetus is conceived."

[46]"'The law of the spirit' means the same thing as 'the spiritual law,' in accordance with a Hebrew idiom." LB, VI, 600B. See also 600E; 613C; 621C-D.

[47]"'First' here has about the same sense as 'especially'; ... in this passage 'Greek' stands for 'heathen'." LB, VI, 562D. See also 572E; 595D; 634B-C; 652D.

[48]The word *dialogismos* does not mean simply thinking, but the thinking of one who uses logic, weighs alternatives and judges among them...." LB, VI, 564E. See also 567C-D; 579B-C; 637B-C.

[49]"Something is 'presented' when it was promised before and is now being offered, or when it was hidden and is now brought forth, as a promissory note would be presented." LB, VI, 628C-D. See also 579B-C; 582F.

[50]"... the allusion is to the grafting on of a shoot, which corresponds to union with the body of Christ. For just as the shoot is plucked from its own tree and shares in the sap of the tree onto which it is grafted, likewise men are grafted onto the body of Christ through baptism and come to share in all of the benefits of Christ." LB, VI, 593E. See also 605D-E.

cal interpretation expressed and applied. Granted all the tools of grammar, we cannot penetrate Scripture with those alone. Many passages, especially of the Old Testament, were meant to be understood allegorically. Some of the things we read there are otherwise either irrelevant or immoral.[51] But what is true of the Old Testament is also true of Paul. There are passages in Romans which cannot be taken literally and must be taken allegorically[52] or tropologically.[53]

Allegory is checked, however, by a principle of interpretation which emerges in Erasmus' practice of exegesis but, so far as I know, not in his theoretical formulations of interpretation, namely, that the simpler interpretation is to be preferred over the more involved. "I am well aware," says Erasmus in one note, "that some men use this passage [Rom. 8:29] as an excellent training-ground to exercise their ingenuity and carry on philosophical disputes about foreknowledge and predestination . . . and I do not mean to criticize their industriousness. But I think that the sense I have explained is simpler and truer."[54]

But even after we have done all that is humanly possible to clarify the texts, much remains unclarified. There are passages in which the Greek is ambiguous and in which no final resolution between alternatives is possible.[55] Erasmus readily admits his limitations, refusing to rule out interpre-

---

[51]See the examples from Scripture cited in LB, VI, 644C-F. It is interesting that this passage was added in 1535, that is, at the time Erasmus was working on the *Ecclesiastes*, in which he voiced his most stringent criticisms of allegorical interpretations.

[52]See LB, VI, 585D-E; 638D. For his use of simile in this connection, see 604E-F.

[53]LB, VI, 585C.

[54]LB, VI, 606F. He might have said at the end, simpler and *therefore* truer. In another passage he writes: "I do not see why we should reject this interpretation, which results from taking the Greek words in their simplest sense. . ." LB, VI, 626F. See also 629B. Schlingensiepen has pointed to this same principle in Erasmus' paraphrase of Matthew ("Erasmus als Exeget auf Grund seiner Schriften zu Matthäus," p. 19).

[55]LB, VI, 598E; 600C; 600C-D; 614F-615B; 636C-D; 639F-640E; 643E. In 584D he simply expounds the differing opinions of several fathers without further comment.

tations that differ from his own.[56] What can we do in these cases? Erasmus suggests several possibilities.

In one passage he suggests that "we do not put the reliability of the Gospel writers to the same test as we would that of other historians."[57] This is not true in the sense that they are not subjected to the same criteria of grammatical, literary, and historical analysis. For we have seen that Erasmus consistently applies the same standards to biblical as to other texts. But it is true in the sense that one can assume truths hidden behind the obscurities of Scripture that cannot be assumed in the case of other books. Sometimes it is necessary to conclude that the meaning of these passages has been hidden from us by God and was not meant to be comprehended.[58] In cases like this, or indeed in any case, we can have recourse to the authority of the Church. This may, in fact, be in spite of the evidence. On Romans 9:5, he writes: "And yet if the Church should teach that we must interpret this passage only in terms of the divinity of the Son, then we will have to obey the Church's decision, although its decision will be of no help in refuting the heretics or in convincing anyone who listens to Scripture alone." However, he goes on to add: "But if the Church further claims that its interpretation is the only one consistent with the wording of the Greek, a mere glance at the passage will be enough to refute that claim."[59]

Much more often, however, Erasmus defers to the authority of the individual Christian rather than to that of the Church. "This phrase can be interpreted in many ways," he says on Romans 1:4. "We will set them all forth simply, as befits our duty. The right to pass judgment on

[56]LB, VI, 582F; 591D.

[57]LB, VI, 556E.

[58]Erasmus draws this conclusion at the end of his long discussions of original sin in chapter 5 (LB, VI, 589E). See also 591C-D.

[59]LB, VI, 611E. Erasmus expressed a similar sentiment in an annotation to Romans 5:12: "A single testimony from Scripture suffices for me; sometimes the authority of the Church suffices, even without Scripture. But to meet the heretics, what use would it be to rule that this passage must not be understood in a different sense, when the evidence cries out that it can be so understood?" (LB, VI, 590A)

them and the power of choosing among them both belong to the reader."[60] Again he writes: "I have shown what sense can be gotten from the Greek words; let the prudent and careful reader follow what he judges to be best."[61] But who is a prudent and careful reader? On what basis does he pass judgment? A criterion is not lacking in Erasmus at this point either. After commenting that he has adopted a particular meaning because it seemed simpler to him, he says that "none of the other interpretations fails to meet the standard of piety."[62] The final criterion is whether or not an interpretation builds up piety. In one of the more moving passages in the annotations, Erasmus writes:

> Truly, Paul's warning to the Jews should be taken to heart even more by us Christians, for if our life is different from that of the heathens only by our profession of the name of Christian and by our ceremonies, while in all other respects it is equal to theirs or even worse, there is a danger that the most holy name of Christ will be polluted and disgraced among the enemies of the faith, ... if they perceive that we are so abjectly subject to lust that we are no more moderate [than they] in thirsting after profit, in our desire for vengeance, in our fear of death, in our longing for life, in the fury of our wars, tumults, and fights—all due to trivial causes.[63]

Be transformed; that is the goal of the Christian, and that becomes the most effective criterion for interpreting the text. "It is more effective," writes Erasmus in a passage that expresses this point beautifully, "to say that since we have as a judge God who justifies us, and since we have the Son of God who died for us and continues to intervene for us, there is no reason why we should fear the charges brought by any man."[64]

[60]LB, VI, 556C. In 606F he concludes: "If anyone prefers another sense, let him take it and use it, for all I care. I am only advising, not trying to establish a precedent; I am only giving you my opinion, not trying to prejudge anyone else's."

[61]LB, VI, 591E-F.

[62]LB, VI, 627D. In 584C he concludes: "Each reading has a pious sense."

[63]LB, VI, 573D-E.

[64]LB, VI, 607F (the passage added in 1522).

The Paraphrase

The paraphrases of the New Testament[65] were not executed in the same way as the annotations. The *Paraphrase of Romans* was the first to appear (1517). It was followed by paraphrases of Corinthians and Galatians (1519); Ephesians, Philippians, Colossians, Thessalonians, Timothy, Titus, and Philemon (1520), and during the same year the epistles of Peter, Jude, and James, as well as the Gospel of Matthew. All the epistles of Paul were published in a collected edition in 1521; the Epistle to the Hebrews appeared during the same year. Erasmus then turned to the remaining gospels and to Acts. His paraphrases of Mark, Luke, John, and Acts appeared in 1523. The paraphrases were published in collected editions in 1524, 1532, and 1534. Like the annotations, however, the paraphrases were revised as they were reissued.

[65]The paraphrases have never been critically edited. A translation into English was prepared in the 1540's under the supervision of Nicholas Udall and published in 1548 and again in 1551. Copies of the paraphrases of the gospels were ordered to be placed in every parish church (See E. J. Devereux, "The Publication of the English *Paraphrases* of Erasmus," *Bulletin of the John Rylands Library*, LI [1969], 348-67). Margaret Roper, the daughter of Thomas More, translated the paraphrase of the Pater Noster into English; this has recently been reprinted with the Latin on facing pages ("Erasmus' Paraphrase of the Pater Noster," *Moreana*, VII [1965], 9-63).

Only four articles have been devoted to the paraphrases: R. H. Bainton, "The Paraphrases of Erasmus," *Archiv für Reformationsgeschichte*, LVII:I-II (1966), 67-76; Joseph Coppens, "Les idées réformistes d'Erasme dans les Préfaces aux Paraphrases du Nouveau Testament," in E. van Cauwenbergh, ed., *Scrinium Lovaniense* (Louvain, 1961), 344-71; Rudolf Padberg, "Glaubenstheologie und Glaubensverkündigung bei Erasmus von Rotterdam dargestellt auf der Grundlage der Paraphrase zum Römerbrief," in T. Filthaut and J. A. Jungmann, eds., *Verkündigung und Glaube: Festgabe für Franz X. Arnold* (Herder: Freiburg, 1958), 58-75; and Hermann Schlingensiepen, "Erasmus als Exeget auf Grund seiner Schriften zu Matthäus," *Zeitschrift für Kirchengeschichte*, XLVIII (1929), 16-57.

Of these studies, that of Schlingensiepen is the most substantial. The article by Padberg, the only one devoted to the *Paraphrase of Romans*, attempts to show that Erasmus understood the Pauline notion of justification by faith and that he stated this before the Reformation began. The texts on the basis of which he makes this case, however, were for the most part added in 1532. Padberg did not bother to collate the various editions of Romans in order to determine just what the 1517 edition omitted, and this largely vitiates his argument.

Why did Erasmus turn first to Paul, and in the Pauline corpus, to Romans, when he began to write paraphrases of the books of the New Testament? There are a number of reasons, all related to his intellectual development discussed in the first two chapters.[66] When Erasmus went to Oxford, he found John Colet lecturing on Paul's epistles. He took great interest in Colet's work, and, either before he returned to Paris or immediately thereafter, he wrote commentaries on Paul (now lost). Colet was doubtless instrumental in turning Eramus toward Paul as a starting point. Then in 1501 Erasmus met Jean Vitrier who, as we have seen, introduced him to Origen. Vitrier's favorite scriptural writer was Paul. In his later life of Vitrier, Erasmus writes:

> He had so thoroughly learned by heart the books of Holy Scripture, St. Paul's Epistles more particularly, that he had the words of his favorite, St. Paul, completely at his finger ends. At whatever passage you set him on, he would, after a moment's thought, go on right through the Epistle without a single mistake. . . . It was his custom to take up St.

[66]There are two reasons given by Erasmus which need not detain us as initiating causes. One is an accident in 1514 resulting in a vow. He describes how his horse, frightened at some linen spread on the ground, swerved in such a way that Erasmus' spine was strained. The pain was so severe that he screamed; he was unable to dismount. His servant helped him dismount and he walked the remainder of the trip. Then he adds: "I made a vow to St. Paul that I would complete my commentary on the Epistle to the Romans if I escaped this danger." (EE, II, 6, lines 18-20; Nichols, II, 152) Feeling better the next day, he offered his thanks to God and St. Paul. This incident recalls the letters from Paris during his illnesses in 1496 and 1498. In this case, however, Erasmus was already preoccupied with Romans; it was on his mind and even partly written. The incident did not turn him to Paul.

A second reason of little weight is Paul's eloquence. Erasmus had said in the *Antibarbari* that Paul was the most outstanding among the apostles for eloquence (EOO, I.1, 122, 130). However, in the preface to the original edition of the New Testament he contrasts the obscurity of the apostolic epistles with the clarity of the gospels (EE, II, 171, lines 181-96). Moreover, in his "Argument" to the *Paraphrase of Romans,* he speaks of Paul as an obscure writer, finding support for this view in Origen and Jerome. (See also LB, VI, 630E; but cf. 608B-D, where he follows Augustine in affirming Paul's eloquence.) In his annotation of I Cor. 4:3, he follows Jerome (in a passage greatly expanded in the 1519 edition) in arguing that Paul's Greek is not elegant (LB, VI, 673E-674D).

Paul, and to spend the time reading him till he felt
his heart grow warm.[67]

Erasmus expressed a similar sentiment in his own person at the end of the *Enchiridion,* exhorting the dissolute
knight to whom he was writing: "Above all, however, make
Paul your intimate friend. Him you should always cling to,
'meditating upon him day and night' until you commit to
memory every word."[68] But perhaps the reason Colet, Vitrier,
and Erasmus were all drawn to Paul had to do with the feeling of rapport each felt with Paul. In the case of Erasmus,
we have seen that very early in his writings the dichotomy
between flesh and spirit appears, and that the contrast between the visible and the invisible world—the heritage of
both the *Devotio Moderna* and Platonism—was natural for
him. Although its meaning changes, this dichotomy is present in his earliest treatises in the monastery and in his correspondence. It is also present in the *Enchiridion,* where
Erasmus is conscious of the difference between his Paulinism
and his Platonism.[69] A further suggestion also appears in the
Enchiridion: Paul is the best of the allegorizers.[70]

Perhaps we can go even one step more and ask: Why
did *Colet* choose Paul? From the end of the patristic period
until the generation of Erasmus there were very few commentaries on Paul's epistles.[71] During the Middle Ages the

[67]EE, IV, 508-9, lines 44-47, 52-54; tr. Olin, *Christian Humanism and the
Reformation,* p. 167.

[68]Holborn, p. 135; Himelick, p. 199. The quoted phrase is from Horace,
Ars Poetica, 269.

[69]See above, p. 57.

[70]See above, p. 54.

[71]There is no single systematic account of the history of Pauline interpretation. For the Greek patristic writers see C. H. Turner, "Greek Patristic
Commentaries on the Pauline Epistles," in James Hastings, ed., *A Dictionary
of the Bible* (New York: Scribner's, 1904), Extra Vol., pp. 484-531. Turner's
article is very useful in illuminating the extent of the work on Paul among
the Greek fathers. He does not, however, deal with the ideas about Paul held
by each father. On the western fathers see Alexander Souter, *The Earliest
Latin Commentaries on the Epistles of St. Paul* (Oxford: Clarendon Press,
1927). Souter deals with the textual problems and with the thought of
Victorinus, Ambrosiaster, Jerome, Augustine, and Pelagius. For a recent
study of the patristic interpretations of Paul, see Maurice F. Wiles, *The Di-*

study of the Bible, insofar as it had been carried on by exegetes like the Victorines, confined itself largely to the study of the Old Testament—Hebrew was much better known and much more studied than Greek—and within the Old Testament, to the historical and prophetic books.[72] The New Testament had not been subjected to critical exegetical study to the same extent. There were perhaps two reasons for this. One was that knowledge of Greek, unlike knowledge of Hebrew, could be used for profane studies and indeed was. Before 1500, only three Greek Psalters were printed. And, of course, Erasmus' version of the Greek New Testament in 1516 was the first. The second reason was the fear that the language used by the heretical Greeks must contain heretical views—and humanists were accused of heresy because of their knowledge of Greek.[73]

Paul, in particular, was considered the property of the theologians or dialecticians, and expositions of Pauline theology came through them rather than through critical biblical study. One interpreter of medieval biblical scholarship writes: "The eleventh- and early twelfth-century masters were inclined to identify exegesis with theology. . . . We find the theological questioning but not the biblical scholarship. It is no accident that the two favorite books for commentators were the Psalter and the Pauline Epistles, their creative energy being centered in the latter; St. Paul provided the richest nourishment to the theologian and logician."[74] But

vine Apostle: The Interpretation of St. Paul's Epistles in the Early Church (Cambridge: Cambridge University Press, 1967). In his bibliography and in chapter 1 of his text, Wiles delineates the sources and more specialized treatments of the interpretation of Paul by the fathers.

On medieval exegesis much work remains to be done. I know of no special studies on the interpretation of Paul during the Middle Ages. But see Henri de Lubac, *Exégèse médiévale: les quatre sens de l'écriture* (Paris: Aubier, 1959-1964), 4 vols.; and Beryl Smalley, *The Study of the Bible in the Middle Ages* (Oxford: Blackwell, 1952; reprinted in paperback by the University of Notre Dame Press, 1964).

[72]Smalley, *The Study of the Bible in the Middle Ages*, pp. 361-62.

[73]See W. Schwarz, *Principles and Problems of Biblical Translation*, pp. 92, 93.

[74]Beryl Smalley, *The Study of the Bible in the Middle Ages*, pp. 76-77.

then suddenly there were a great number of commentaries on the Pauline Epistles, among them Colet (1496-1499), Lefèvre d'Etaples (1512), Luther (1515-1516), Erasmus (1517), Calvin (1539). It may be that the revival of Paul by the Christian humanists of Northern Europe was related to the Platonic revival in Italy a generation earlier. But it may also be that for those who wanted to return to the sources of Christianity, and in doing so to remove the distortions brought into being by scholastic theology, Paul seemed to be one most in need of rehabilitation.

There is still another consideration worth pondering. For both the humanists and the Protestant Reformers the central position accorded Paul rested on his psychology of faith, that is, on his understanding of the law as that which binds man and from which he must be freed (the Reformers) and on the dichotomy between flesh and spirit (the humanists). This is true even if, as has been cogently argued, Paul's understanding of what he was saying was quite different from what his sixteenth-century interpreters believed he was saying.[75] Paul was instrumental in the development of new ways of orienting the Christian consciousness to God and the world; indeed, he more than any other Christian thinker addressed himself—in the eyes of sixteenth-century interpreters—to the kinds of concerns that pressed religious persons during this period. And he not only spoke to them; he also resolved them. It was for this reason, perhaps, that so many found sustenance in Paul.

Erasmus began work on a commentary on Romans for the second time in 1514.[76] But he actually executed it between May and July, 1517. On May 30 of that year, he wrote to Thomas More that he and Peter Gilles were planning to present him with portraits of themselves painted by Quentin Matsys, though the ill health of each of the subjects was slowing down the artist's work.[77] The portraits were com-

---

[75]See Krister Stendahl, "The Apostle Paul and the Introspective Conscience of the West," *Harvard Theological Review*, LVI (1963), 199-215.

[76]See above, pp. 46, 129.

[77]EE, II, 576, lines 6-14; Nichols, II, 559.

pleted by September 8, when Erasmus writes to More that he is ready to send them to England.[78] More wrote to Erasmus and Peter Gilles separately, thanking them profusely for their gifts. In his letter to Gilles he comments that Erasmus is "represented as beginning his Paraphrase on the Epistle to the Romans. . . ."[79] Contemporary with More's letter to Gilles is one by Erasmus to Gilles in which he comments: "The Paraphrase which I was beginning in the picture [by Matsys] is already finished, and is being printed."[80] Letters dated November 2 and November 19 indicate that the *Paraphrase* is still in press.[81] On November 30, Erasmus sends a copy to Thomas More.[82] Hence, it issued from the press of Thierry Martens at Louvain toward the end of November, 1517.

As the printing nears completion, Erasmus makes passing references in his letters to the labor it has cost him. In one letter in mid-November, he comments: ". . . my Paraphrase of the Epistle to the Romans is in the press here—a work of more labor than is seen on the face of it."[83] He confirms this judgment in another letter written about the same time, commenting that the paraphrase "is a small book, but no one would believe without making the experiment, what toil it has cost me."[84] Once he had completed the paraphrase, however, and had returned to the immense labor of revis-

---

[78]EE, III, 76, lines 1-4; Nichols, III, 41. By September 16 they had been sent (EE, III, 92, line 1; Nichols, III, 69).

[79]EE, III, 105-6, lines 11-15; Nichols, III, 92. From More's description of the paintings we know that the representations of Erasmus now extant are not the original, though Matsys' original of Peter Gilles is extant. See Alois Gerlo, *Erasme et ses portraitistes* (Nieuwkoop: B. de Graaf, 1969), p. 16, n. 19.

[80]EE, III, 110, lines 15-16; Nichols, III, 98.

[81]On November 2 he writes: "The Paraphrase on the Epistle to the Romans is being elegantly printed. It is only right that Paul should speak to the *Romans* in tolerable Latin. This work is wonderfully approved by the learned." (EE, III, 120, lines 29-32; Nichols, III, 118) For the letter of November 19, see EE, III, 148, lines 3-4; Nichols, III, 145.

[82]EE, III, 153, line 2; Nichols, III, 166.

[83]EE, III, 134, lines 14-16; Nichols, III, 106.

[84]EE, III, 144, lines 7-9; Nichols, III, 153. See also EE, III, 147, lines 2-4; Nichols, III, 157.

ing his first edition of the text of the New Testament, he judged the labor of the paraphrase in retrospect to have been a means of relaxation! Scarcely one week after the publication of the paraphrase he wrote to one correspondent: "I send ... our Paraphrase on Paul's Epistle to the Romans, which is our latest offspring. For since I am now engaged in the most difficult of all literary labors, that is, the revision of the text of the New Testament, I am wont to refresh my mind with such relaxations. As often as satiety tempts me to steal away, this serves as my ball or my die, sending me back to work with fresh vigor."[85] Reflecting in March, 1518, on the enthusiastic reception of the paraphrase, as opposed to the many critical strictures against his work on the text of the New Testament, Erasmus comments: "It must however be admitted that our paraphrase is applauded by everyone. It is some satisfaction to have produced even a single book which pleases such surly critics. I only wish that I had confined myself to like fields, in which much more credit was to be had with much less labor."[86]

In the letter to More accompanying his paraphrase, Erasmus says: "I send you the book of Paraphrase, rightly so entitled." Before sending it to the press, all his references to it used the word "commentary" rather than "paraphrase." He does not say whether or not he consciously changed the plan of his work from commentary to paraphrase.[87] And he does not comment upon the distinction between the two until he has been engaged in the task of writing paraphrases for some time. In a letter written in 1522 he says: "For a paraphrase is not a translation but a certain freer kind of continuous commentary with the integrity of the persons

[85]EE, III, 150, lines 8-14; Nichols, III, 163. He repeats the same judgment two weeks later; EE, III, 168, lines 7-10; Nichols, III, 195.

[86]EE, III, 249, lines 78-83; Nichols, III, 305.

[87]In the 1516 edition of the *Novum Instrumentum* Erasmus says in a note to Romans 1:11 that he will write a fuller commentary on Paul at a later time. He omitted this statement for the first time in the 1527 edition. Apparently then, as late as 1516 Erasmus did intend to write a larger commentary on Paul, something more ambitious than the paraphrases. (The passage from the 1516 edition is quoted in Allen, III, 115, n. 28.)

speaking maintained."[88] And in his prefatory letter to his Paraphrase of the Gospel of John, he says: "However, I do not wish that anyone grant more to this paraphrase than would have been granted to a commentary, as if I had written a commentary—although a paraphrase also is a kind of commentary."[89]

Erasmus was not satisfied with the first edition of his work. Writing to Cardinal Grimani on April 26, 1518, he states that even though the paraphrase had been dedicated to him, he had not sent him a copy in part because "I was not quite pleased myself with the first edition."[90] Barely two weeks after the first edition had come off the press, he sent Beatus Rhenanus, who worked at the Froben Press in Basel, a revised copy. And although he says that it would not be fair to the Louvain publisher to reprint the work immediately,[91] Froben could hardly be said to have delayed, for the first of his many editions appeared in January, 1518.[92] This was reprinted in April and November of the same year and again in 1519 and in 1520. Thereafter it was published to-

[88]EE, V, 47, lines 37-39.

[89]EE, V, 172, lines 395-97. Nichols points out (III, 166) that the Greek *Paraphraseos,* used in the letter to More, can mean either a running *alongside* the text or a going *beyond* it, and that Erasmus never clarifies which he intends. Allen, in his introduction to Erasmus' prefatory letter dedicating the *Paraphrase of Romans* to Cardinal Grimani, says: "In this [paraphrase] he would be free on the one hand from the restrictions of a literal translation such as he had previously carried out, and on the other from the severities of a scholarly commentary, which he had discovered to be less easy to him than paraphrase: as indeed it was alien to his genius." (EE, III, 136) The evidence Allen cites in support of this assertion, however, does not in fact support it.

[90]EE, III, 305, lines 4-5; Nichols, III, 371. The source of Erasmus' dissatisfaction is not clear, for he made few substantive changes in the second edition, and the printing errors were not numerous.

[91]EE, III, 160-61, lines 18-20; Nichols, III, 182.

[92]P. S. Allen points out that Froben consistently issued the works of Erasmus first published by Martens almost immediately after Martens published them and that Erasmus connived at this. Probably for this reason, Martens' edition was small and today is extremely rare. *(Erasmus: Lectures and Wayfaring Sketches* [Oxford: Clarendon Press, 1934], p. 137)

gether with paraphrases of other epistles and after 1524 in the collected editions.[93]

Erasmus made forty-three substantive changes (usually additions) to the paraphrase in editions subsequent to the first, of which two were made in 1521 and forty-one in 1532. Viewed together, two things are striking about these changes. The first is the more explicit connection of righteousness with faith in Christ. The significance of this for Erasmus' theology will become clear in the following chapter, but the fact itself should be noted here. Note the following passages, in each of which the italicized portion was added in 1532:

> 2:10: Contrariwise glory, honor, and peace will be repaid equally to all, whoever *through faith* has lived well. . . .
>
> 2:20: Do you think that all of this [the law] is enough to give you preference over the heathen, *under the grace of the Gospel?*
>
> 2:26: and if he *trusts and* obeys Christ who is the fulfillment of all laws.
>
> 3:22: Righteousness, I say, not of the Law . . . but through faith *and trust* in Jesus Christ. . . .
>
> 3:25: He declares his righteousness for men on these conditions: *through his Son* he forgives the errors of their former life. . . .
>
> 3:26: . . . it is a new law which considers nothing except faith *in the Son of God.*
>
> 3:28: For in our opinion . . . in the future anyone at all will be able to attain righteousness *through faith.* . . . That Law was peculiar to the Jewish nation, but this favor *of the grace of the Gospel* proceeds from God. . . .
>
> 4:25: . . . Christ who voluntarily surrendered himself to death so that *through faith* our crimes might freely be wiped away.
>
> 5:11: Thus it is clear that the whole of this benefit should be ascribed to none other than God himself *and his only Son.*

[93]The *Bibliotheca Erasmiana* (Gand, 1893; reprinted, 1961), Part I, p. 145, lists an edition of the *Paraphrase of Romans* published separately at Louvain in 1527. Allen, on the contrary, remarks that Romans was never published separately after 1520 (EE, III, 137). Moreover, I have been unable to locate any copy of the 1527 edition. I doubt that such an edition exists.

8:25: ... *but we are finally rendered acceptable to God by our faith* if we discern with the eyes of faith things which cannot be seen with the eyes of the body....

9:5 [1517]: ... God of the whole world protecting all men, to whom alone praise is owed for all eternity.

[1532]: [Christ is] a God who is one with the Father. He protects all men, and all things are carried out by his inscrutable wisdom. Because of such an unusual love for the human race, praise and thanksgiving are owed to Christ alone for all eternity.

This represents one-fourth of all the changes made in the *Paraphrase of Romans*. How are they to be explained?

The answer to this question includes the explanation also of the second striking feature of Erasmus' changes: the accommodation of several of them to viewpoints characteristic of the Protestant Reformers. Note, for example, the following additions, also made in 1532.[94] Again, in each case the italicized portion represents the addition:

1:7: ... *grace, that is, the free gift of the truly justifying faith of the Gospel.*

1:13: *By the Gospel I mean justification through*

---

[94]Robert Kleinhans has put forward the hypothesis that Luther influenced a change in Erasmus' view of baptism in the paraphrases. He states: "In early writings Erasmus clearly contrasted salvation in Christ with the false doctrine of salvation through adherence to the Law or philosophical learning, but with the publication of the Paraphrase on the gospel according to St. Mark (Dec. 1523) there is an almost Lutheran stress on the free forgiveness of sin as opposed to ceremonial religion." On the basis of his observation of this difference Kleinhans suggests that Erasmus first seriously read Luther between January 1522 and the publication of the paraphrase of Mark in 1523 *(Erasmus' Doctrine of Preaching, pp. 114-23)*.

On the basis of my study of Romans, I believe that both of Kleinhans' theses are incorrect. As to the first, it is clear that in his 1523 edition of Romans there are no changes in a Reformation direction. There are such changes in the annotations in 1527 and again in 1535 (LB, VI, 559C-D; 578E-F; 587B), and in the paraphrase of 1532. We could just as well prove a "Lutheran" influence in 1527 or 1532 or 1535 as 1523. The same holds for his second hypothesis. Perhaps Erasmus did not read Luther seriously until 1527 or later! If there was a Lutheran influence on Erasmus, which I doubt, it must be demonstrated on other grounds.

faith in Jesus Christ, whom the Law promised and prefigured.

2:7: . . . namely those who now *rely on the promises of the Gospel* and persevere in pious works. . . .

3:26: *He does not forgive because men have merited it, but because he himself had promised forgiveness.*

3:30: And so it is not the case that there is one God who justifies the circumcised by faith in the law *which promised them a savior,* and who leads them to faith *in the promises* of the Gospel. . . .

8:39: But we are not afraid, neither of any common angel . . . nor of some preeminent angel . . . *even if miracles come forth from heaven or the terrors of hell threaten us.* . . .

10:15: . . . not circumcision and the keeping of the sabbath, but 'peace,' which *through faith after our sins have been abolished,* welds us together by mutual love in Christ.

11:26: *When they cease relying on works and become strong through faith, they will succeed in gaining the Lord's blessing.*

It would be incorrect, I believe, to conclude from both these groups of changes—which constitute about half of all the changes made in the paraphrase—that Erasmus was becoming more conservative in his old age or that he never could decide whether he was a Catholic or a Protestant. Rather, the explanation is to be sought in Erasmus' passionate interest in Christian unity. He had shown in a colloquy written in 1524, just a few months before he composed his diatribe on free will against Luther, that Lutherans were essentially Catholic in their beliefs and that these should not become the basis for the division of Christendom.[95] Likewise, he could show in 1532 that his own position was flexible enough to include the assertions of the Reformers without distort-

[95]See "An Examination Concerning Faith," in C. R. Thompson, *The Colloquies of Erasmus,* pp. 177-88. See also Thompson's critical edition and study of this colloquy: *Inquisitio de fide* (New Haven: Yale University Press, 1950). See further *De Amabili ecclesiae concordia,* 1533 (LB, V, 469-506); tr. "On Mending the Peace of the Church," in J. P. Dolan, *The Essential Erasmus,* pp. 327-88.

ing his basic perspective. Indeed, in a number of his changes, he added an emphasis characteristic of the Reformers to one of his own. For example, after he says in Romans 1:7 that we are justified by the free gift of the Gospel, he adds: "Then, after this faith has completely abolished all the sins of your former life, I wish you the peace of a secure conscience and a steadfast friendship with God." This would not have been said by Luther. He goes on to conclude that these two things are not gotten through the Law, but through the generosity of God in Christ.[96] Moreover, there are also a number of additions which reinforce his tropological interpretation.[97] Erasmus did not change his perspective, nor was he "influenced" by the Reformers; nor did he simply grow old. He maintained an interpretation of Christianity which he believed could be universally accepted by all Christians and, if accepted, would bring about the reform of Christendom. He never deviated from this belief, and he never ceased to express it in his writings.

The thought of all great men is capable of taking much into itself without losing its coherence. Indeed, that is one of the characteristics of a great mind. Erasmus has been called "great" on a number of counts, but few are willing to grant him that title in the arena of religious thought. But if we analyze his theology as it appears in his work on Romans we may perhaps realize more than has been done in the past the religious vision and power which Erasmus' thought embodied.

[96]See also 2:7.

[97]See the changes in 1:16; 2:1; 5:21; 6:21; 8:6; 8:26; 9:16; 9:21; 9:28; 12:12; 12:19. The one change made in 1521 (Rom. 9:6) is also tropological in its emphasis.

V

HUMANIST RELIGIOUS CONSCIOUSNESS: THE THEOLOGY BEHIND THE METHODOLOGY[1]

For Erasmus theology did not begin with true propositions but with the life experiences of persons; it did not end in a systematic formulation which could answer intellectual criticism but in a life directed or redirected toward religious ends. When he speaks about the nature of God or the actions of God in Christ, a kind of human response is also part of the assertion. This dialectic provides the most congenial organizing motif for our discussion of Erasmus' religious consciousness.

The Nature of God and His Meaning for Human Existence

There is no more dramatic instance of Erasmus' transformation of scholastic propositional theology than his modi-

[1] I have profited from reading in manuscript a paper by John B. Payne, "Erasmus: Interpreter of Romans," subsequently published in *Sixteenth Century Studies and Essays*, Vol. II, ed., C. S. Meyer (Foundation for Reformation Research, 1971). His discussion of Erasmus' theology follows the outline of Romans and makes no attempt to provide an overarching frame of reference into which Erasmus' ideas fit. Perhaps in part for this reason, his conclusions are a much more accurate index of Erasmus' theology than the one earlier attempt apart from this chapter to provide such a framework. See above, ch. IV, note 65.

fication of the attributes of God. Except for the notion of omnipotence, which he uses in his own way, he never discusses the existence, simplicity, perfection, goodness in general, infinity, immutability, eternity, and unity of God, as does St. Thomas at the beginning of his *Summa Theologica.* The attributes which Erasmus emphasizes throughout are the notions of God as loving, persuading, promising, truthful in fulfilling his promises. And each of these calls to mind a human response.

God's nature is preeminently that of a loving benefactor. Had he not loved us with a very great love he would never have sent his only son to take on a mortal body and die for men who were still lost in sinful desires. Only a deep love can reclaim persons unworthy of such loyalty[2] and sustain them to the point that nothing can overcome them when that love is operative.[3] God breathes into us the strength of love, and for such strength nothing is difficult or unpleasant.[4] Nothing can restrain us from responding to a love so overpowering in its goodness, whether human wickedness, perplexity or suffering, hunger or want, danger or persecution.[5] Love is a human possibility because its deepest expression has been made possible by a loving God. Love as an attribute of God, therefore, is not so much a true proposition as it is a statement about the possibilities of human life.

A loving God is one who persuades; he does not compel. God invites everyone but forces no one.[6] Man's response is therefore a matter of free choice. He responds because he is persuaded, not because some necessity drives him. Erasmus' view of predestination follows from or is a part of his notion of God as one who persuades. God makes his mercy available to everyone.[7] Hence, it is true to say that there is no

[2]LB, VII, 792D.

[3]LB, VII, 805D.

[4]LB, VII, 802B-C.

[5]LB, VII, 805C.

[6]LB, VII, 788E.

[7]The distinction between Christ and Moses is that Christ makes available for *all* what Moses made available for only one nation, as I shall point out in more detail below.

salvation apart from the kindness of God. But it is not true to say that a refusal of the kindness of God is attributable to God.[8] God did not harden Pharaoh's heart, but he *did* show his power through Pharaoh when Pharaoh's *own will* prevented him from believing.[9] God does have power. He is omnipotent. But he does not use his power to overwhelm human will, even though human will cannot thwart the purposes of God.

The purposes of God are revealed through his promises. God promised Abraham that Christ who would be born from his seed would bless all nations.[10] Abraham believed God, proving that "God was truthful—since he was unwilling to deceive anyone, and omnipotent—since he was able to fulfill whatever he had promised, however much this exceeded human strength."[11] The Gospel is Abraham's final vindication, for it displays for us that what God promised he fulfilled.[12] God is therefore one—the only one—in whom ultimate trust can be placed.

To trust that the promises of God are true is to be a person of faith as Abraham was.[13] Faith here has the double meaning of something received from God [*fides qua creditur*] and a human response [*fides quae creditur*]. In a note to the 1527 edition of his New Testament Erasmus writes:

> Sometimes "the faith of God" is mentioned, by which we trust in him rather than in man; it is said to be [of God] also because it is given by him; not only because it is directed at him. Sometimes [faith is] reciprocal, as in "the righteous man shall live by faith:" [such faith is] of God because he does not deceive in what he has promised, and also of the man who has faith in God. The phrase under consideration, "through faith for faith," has this same double significance. For God at appointed times

[8]LB, VII, 807E-F.
[9]LB, VII, 808A.
[10]LB, VII, 789B-C.
[11]LB, VII, 791B-C.
[12]LB, VI, 644D; LB, VII, 795B.
[13]LB, VII, 807A; 811E.

began to reveal his nature and to fulfill his promises; and likewise man's understanding of and trust in God increased by steps. Few believed in prophets until God actually revealed to their eyes what he had promised.[14]

Sometimes Erasmus speaks as if trust [*fiducia*] is the human response to the faith [*fides*] given by God.[15] He does not follow this formulation systematically,[16] but it is nonetheless discernible that his understanding of faith embodies both divine action and human response.

Abraham, to be sure, was given the sign of circumcision as a warrant of righteousness, but Abraham's faith was not based on this sign, since he was commended for his faith prior to the sign.[17] Faith is taken in not by the eyes but by the obedient spirit.[18] Obedience to faith means simple and tacit obedience, not that of Jews who demand signs—they should be confronted with the example of Abraham,[19] or of Christians who are more addicted to their ceremonialism than the Jews ever were,[20] or of philosophers who flaunt their subtle arguments, or of scholastic theologians who pose questions for themselves which have no relationship to piety.[21]

Trusting God in one's heart is spiritual worship; demanding from him a sign is carnal worship. These two forms of religion are mutually exclusive. Formal religion, which places reliance on ceremonies, e.g., certain rituals or the observance of fast days, is carnal. Adherence to religion in this form means rebellion against God[22] in the sense that it de-

[14]LB, VI, 562F-563B.

[15]For example, in the 1532 addition to the paraphrase of Romans 3:22, "the righteousness of God through faith for all who believe," he writes *per fidem ac fiduciam,* "through faith *and trust.*" LB, VII, 786E.

[16]He uses both terms in different passages in referring to Abraham's faith: *fidei commendatione* in 4:13 (LB, VII, 790A); *fiduciae commendatione* in 4:24 (LB, VII, 791D).

[17]LB, VII, 789C.

[18]LB, VII, 812B-C.

[19]LB, VII, 787F-788A.

[20]LB, VI, 638F-639B.

[21]LB, VI, 558D.

[22]LB, VII, 801D.

nies trust as the foundation of all true religion. Formal religion makes true righteousness impossible, since righteousness depends upon faith rather than upon ceremonies.[23] Purity of heart, not obedience to formal law, is the essence of true religion:

> After the law began to be spiritual, God demanded the sacrifice of spiritual victims. Sacrifice your disposition to pride rather than a young calf, strangle your boiling anger instead of a ram, immolate your passion instead of a goat, sacrifice to God the lascivious and deceitful thoughts of your mind instead of pigeons and doves. These are the sacrifices truly worthy of a Christian, these are the victims pleasing to Christ. God is spirit, and he is won over by gifts of the Spirit. He demands to be worshiped not by ceremonies but by a pure state of mind. Cut away from your mind your superfluous and disgraceful passions instead of cutting away your foreskin from your body. The sabbath is for you a mind unoccupied by the tumult of disorders.[24]

In a past dispensation God allowed carnal sacrifices to count as sufficient. Through Moses he provided the Jews with a carnal law. This law, however, was given only for a time,[25] and its authority extended only to the people to whom it was given.[26] God, however, promised Abraham that he would be the source of blessing for all nations. Hence, a new dispensation was necessary, in which the carnal would be transcended by the spiritual. This is the dispensation of Christ. Moses is the conveyer of the carnal law which was temporary; Christ is the conveyer of the spiritual law which is eternal.[27] Now that the spiritual law has come, the carnal law leads not to life but to death.[28] Those who continue to hold to the carnal understanding of the law even after the arrival of the new dispensation of the spiritual law cannot

[23]LB, VII, 781B.

[24]LB, VII, 817C-D.

[25]LB, VII, 810E; 811A.

[26]LB, VII, 790B-C.

[27]LB, VII, 800F-801A.

[28]LB, VII, 801C-D.

be pleasing to God. In order for that to happen they must go over to the spirit.[29] The carnal law prefigured the spiritual law in types and shadows.[30] But now shadow has given way to substance. We live in the reign, not of Moses, but of Christ.[31]

The Nature and Work of Christ and of the Christian Believer

It is Erasmus' picture of Christ that gives content to his notion of the spiritual worship of God. Who is Jesus Christ? "He is a man in such a way that at the same time he is also God . . . of the whole world, and a God who is one with the father."[32] He is a man according to the flesh, son of God and God according to his virtue and holiness.[33] From David he received the infirmity of the flesh[34] and hence the power to die;[35] from the Father his eternal sonship through the spirit[36] and hence the power to make us immortal.[37] Erasmus makes no clear distinction between Christ as eternal Son of God and Christ as adopted to sonship through his virtue and holiness. The unity of the two notions is the heavenly character of the resurrected Christ.[38] His life on earth provides the attributes of the heavenly figure. Thus Erasmus can say that Christ "is nothing other than love, truth, temperance, and the other virtues;"[39] and that "he is chastity, sobriety, peace, love."[40] He does not intend by such assertions to reduce Christ to a personification of the virtues of classical and

[29]LB, VII, 801E; 815F.
[30]LB, VII, 827D.
[31]LB, VII, 801B.
[32]LB, VII, 806D.
[33]LB, VI, 555D.
[34]LB, VII, 779B-C.
[35]LB, VI, 556B.
[36]LB, VII, 779B-C; 815F-816A.
[37]LB, VI, 556B.
[38]LB, VII, 779B-C; 793D; 798D-E.
[39]LB, VII, 801F.
[40]LB, VII, 822C; see also *Enchiridion* (ed. Himelick), p. 49, n. 3.

Christian antiquity. What Erasmus means is that the virtues exemplified by the Son on earth are part of the nature of the resurrected Son. Hence it is less misleading to say, as Erasmus does at another point, that Christ "was the source of all virtues."[41]

This Jesus Christ, man according to the flesh and Son of God and God according to the spirit and his adoption, makes possible a reconciliation between God and men. Appropriation of his life, death, and resurrection frees us from servitude to sin which is death, leads us to fulfillment of the spiritual law which is true righteousness, and promises full salvation which is immortality. This is the work of Christ, accomplished for all men. But its effect on each of us depends upon our response to it. The dialectic with which we began between the nature of God and the human response for which it calls, becomes now an explicitly Christian dialectic in which trusting God in faith is appropriating the work of Christ through imitation. Consideration of each of the aspects of Christ's work makes clear the various strands of this dialectic.

Sin and death entered the world because men turn away from God. This turning away began with the sin of Adam in which all his posterity follow since "no one failed to imitate the example of the first parent."[42] Erasmus refuses to make Adam responsible for the sin of all his descendants. We do indeed follow Adam, and there does seem to be a natural propensity in man to sin. But this propensity results more from imitation than it does from nature. Although insistence on this point leaves human freedom intact and assures man's responsibility before God, nonetheless sin is pervasive. All men are in fact sinners, and sin leads to death inasmuch as it separates men from God the lifegiver. Because of sin, death reigned. Christ freed us from this servitude to death[43] by taking it upon himself. For

[41]LB, VII, 826E-F.

[42]LB, VII, 793B; see LB, VI, 585B-590B.

[43]LB, VII, 794D.

> it had to follow that flesh destroy flesh, and sin be conquered by sin, and that death should overcome death. Therefore God, eager for human salvation, sent his own son. Even though he is a stranger to all contagion of sin, nevertheless he was dressed in the same flesh in which other sinners are clothed. For he assumed the nature common to all men and lived as a sinner among sinners. Indeed, he was crucified as a criminal among criminals. . . . And since he died in this way in accordance with the flesh which he had put on, he conquered death, which had been our master through the passions of the flesh and the carnal law. . . ."[44]

Thus, "just as sin originated through one man, so through the one Christ, in whom we are all born again through faith, innocence and life, the companion of innocence, have been brought back; and this happiness has proceeded from the one leader of the new race."[45] The movement here is man-death-Christ-life. "His death has taken away our sin, his life will protect our innocence. His death rescued us from the power of the Devil; his life will insure his Father's love toward us."[46]

From a human point of view, to say that Christ has destroyed the reign of sin and death and restored us to life means that he has bestowed his mercy upon us,[47] absolved us from the guilt due to our sin,[48] and restored us to righteousness.[49] Everything, then, we owe "to the kindness of God towards us. He has snatched us from such great evils, not through the Law or circumcision, but through Jesus Christ our Lord."[50] Nothing we have received is a reward for something *we* have done. It is rather a benefit from a kind father credited to Christ, "for the Father has wished that what-

[44]LB, VII, 801A-B.
[45]LB, VII, 793B.
[46]LB, VII, 792F.
[47]LB, VI, 578E; 626D.
[48]LB, VII, 805B.
[49]LB, VII, 794A.
[50]LB, VII, 800D.

ever he has bestowed upon us should be accredited to Christ. . . ."[51]

The first act of human righteousness is to acknowledge that whatever good is in us comes from and through Christ. This is the sense in which Abraham was righteous, as we have seen; he believed that Christ would be born from his seed.[52] So also Paul was proud of Christ, humble about himself;[53] what he did he acknowledged to be the strength of God in him.[54] We also must acknowledge that what is good in us is from God; only what is evil comes from ourselves alone.[55] To give all credit to God and Christ is to have faith and to be righteous.

Conversely, to be made righteous by God is not a reward but a favor. Wages are paid for deeds; a favor, on the other hand, is something spontaneously granted to undeserving persons. If a payment is reckoned as due in return for works, then the favor ceases to be a favor and has to be called a reward.[56] We can speak of "reward," then, only in terms of

[51]LB, VII, 797D-E. Margaret Mann Phillips points out in a recent article that Erasmus abandoned his youthful enthusiasm for Seneca and turned more toward Cicero in his mature years, so far as his classical interests were concerned. She quotes the following from Erasmus' preface to a new edition of Seneca in 1529: " 'He says the wise man owes his happiness to himself alone, and has no need of the gods, indeed that the gods themselves owe something to the sage. But our faith tells us that sparrows and lilies are in the hand of God; and that man has nothing good in himself, but owes everything in the way of happiness to the free gift of Providence.' The self-confidence of the Stoic was as alien to the mature Erasmus as to the mature Montaigne." ("Erasmus and the Classics," in T. A. Dorey, ed., *Erasmus,* p. 16) This conclusion supports my interpretation of Erasmus' theology in the *Paraphrase of Romans* and requires, I believe, a modification of the judgment expressed by Eugene Rice that "Erasmus and Vives tend to see virtue as a natural human acquisition." The evidence Rice cites is all taken from earlier works of Erasmus. The thought of the mature Erasmus, while not metaphysically speculative, was also not ethical in a naturalistic sense. (*The Renaissance Idea of Wisdom* [Cambridge: Harvard University Press, 1958], pp. 156-63.)

[52]LB, VII, 789B-C.

[53]LB, VI, 648E.

[54]LB, VII, 828C.

[55]LB, VII, 808D-E; 816F-817A.

[56]LB, VII, 813D.

something that comes to us as a benefit, not as something that is due us or that we earn by our own efforts. The notion of "merit" is properly understood only in this context. Erasmus can speak of faith as merit;[57] he even says that we are encouraged to perform meritorious actions.[58] But he clearly means in these cases that actions are meritorious as seen by God; from our side they are the results of God's favor toward us and represent nothing that we can claim for ourselves. Merit, in other words, is something God can grant to us, but that we can never grant to ourselves. Whatever *we* do is the result of God's goodness in us, however God may regard it.

In freeing us from servitude to sin and death and for faith, Christ transforms us from persons of the flesh to persons of the spirit. Here we return, in an explicitly Christian context, to the contrast between Christ and Moses. Christ is like Moses in the sense that he is a lawgiver. There is a law of Christ, just as there is a law of Moses.[59] But there the similarity ends. For the Mosaic law was carnal, based on the observance of rites and ceremonies; righteousness was judged in terms of adherence to these proper forms of religion. The law of Christ is spiritual; it speaks to the human heart. In one sense, then, Christ is in direct continuity with Moses, for like Moses he brings the law of God to men.[60] But in another sense, he abrogates the law of Moses, for now that the law of the spirit has arrived, the law of the flesh ceases to have any power or authority.[61] Its temporally and geographically restricted dominion has been superseded by an appeal to the human heart which is eternal and universal. Henceforth, salvation is possible only through adherence to Christ and the law of the spirit.[62]

The law of the spirit which we are to follow was exemplified in the life of Christ. To understand its content and meaning we need to probe the question: What manner of

[57]LB, VII, 809A.
[58]LB, VII, 796C.
[59]LB, VII, 779D.
[60]LB, VI, 617E.
[61]LB, VII, 798B-C; 800F-801A; 801B; LB, VI, 600C-D.
[62]LB, VII, 787B-C; 801E.

man was Christ? He was a man who lived continuously in the presence of God.[63] He was innocent, in the sense that he was free from sins; he was righteous, in the sense that he trusted God.[64] Christ perfectly exemplified all the virtues of which he is also the source: chastity, sobriety, peace, truth, temperance, love.[65] Love is perhaps a summation of them all: The whole law of the spirit is expressed in the love of Christ[66] because of which he redeems unworthy men,[67] encourages us and persuades us to acts of charity;[68] sustains us in our perseverance to love as he loved.[69] It would be a mistake to assume that in Christ's life there was no struggle, that he moved through life on earth without any perceptible connection with finite human existence. Christ endured much, and through his endurance he gained in humility and glory.[70] Indeed, he "achieved the position of good by bearing evil, he came to rule through obedience, he came to glory through dishonor, he came to immortality through death."[71]

Although Erasmus does not say so directly, it might be true to conclude that Christ earned his adoption to glory through his actual winning out over the evils of the world. His eternal sonship would then constitute the condition of his possibility of winning out, that is, the grace of God in his life. Erasmus' discussion of the life of the believer as "the imitation of Christ" suggests this analogy. For he asserts that "one who has Christ must imitate him."[72] We must follow the example of his innocence and righteousness; we must live continuously with God; we must bear evil, achieve glory through dishonor and immortality through death; that is, we

---

[63]LB, VII, 795F-796A.

[64]LB, VII, 794B-C.

[65]LB, VII, 801F; 822C; 826E-F.

[66]LB, VII, 809D.

[67]LB, VII, 792D.

[68]LB, VII, 796C.

[69]LB, VII, 805C; 805D.

[70]LB, VII, 827A.

[71]LB, VII, 802E.

[72]LB, VII, 802F.

must suffer with him to reign with him. The world will conspire against us as it did against him to prevent our imitating his example. We will be insulted by evil men and lured away by one or another temptation of the flesh. But we can persevere and be adopted into sonship. The love of Christ in overcoming sin and death constitutes the condition of the possibility of our achieving sonship. But that sonship is not guaranteed by any action of Christ as, by analogy, Christ's eternal sonship did not guarantee his adoption. Thus Erasmus can say that "through Christ we have attained the right to a common inheritance. However, the possession of this inheritance becomes ours only if we travel toward it on the same road by which Christ himself reached it."[73] If a believer, having received the grace of God, does not persevere in living out the implications of that grace in his life, he may lose what he has received. He may alienate God through ingratitude and arrogance.[74] "God withdraws from the ungrateful what he has freely bestowed, unless you acknowledge his kindness and rightly use the divine gift. Your ingratitude would destroy what the goodness of God has given you. Arrogance would destroy what obedience has gained. Unless you are careful, you may fall away again from the tree onto which you have been grafted."[75]

But the converse is also true. If one perseveres, he may also be an agent of regeneration for others. For "just as Christ lowered himself to our level so that he might slowly raise us to his own height, so it is proper for us to strive to imitate his example in alluring our neighbor to true piety."[76] The Christian, by imitating the virtues of Christ, just might help bring about the true reform of Christendom. In turning men to a more regenerate life he becomes like Christ, and, in doing so through persuasion and example rather than force and violence, he emulates the nature of God. Here is the point of fusion in the Erasmian notion of

[73]LB, VII, 802E.
[74]LB, VII, 815B.
[75]LB, VII, 815D.
[76]LB, VII, 827A.

reform between the transformation of the individual and that of society. We have come to see the process of *social* change as something very different from that of individual conversion and behavior, but for Erasmus the two were inextricably linked; one followed from the other.[77]

Just as Christ's nature did not dictate his response to God, so Christ's actions in our behalf do not dictate our response to God. Our nature remains what it was. What the nature of Christ made possible for him and his actions make possible for us is a change in our actions which would reflect, not a *change* of nature, but, a *redirection* of our natures. Thus, "good" and "evil" do not refer to nature but to actions. Commenting on Romans 12:12, "overcome evil with good," Erasmus says:

> "Good" and "evil" do not refer here to a bad or a good man but indicate actual kindness or injury. Therefore, a man is conquered by evil if he does not restrain his spirit when provoked by injury but is driven to return injury for injury. A man conquers evil with good if he pays back evil acts with good acts and causes his enemy to come to his senses and to become his friend.[78]

He goes on to comment that Christ teaches the same thing in the gospels, even as a heathen like Socrates taught heathens before Christ. The emphasis on Christ as having made possible a consistent new way of behaving rather than as having changed our natures constitutes the fusion of classical and Christian elements in Erasmus' theology.

His theology is Christian rather than classical, however, in two important respects. First, as we have had occasion to see in other contexts, Christ makes possible *universally* what was revealed only to and for a few by Socrates (as by Moses in another culture). Christ is for everyman; through him everyman is a potential Socrates, that is, a knower and doer of the good. This aspect of Erasmus' Christology throws light on the blend of what we might call aristocratic and demo-

---

V

153

[77]See above, pp. 81-83.

[78]LB, VI, 634B-C.

cratic elements in him. On the one hand, Erasmus believed in a hierarchy of authority and in the special responsibility of those in power to set proper examples for others. As we have seen in *The Praise of Folly* and numerous other writings, he is harsh on men in power who fail to set a proper example for those below them, since the way in which they act influences the lives of many others. At the same time, there is in Erasmus the idea that all men are equal before God and have the same responsibility before God. No man can depend upon the faith of someone else to save him or rest in the easy exercise of formal religion. There is also the implication that true greatness, that which stands above even the power and authority of kings and bishops, is the greatness of faith. It is faith—the union of belief in Christ and acting out belief—that makes men great. Kings and popes fail to achieve greatness, even though they have easy access to it, when they lead men away from a righteous life of peace and love. Ordinary persons like Socrates achieve greatness without having been born into it when they lead men to self-knowledge and righteous behavior. There is a clear analogy here between Christ's nature and work and the society in which Erasmus lived. Christ was born the eternal son of God, just as the eldest sons of kings are born to power. But it was Christ's actions on earth which led to his adoption to glory and to the realization of his eternal nature. So also must the potential of those born to glory here on earth be realized through their actions—or not at all. And contrariwise, the actions of those not born to glory can raise them to glory. This is the possibility which Christ has unleashed in the world.

Second, Erasmus recognizes the limitation of ever fully doing the good or achieving its complete blessing in this life. An essential part of doing the good is knowing that what is striven for in a partial way in this life will be consummated only in the life to come. The Christian's life is never separated from this hope. His hope is based on the trustworthiness of God in fulfilling his promises of which Scripture gives evidence. Christ was foretold in the Old Testament, and the prophecy was true. Since we have proofs of God's truthfulness toward us, we can trust that the promises made in the New Testament which are not yet fulfilled, e.g., our resurrection and ascension and our participation in the glory of God, will also be fulfilled.[79] Our future hope keeps us on the proper path and limits the power of temptations of the present to deter us from the good to which we are constantly called.

[79]LB, VI, 644C; LB, VII, 792A; 795B; 803D-E.

VI HUMANIST RELIGIOUS CONSCIOUSNESS AND EVANGELICAL PROTESTANTISM: A COMPARISON OF ERASMUS AND LUTHER ON ROMANS

One year before the appearance of Erasmus' *Paraphrase of Romans,* Luther completed a series of lectures on Romans which spanned three semesters: summer, 1515; winter, 1515-1516; and summer, 1516; in other words, from Easter, 1515 through September, 1516. Before 1905, when Luther's personal copy of his *Lectures on Romans* was discovered in the Royal Library of Berlin, the lectures were known through a copy made by Johann Aurifaber for Ulrich Fugger which eventually found its way into the Vatican Library, and through several students' notebooks based on what Luther had dictated in his class lectures. Three years after the discovery of Luther's manuscript, Professor Johannes Ficker published a provisional edition of the lectures; in 1938, he published the definitive edition.[1]

Already in 1904 Heinrich Denifle, making extensive use of the Vatican manuscript of Luther's *Lectures on Romans,*

---

[1] *Römerbriefvorlesung* (Weimar: Böhlau, 1938). Recently Professor Wilhelm Pauck translated the *Scholia* of Luther's lectures in their entirety, together with the interlinear and marginal glosses referred to in the *Scholia* (*Luther: Lectures on Romans* [Philadelphia: The Westminster Press, 1961]). My citations of *Lectures,* followed by page numbers, refer to this edition.

had sought to prove[2] that Luther knew nothing of scholastic theology and that, far from being a theologian, he was a psychotic moral degenerate whose principal goal was to destroy Christian morality through undermining the law. Denifle's picture of Luther, although reputedly based on the newly discovered source material, was in fact very similar to that of all Roman Catholic biographers of Luther since the time of the Reformer himself. A Roman Catholic scholar, Adolf Herte, demonstrated[3] that Denifle's picture of Luther, as that of the generation of scholars who followed him,[4] was based on the early vilification of Luther by Johannes Cochlaeus, a convert who turned against Luther and sought to portray him in the worst possible light.

Spurred by Denifle's attack, by discovery of the new source material, and by the approach of the 400th anniversary of the beginning of the Reformation, Protestant scholars took up the task of reinterpreting Luther. Karl Holl, in an important essay written in 1910,[5] proved that there is a strong notion of man's being nurtured in the Christian life through a growth of repentance that is not complete until the resurrection. Holl went further, however, and identified this nurture in justification with an actual righteousness. This makes the answer to Denifle's charge of antinomianism more decisive, but, as later scholars have pointed out, this is a return to the Catholic doctrine of justification in which man has a claim before God. Luther is adamant here and elsewhere in his writings that such a claim never obtains; the sovereignty of God's grace means that man never has a claim before him.[6]

---

[2] See *Luther und Luthertum in der ersten Entwicklung quellenmässig dargestellt*, 2 vols., Mainz, 1904.

[3] See *Das katholische Lutherbild im Bann der Luther-kommentare des Cochlaeus*. Munster, 3 vols., 1943.

[4] For example, Hartmann Grisar, *Luther*, 3 vols., 1913-1917.

[5] "Die Rechtfertigungslehre in Luthers Vorlesung über den Römerbrief mit besonderer Rücksicht auf die Frage der Heilsgewissheit," reprinted in his *Gesammelte Aufsätze zur Kirchengeschichte* (Tübingen: J. C. B. Mohr, 1932) , I, 111-54.

[6] See Regin Prenter, *Spiritus Creator*, tr. John M. Jensen (Philadelphia: Muhlenberg Press, 1953) . This has not deterred an English Protestant writer

A subsequent generation of Roman Catholic scholars, following the lead of Joseph Lortz, have contended that there was indeed in his earlier years a "Catholic" Luther, but that he later became a "Protestant," i.e., a religious individualist. Lortz himself believes that the first expression of Luther's Protestantism was his commentary on Romans.[7] One of Luther's most recent Catholic interpreters, Jared Wicks, S.J., has argued that the "Catholic" Luther is present even in the *Lectures on Romans* but that he disappears in 1518 when a decisive shift from a man yearning for grace to a man certain of the forgiveness of his sins takes place. Wicks argues (almost completely reversing the position taken by Denifle at the beginning of the century) that the yearning for grace is thoroughly Catholic, the certainty of salvation Protestant.[8]

Protestant scholars, ever since the beginning of the Luther Renaissance which began with the recovery of the *Lectures on Romans,* have agreed with their Roman Catholic counterparts at least to the extent of recognizing the pivotal importance of these lectures for the interpretation of Luther. Not all would agree with the judgment of Karl Holl that this is the greatest of all Luther's achievements, but there is a growing consensus that in these lectures we find for the first time clearly stated all the ideas that were later regarded as so characteristic of Luther.[9]

from making essentially the same mistake as Holl in a recent interpretation of Luther's *Lectures on Romans* (A. S. Wood, "The Theology of Luther's Lectures on Romans," *Scottish Journal of Theology,* III, [1950], 1-18, 113-26; see especially p. 116).

[7] See Joseph Lortz, *The Reformation in Germany,* tr. Ronald Walls (New York: Herder and Herder, 1968), I, 210. See also Lortz's later article on these lectures, "Luther's Römerbriefvorlesung—Grundanliegen," *Trierer theologische Zeitschrift,* LXXI (1962), 129-53, 216-47.

[8] Jared Wicks, S. J., *Man Yearning for Grace* (Washington: Corpus Books, 1968). For a succinct survey of the shift in Catholic views of Luther, see Fred W. Meuser, "The Changing Catholic View of Luther," in Fred W. Meuser and Stanley D. Schneider, eds., *Interpreting Luther's Legacy* (Minneapolis: Augsburg, 1969), pp. 40-54.

[9] See, for example, E. G. Rupp, *The Righteousness of God* (London: Hodder and Stoughton, 1953), p. 158; Heinrich Boehmer, *Martin Luther: Road to Reformation,* tr. J. W. Doberstein and T. G. Tappert (New York:

When Erasmus' edition of the *New Testament* first made its appearance in March, 1516, Luther had completed his lectures on the first eight chapters of Romans. He made use of Erasmus' text, translation, and annotations from chapter 9 forward. It is evident in the use Luther makes of Erasmus' work that the younger man had great respect for his older and renowned colleague. On many occasions he follows the readings of Erasmus on various texts,[10] and at one point he goes out of his way to concede agreement with "Erasmus and his followers" when his primary emphasis differs from Erasmus'.[11] Still further, Luther's discussion of the needless proliferation of holy days and the desirability of curtailing their number is doubtless directly dependent upon Erasmus' annotations, where the same subject is discussed and the same conclusion reached.[12] In all this there was no awareness

Meridian Books, 1957), p. 136; and Wilhelm Pauck, "Introduction," to *Lectures,* lxv.

The literature on Luther's *Lectures on Romans* is very large. The most complete listings are in the editions by Ficker and Pauck. There are, however, several items to which any reader should be initially referred regarding Luther's exegetical method and his theology. On his exegetical method see, in addition to Pauck's "Introduction" to the *Lectures,* R. W. Doermann, "Luther's Principles of Biblical Interpretation," in F. W. Meuser and S. D. Schneider, eds., *Interpreting Luther's Legacy,* 14-25; Gerhard Ebeling, "Die Anfänge von Luther's Hermeneutik," *Zeitschrift für Theologie und Kirche,* XLVIII (1951), 172-229; K. A. Meissinger, *Luthers Exegese in der Frühzeit* (Leipzig, 1910); Jaroslav Pelikan, *Luther the Expositor,* companion volume, *Luther's Works* (St. Louis: Concordia Publishing House, 1959); Warren A. Quanbeck, "Luther's Early Exegesis," in *Luther Today* (Decorah, Iowa: Luther College Press, 1957). On Luther's theology in the *Lectures,* see the titles already mentioned by Boehmer, Holl, Lortz, Rupp, Wicks, and Wood. I would especially recommend Rupp as a good starting point.

[10]Luther, *Lectures,* pp. 272, 289, 295-96, 300, 313.

[11]Luther, *Lectures,* p. 419.

[12]No attention is called to this fact in the translation of Luther's *Lectures,* but the affinities can easily be seen by comparing Luther (*Lectures,* pp. 384ff.) with Erasmus (*Annotations,* LB, VI, 639E-640E). Erasmus' discussion, in fact, seems to have triggered in Luther a discussion of similar abuses; the decretals, pomp, ritual, vestments, monks. The abolition of holy days is one among a number of recommendations Luther makes for church reform in his *Open Letter to the German Nobility* (*Three Treatises* [Philadelphia: Muhlenberg Press, 1947], p. 73). For further examples of Erasmus' influence, see W. Schwarz, *Principles and Problems of Biblical*

of the imminent eruption of controversies that were to separate them and rend Europe into opposing religious factions. All the more, then, might we expect to understand the different sensibilities which exploded the Middle Ages by comparing these two interpreters of Paul.[13]

We have already seen in our discussion of Erasmus' *Paraphrase* that Christology, especially the work of Christ and its implications for the life of the believer, constitutes the core of the Christian religion as Erasmus understands it. The same is true for Luther, but as we shall now see, the righteousness of Christ is interpreted by each in relation to views of the nature of man which are quite different, and this leads in turn to alternative views of the nature of God, the law, and Christ.

The Righteousness of Christ and the Nature of Man

For Erasmus, as we have seen, the end of human life is righteousness, which may be defined as "the harmony and

---

Translation, pp. 186-89. See also the same author's "Studies in Luther's Attitude Towards Humanism," *Journal of Theological Studies,* VI:I (April, 1955) , 66-76, especially 72-76.

[13]So far as I know there has never been a comparison of Luther and Erasmus based on their theological writings prior to the outbreak of the Reformation. All of Erasmus' biographers deal with the relationship between the two men from the beginning of the Reformation until their exchanges on free will largely through analysis of their correspondence. For two good accounts in English, one of which stresses the differences and the other the affinities between the two, see M. M. Phillips, *Erasmus and the Northern Renaissance* (London: English Universities Press, 1949) , ch. 5; and Roland Bainton, *Erasmus of Christendom* (New York: Charles Scribner's Sons, 1969) , ch. 7.

On the debate concerning free will, there is an immense literature, most of it written from one or another confessional point of view. This debate and the literature surrounding it are not part of my subject here. Indeed, my intention is to throw light on the later controversy through comparing the two men on a subject of mutual inquiry undertaken before they knew one another and found themselves in the maelstrom of the Reformation. Let me mention only the recent translation of Erasmus' diatribe and Luther's response, accompanied by introductions: E. G. Rupp, *et al., Luther and Erasmus: Free Will and Salvation* (Philadelphia: The Westminster Press, 1969) .

concord of all virtues."[14] Christ is the source of righteousness, hence of all the virtues.[15] He is the source of *faith*, for
he is the gift of a kind father through whom grace comes.[16]
He is the source of *hope*. "Christ was resurrected, he as-
cended into heaven, he sits at the right hand of the Father.
These things have already been accomplished in Christ; and
they are what we must finally hope for, if only we keep
emulating them as far as it is given to us and, as it were,
meditating on them."[17] And he is the source of *love*. "For
whoever loves his neighbor with sincere and Christian love
possesses the basis of the whole Mosaic Law [Christ]; if love
is present, there is no need for other laws, since this alone
prescribes more efficaciously whatever is ordered by innu-
merable prescriptions of laws."[18] Faith, hope, and love are
the highest virtues, and each is grounded in Christ. All human virtues follow from these. In embodying any virtue
whatsoever, the Christian progresses "from virtues to greater
virtues," imitating Christ—the perfect expression of all virtues—and so becoming more like him. Virtue follows from
faith, and faith is expressed through participation in
virtue.[19]

For Luther also the end of human life is righteousness,
and Christ is the source of righteousness. Moreover, Christ
is the perfection of all virtues, both divine and human. But
the Christian does not attain righteousness by emulating
these virtues *because he cannot*. According to Aristotle,
Luther writes, "righteousness follows upon and flows from
actions. But according to God, righteousness precedes works
and works result from it."[20] Therefore, "it is wrong to define
virtue in the way of Aristotle. It makes us perfect and produces laudable acts only in the sense that it makes us per-

---

[14]LB, VII, 796C-D.
[15]LB. VII, 826E-F; see above, pp. 146-47, 150-52.
[16]See above, pp. 136-39, 148-49.
[17]LB, VII, 795B; see above, pp. 151-52, 154-55.
[18]LB, VII, 821D-E; see above, pp. 141-42, 150-51.
[19]LB, VII, 795A-B; see above, pp. 151-52.
[20]Luther, *Lectures*, p. 18; see also p. 228.

fect. . . . before men and in our own eyes. Before God this is abominable, and the opposite would please him much more."[21] Virtue, then, does not consist in *doing* anything—even emulating Christ—but rather in *being* before God in a certain way. "Being," says Luther, "comes before doing."[22]

For Erasmus it is possible to do the good because a natural knowledge of the good is implanted in man's mind. In discussing our natural knowledge of God, he comments on Romans 1:20—the principal passage of Scripture to which later theologians have referred in discussing this topic: "Even though God himself is invisible, nevertheless *he is seen by the intellect* in this world [which is] so marvelously founded and so wonderfully administered."[23] Our minds, however, while not completely corrupted, have been led astray by the power of the inclination to sin in us.[24] But through the sacrifice of Christ for our sins, we boast that we now have peace with God and a certain hope of future glory. The goodness of Christ altogether conquers sin and restores us to righteousness.[25] With the advent of Christ we have two choices: either servitude to sin or servitude to Christ. And it has been left up to us to decide which to embrace; we choose our own authority and yield to the one to whom we have made ourselves servants.[26] Thus, grace perfects our nature.

But for Luther, man is not both rational and sinful; rather, he is first and last a sinner. The scholastic theologians, he asserts, define original sin as "the privation or lack of original righteousness," that is, as the loss of grace, though

[21]Luther, *Lectures*, p. 266; see also pp. 4, 44.

[22]Luther, *Lectures*, p. 321, n. 1.

[23]LB, VII, 781D, emphasis added. Note that Paul says in this verse that God's eternal deity "has been clearly perceived in the things that have been made." Luther follows Paul here, asserting that "men measure God in terms of the benefits they receive from him." Luther, *Lectures*, p. 24.

[24]LB, VII, 800C-D; see above, pp. 147-48.

[25]LB, VII, 793E; see above, p. 148. Erasmus says in another passage that Christ died "in order that he might kill the guilt in us." See also LB, VII, 801A-B.

[26]LB, VII, 796C-D; see above, pp. 151-53.

not as the loss of reason. This, however, is not nearly radical enough. For

> according to the apostle [Paul] . . . it is not merely the privation of quality in the will, indeed, not merely the loss of light in the intellect or of strength in the memory, but in a word, the loss of all uprightness and of *the power of all our faculties of body and soul* and of the whole *inner and outer man.* Over and beyond this, it is the proneness toward evil; the loathing of the good; the disdain for light and wisdom but fondness for error and darkness; the avoidance and contempt of good works but an eagerness for doing evil.[27]

Even if we could be outwardly righteous, formally meeting the commandments of God, we could not do so inwardly. For no one "does the good and avoids evil from such a mind that he would persist in thus doing and not doing even without a commandment or prohibition. I believe that if we really analyze our heart, nobody . . . but if he could . . . would leave much good undone and do evil. This is what it means to be in sin before God."[28] But suppose someone claims that he *would* do the good, even if no one were looking. "If he says he would, he is proud as he is bold, because he could not avoid being self-satisfied in his own boasting vainglory. This is because man cannot but seek his own and love himself above everything. This is the sum and substance of all his faults."[29] Therefore, it is not a question of perfecting the nature we already have, but of replacing the nature we have with a new nature. For Luther, grace does not perfect nature; it is a new kind of nature replacing the natural man.

> For grace sets before itself no other object than
> God to whom it is moved and directs itself; it sees

[27]Luther, *Lectures,* pp. 167-68, emphasis added.

[28]Luther, *Lectures,* p. 87.

[29]Luther, *Lectures,* pp. 88-89. See also pp. 263-64: "If someone were to say: But I do not love my life in this world, because I seek what is good for it in the world to come, I answer him as follows: You do this from self-love, which is a love of this world; therefore, you thereby still love your life in this world."

him alone; it seeks him alone and moves toward him in all things, and everything else it sees in between itself and God it passes by as if it did not see it, and simply turns to God. . . .

Nature, on the other hand, sets before itself no other object than the self, to which it is moved and directs itself; it sees and seeks only itself and aims at itself in everything; everything else, even God himself, it bypasses as if it did not see it, and turns to itself. . . .[30]

The consequence of Erasmus' view is that either we are in sin or out of sin. Commenting on Romans 6:11 he writes: "Just as Christ has once for all been raised from the dead and will not suffer again any tyranny of death, so also you must struggle *lest sin, once destroyed, should recover its lost tyranny over you* and should renew its authority over death."[31] Once grace has been restored to nature, there is a real possibility of actual righteousness, but at the same time righteousness can be lost again through human actions.[32]

But the single-mindedness with which Luther looks into the depths of man's sinful nature makes such a conclusion incredible to him. The self is so corrupted that even knowledge of its corruption must be revealed from outside. "By faith alone we must believe that we are sinners, for this is not obvious to us; indeed, quite often *we are not even conscious of it.*"[33] Because we can know our sin only insofar as God chooses to reveal it to us, we can never achieve actual righteousness through our behavior. For man remains "a sinner in fact but righteous by virtue of the reckoning and the certain promise of God that he will redeem him from sin in order, in the end, to make him perfectly whole and sound."[34] Thus "there comes about a *communio idiomatum:*

---

[30]Luther, *Lectures*, p. 219.

[31]LB, VII, 795F-796A, emphasis added.

[32]See above, p. 152.

[33]Luther, *Lectures*, p. 81, emphasis added. See also p. 105 and especially p. 79: "For it would be impossible for man to know from his own self-knowledge that he is a liar before God unless God himself revealed it to him."

[34]Luther, *Lectures*, p. 127.

one and the same man is spiritual and carnal, righteous and sinful, good and evil."[35]

It is because reason is not destroyed and actual righteousness is therefore possible that for Erasmus "those who imitate and fulfill the law by their deeds and habits" are "considered righteous in God's judgment."[36] God wants the sacrifice of our pride, passions, and deceitful thoughts.[37] But because man is *finite,* because "this body is subject to death and sorrows," the harmony between nature and grace cannot be achieved in this life. It is completed in the resurrection "when we will leave behind the pain of this whole mortal existence and reign forever with the immortal Christ."[38]

But if what must be overcome is not our *mortality* but our sin, then what we need is a new nature, for unlike a disordered reason, a disordered will requires a complete turning, a transformation. Commenting on I Samuel 10:6, "and you shall be turned into another man," Luther says: "He does not say: Your sins shall be turned into something else, but you shall first be changed and when you have turned into another man, also your actions will be entirely changed."[39] And he continues: "Hence, we can only marvel at the foolishness of the hypocrites who weaken themselves by their many efforts to change their works instead of humbling themselves enough to pray that their *persons* might be changed by grace."[40]

Thus, it is not the sacrifice of our *passions* that God wants, but rather the sacrifice of *ourselves.*[41] Moreover, the depth of sin renders its complete removal in this life out of the question. ". . . all the apostles and saints confess that sin and concupiscence remain in us until the body is turned to ashes and a new one is raised up that is free from concu-

---

[35]Luther, *Lectures,* p. 204.

[36]LB, VII, 783D-E.

[37]See above, p. 145.

[38]LB, VII, 803A; see also LB, VII, 783B-C; and above, pp. 154-55.

[39]Luther, *Lectures,* p. 194.

[40]Luther, *Lectures,* p. 195, emphasis added.

[41]Luther, *Lectures,* p. 323.

piscence and sin. . . ."[42] Luther even goes so far as to say that sin is so much the definition of man that if we should lose it we would cease to be earthly creatures: "For if such remnants of sin were not in us and we could seek God with a pure heart, then what is human in us would certainly soon be dissolved and our souls would fly to God."[43]

The Revelation of the Law

How, according to Luther, does man become a new self? He does so first through the law. What is the law? It is "every teaching that prescribes what constitutes the good life, whether it is to be found in the Gospel or in Moses."[44] The law has the power to change man because it comes to him as a *revelation* from God. What does it reveal? First, it reveals *that* we are sinful (a knowledge, let us remember, which we cannot have within ourselves because of our complete corruption). ". . . we cannot know the old man in us, before the law is made known and proclaimed, for he is born, so to speak, when the law is proclaimed. And thus it is through the law that we are subject to the old man in us and to sin (i.e., we know by the law that we are subject to them) and thus sin had dominion over us through the law. . . ."[45] Second, the law casts us into despair over our sin. "The truly righteous . . . implore God with groanings for his grace, not only because they see that they have an evil will and are thus sinful before God, but also because they see that they cannot possibly ever penetrate and confine the evil of their will."[46] In Luther, the revelation of the law is a

[42]Luther, *Lectures*, p. 178.

[43]Luther, *Lectures*, p. 112. The medieval notion of the beatific vision, according to which the soul could begin its ascent to God in this life but would see God face-to-face only in the next life, is affirmed by Luther only in its conclusion. For him, there is no way to "progress" toward that end in the present life. The later Protestant notion of sanctification as a moment separate from justification and implying "growth in grace," always remained foreign to Luther. See Rupp, *The Righteousness of God*, p. 184.

[44]Luther, *Lectures*, p. 197.

[45]Luther, *Lectures*, p. 196, n. 5; see also p. 171.

[46]Luther, *Lectures*, p. 87; see also p. 298.

negative revelation. Its function is to cancel out any claims that the self would make for itself before God.[47]

For Erasmus also the law is a revelation from God, a revelation which is both fleshly and spiritual. The law interpreted carnally is all the prescriptions which belong to the Jews as an historical people but which no longer have validity;[48] and by extension decrees having to do with formalized religious practice or ceremonialism.[49] The spiritual law is the moral law, whether in the Old Testament or the New Testament, and its validity is not historically conditioned. When Erasmus speaks of this law, he can say (as Luther does) that the law makes sin known.[50] But the uniformity and timeless character of the moral law lead him to emphasize the continuity between Old Testament and New Testament. Commenting on Romans 3:2 he says: "... the man who holds the promises of the Law appears to be much more prepared for the faith of the Gospel. And the man who holds the image of the truth has certainly made an advance: *for the law of Moses and the oracles of the prophets are indeed an advance toward the evangelical preaching of Christ.*"[51] It is as if the gospel is the logical outcome of the law, as if one flows into the other as a stream into a river.

Luther's stress on the wrath of God, which one *never* finds in Erasmus,[52] grows out of their different interpretations of the law. The law for Luther is the wrathful side of God's nature, that by which he casts us down in order that he might build us up.[53] For Erasmus, the law is simply an extension of the kind and persuasive mind of God. On

---

[47]"For he [God] cannot demonstrate his power in his elect, unless he first shows them their weakness by concealing their power and reducing it to nothing so that they cannot glory in their own power." Luther, *Lectures*, p. 275.

[48]See above, p. 145.

[49]See above, pp. 144-45.

[50]LB, VII, 793C.

[51]LB, VII, 785C-D, emphasis added.

[52]See above, pp. 142-43.

[53]"... it is [God's] nature first to destroy and to bring to nothing whatever is in us before he gives us of his own. ..." *Lectures*, p. 240.

Romans 2:4, Luther writes: "... the godless man does not know that the goodness of God leads him to repentance, but the righteous man understands that the severity of God also works toward his salvation. For he [God] breaks down and heals, 'he kills and makes alive' [I Samuel 2:6]."[54] Commenting on the same passage, Erasmus says that the gentleness of God should not arouse the false hope of escaping punishment for wickedness but rather should entice and invite you "to repent and to come to your senses, in order that you may be overwhelmed by his kindness and finally begin to be displeasing to yourself."[55] Again, in commenting on Romans 8:15, Erasmus says we should be confident in addressing ourselves to God as our father, for he listens as a parent. And if there is any doubt about his view of parents, he adds in commenting on 8:16: "We would not have dared to beseech him with this word unless we considered ourselves his sons and him our *kind father*.[56] Luther, commenting on the same passage, remarks at one point: "[Some men] say secretly in their heart: God acts like a tyrant; he is not our father but our enemy. And this is true. But they do not know that one must agree with this enemy and that thus and only thus does he became a friend and father."[57]

The Revelation of Christ

Christ, for Erasmus, is like God in nature. He is gentle and loving, and he builds on the past, completing the best in it, discarding the unnecessary. Christ's relation to Moses

---

[54]Luther, *Lectures*, p. 42.

[55]LB, VII, 783A. In his paraphrase of the following verse (LB, VII, 783A-B), Erasmus makes it clear that God's wrath *follows* his love at the end of time for those who have rejected God's gentleness. Erasmus says later on Romans 5:10 that before Christ's death for us we were confronted with an angry and hostile God, but that since Christ we have obtained God's kindness. Christ's death rescued us from the power of the devil; his life will insure his father's love toward us (LB, VII, 792E-F). But there is nowhere in Erasmus the suggestion that the wrath of God belongs to the Christian view of the divine.

[56]LB, VII, 802D, emphasis added.

[57]Luther, *Lectures*, p. 233.

is a good example. Like Moses he is a lawgiver, and the law he gives, while abrogating the carnal law of Moses,[58] also completes the Mosaic law, in the sense that it fulfills completely what the Mosaic law could achieve only partially.[59] Christ does not cut away what existed before so much as he fills up what was partial with his own more complete nature. This sense of continuity is maintained throughout in Erasmus' Christology. Christ brought the mercy of God to men, in the sense that he bestowed a favor upon them in granting a grace men did not deserve. In doing so, however, he did not overcome God's wrath; rather he made manifest the loving nature of God even more fully than it had been realized before. In this way, he awakes in us the possibility of love. He does not change our nature from one of total corruption to goodness through grace. Rather, he builds on the goodness in us to make us more like himself. And the goodness which is thus manifest is real in us; the glory and the gift are from God, but the righteousness given us through them is ours.

Luther's picture of Christ is very different, because where Erasmus sees continuities Luther sees contrasts. First of all, Christ like the law is a revelation of God, but the two revelations are of completely different aspects of God. The law is the revelation of God as wrathful; its effect is to cast us into despair. Christ is the revelation of God as merciful; its effect is to give us life and hope. Thus, Christ and the law, even though both are revelations of God, are entirely different things. For Christ cancels out or abrogates the law. The law reveals us to ourselves as sinful; but "sin is covered by Christ when he dwells in us...."[60] To be in bondage to Christ is to be freed from bondage to the law. Thus, while

---

[58]See above, pp. 145, 150.

[59]LB, VII, 800F-801A. On Romans 16:25-27 Erasmus writes: ". . . . and through one Gospel, the Law of Moses has not been totally repealed; instead, the mystery which was formerly hidden for many ages is now revealed according to the oracles of the ancient prophets and made known by the radiant Gospel." LB, VII, 832B.

[60]Luther, *Lectures*, p. 132; see also p. 134. In another passage he writes: ". . . the difference between the two testaments: Where we increased sin, there was the earlier testament. But where God has taken sin away, there is the new testament." *Lectures*, p. 316.

Luther can say, as does Erasmus, that Christ alone fulfills the law,[61] he means by this, not that Christ is the completion of the law, but rather that Christ abrogates the law.[62] Christ is not in continuity with Moses; he stands over against Moses.

> The real difference between the old and the new law is this: The old law says to those who are proud in their own righteousness: You must have Christ and his spirit; and the new law says to those who humbly recognize that they lack all righteousness and who seek Christ: Behold, here is Christ and his spirit! They, therefore, that interpret the gospel as something else than 'good news,' do not understand the gospel. *Precisely this must be said of those who have turned the gospel into a law rather than interpret it as grace, and who set Christ before us as a Moses.*[63]

Christ, then, brings the mercy of God into the world for the first time. Apart from him God is wrath alone. In him, wrath is overcome and a new era dawns in the life of men.

In this connection, it is important to remember that in the medieval piety in which Luther was raised, Christ was viewed primarily as the *judge.* Hence the cult of the saints, especially that of the Virgin Mary, who could intercede with the judging son to obtain mercy for the faithful. Luther made Christ immediately available to the believer. While it may be true, therefore, as Erik Erikson says, that "wherever Luther's influence was felt, the Mother of God . . . was dethroned,"[64] it is also true that Jesus in Protestant piety embodied the chief characteristic of Mary in medieval piety: the agent of mercy.

In bringing mercy into the world Christ restored men to a lost humanity. He did not (as he did for Erasmus) build on a humanity already present. Rather, he made us men for the first time. Apart from God in Christ, says Luther, man cannot know himself at all.[65] For before revela-

[61] Luther, *Lectures,* p. 114.
[62] Luther, *Lectures,* p. 117.
[63] Luther, *Lectures,* p. 199, emphasis added.
[64] *Young Man Luther,* p. 71.
[65] Luther, *Lectures,* p. 308.

tion "there is available only a tiny bit of that will which would be needed in order that what was commanded actually be done."[66] But "this tiny motion toward God (of which man is naturally capable) . . . has no effect at all."[67] When Luther writes that " 'to will' . . . means to demonstrate with all our powers, efforts, prayers, works, sufferings, that we long for righteousness but that we do not yet have what shall be,"[68] we are already on the other side of revelation. God has turned to man through the law, but then, also through Christ, since it is only through mercy that we are able to face wrath. And what was not possible, namely, man's willing, before grace, is possible after grace. "The power of free decision insofar as it is not under the sway of grace has no ability whatsoever to realize righteousness, but it is necessarily in sins. . . . But when it has received grace, the power of decision really becomes free, at all events in respect to salvation."[69] This is what it means to be restored to our humanity.[70] Luther was, I believe, the first Christian thinker

[66]Luther, *Lectures,* p. 222.

[67]Luther, *Lectures,* p. 130.

[68]Luther, *Lectures,* p. 135.

[69]Luther, *Lectures,* p. 252.

[70]The problem in Protestant forms of religious consciousness is not whether man can turn to God before grace, but rather, since grace is that which makes a man human, knowing that one is in grace and lives out of grace. Otherwise, one's being is threatened. This is why Luther can say that "the people of faith spends its whole life in search of justification" (*Lectures,* p. 119). The problem is to know how one stands before God.

Luther speaks to this problem in these lectures time and again. The following is his characteristic response: ". . . if a man is overwhelmed by the fear that he is not one of the elect or if he is assailed and troubled about his election, let him give thanks for such fear and let him rejoice over his anxiety. . . . He himself is aware of the fact that he is 'troubled.' He should be bold, therefore, and unhesitatingly rely on God's truthfulness and accept his promise and thus free himself from his former notion that God only frightens, and thus he will be saved and elected. It is certainly not characteristic of the reprobate, at least in this life, that they tremble at the hidden counsel of God, but this is characteristic of the elect." (*Lectures,* pp. 254-55) Luther even goes so far as to say that dissatisfaction with oneself is an *infallible sign* "that one really has the word of God and that he carries it in his heart. . . ." (*Lectures,* p. 298, emphasis added)

But what in Luther was a "quest" became in later Protestant thought a "state." Justification and sanctification became particular moments in the

to identify being human with being Christian.[71]

Parenthetically, the function of Luther's doctrine of predestination is clarified by the preceding discussion. About the notion of predestination he writes:

> For how these two statements can be reconciled and by what criterion they are correct, namely, that God wants to bind me and all other men to himself and yet gives his grace only to whom he wills to give it, and, moreover, that he does not will to give it to all but reserves it for himself to elect some among them—this, I say, we shall see only in the future. Now we can only believe that this is just, because faith is the conviction of things unseen.[72]

This has no effect on the goodness of God because, as Luther says, if God wills it so, it is not wicked. "For everything is his as the clay is the potter's! ... We must therefore, have a mind about God different from that which we have about man. For he does not owe anyone anything."[73] In the light of our preceding discussion, it is clear that the function of this doctrine is to remind man that he cannot save himself, that "relying on our free will, we feel secure and doze, for we think that it is in our power to awaken in us a pious intention whenever we want to."[74]

The effect of Luther's identification of Christ with our humanness is to make our righteousness forever outside us in Christ and our humanity dependent upon clinging to

---

life of the believer. Jared Wicks, S. J., has argued in his recent study of Luther's early writings that Luther's "quest" ended in 1518 when a decisive shift occurred in his writings and the "state" of the certainty of the forgiveness of sins replaced his earlier sighing for forgiveness. (*Man Yearning for Grace, passim*)

[71]In contemporary theology, Rudolf Bultmann exemplifies the same stance, as in the statement: ". . . the only reasonable attitude for man to adopt apart from Christ is one of despair, to despair of the possibility of ever achieving authentic being." (*Kerygma and Myth*. London: SPCK, 1957, p. 30) This is probably the most radical apologetic stance possible for a Christian thinker.

[72]Luther, *Lectures*, pp. 29-30; see pp. 248, 275.

[73]Luther, *Lectures*, p. 253; see also p. 252.

[74]Luther, *Lectures*, p. 389.

Christ in faith. As soon as we let go of Christ (or more precisely: are let go by him) we are nothing. Righteousness is never a human attribute; it is always alien to us, belonging only to God. "For God does not want to save us by our own but by an extraneous righteousness which does not originate in ourselves but comes to us from beyond ourselves, which does not arise in our earth but comes from heaven. Therefore, we must come to know this righteousness which is utterly external and foreign to us. That is why our own personal righteousness must be uprooted...."[75] We are righteous "only by virtue of the fact that God reckons us so...."[76] That is, we are righteous only insofar as we depend upon the righteousness of God.

The Life of the Believer

The dichotomies between the wrath and the mercy of God, human and divine righteousness, law and gospel, Luther pursues in his discussion of the life of the believer. The Christian upon whom God has bestowed his mercy is wrenched away from the world; his allegience is transformed. Hence, Luther's language about hatred of self. He goes so far as to say that the man who "hates himself in his heart, really loves God above everything."[77] This does not mean rejection of oneself in the sense in which Nietzsche and since him many psychologists have accused Christians of basing love on self-rejection. Luther writes: "He ... that hates himself and loves his neighbor loves himself truly. For then he loves himself outside himself and thus he has a pure love for himself as long as he loves himself in his neighbor." And he adds: "Consequently, you do evil if you love yourself; you will be free from this evil only if you love your neighbor in the same way in which you love yourself, i.e., if you cease to love yourself."[78]

[75]Luther, *Lectures*, p. 4.

[76]Luther, *Lectures*, p. 124.

[77]Luther, *Lectures*, p. 222. Again: " 'To love' means to hate and condemn oneself. . . ." (*Lectures*, p. 263; see also pp. 70, 201, 330, and *passim*)

[78]Luther, *Lectures*, pp. 407, 408.

This is the depth of the human condition: **Man is so much a sinner that his total being is corrupted, and he is unable to love anyone else for their sake rather than for his own.** He can only love others if he is taken outside himself and *becomes* the love of God in him. Then he has God; and having God he can *be;* and being, he can *do* for others. Thus "one must first seek God and then not what concerns one's own self but that which concerns one's neighbor."[79] For that is what freedom means: the ability to get outside one's own self-concern and be concerned about others. " 'Love seeks not its own,' i.e., it causes man to deny himself and to affirm his neighbor, to put on affection for others and to put off affection for himself, to place himself in the position of his neighbor and then to judge what he would want him to do to himself and what he himself and others could do to him. Thus he will find by this infallible teaching what he must do."[80]

Love will always mean to bear with the neighbor, that is, to make "one's own the sins of all men and to suffer with them."[81] We are free even to give up our freedom when by doing so we can aid a brother.[82] "For although one is free to do anything, he must not make a display of his freedom, and this for the sake of the salvation of his brother. It is better for him to be outwardly deprived of his freedom than that the weak brother should perish."[83] Already in these lectures Luther has reached the conclusion which he summarizes so beautifully in his *Treatise on Christian Liberty* four years later: "A Christian man is a perfectly free lord of all, subject to none. A Christian man is a perfectly dutiful servant of all, subject to all."[84]

The Christian who lives outside himself for his neighbor leads an "unworldly" life or, conversely, a "godly" life.

[79]Luther, *Lectures,* p. 399.

[80]Luther, *Lectures,* p. 369.

[81]Luther, *Lectures,* p. 403.

[82]Luther, *Lectures,* p. 382.

[83]Luther, *Lectures,* p. 394.

[84]Martin Luther, *Three Treatises,* p. 251.

For God and the world are opposed to one another. The consequence Luther draws is that to be a Christian in the world means to suffer. "For nothing proves more truly that one's opinions, words, or actions are from God than when they are criticized or reproved. Everything that comes from God is, as one can see in Christ, rejected by man as are stones by the builders."[85]

So it was also with Christ. "For even Christ suffered damnation and dereliction to a greater degree than all the saints. And his sufferings were not, as some imagine, easy for him. For he really and truly offered himself for us to eternal damnation to God the Father. . . . All his saints must imitate him in this. . . ."[86]

Thus it is that the highest rank among Christians belongs to those who "in actual reality resign themselves to hell if God wills this. . . ."[87] Indeed, *"unless* one experiences in himself that should God want it so, he does not wish to be saved or refuse to be damned," he cannot know whether he loves God with a pure heart.[88] Therefore, "we should be best pleased when something happens to us that is most unpleasant to us, for there is in it most certainly the acceptable will of God, i.e., a very gentle and pleasing will. And we should be most confident when something desperate and hopeless befalls us, for the perfect will of God is in it, perfecting everything and bringing full salvation."[89]

Finally, for Luther, the fact that the Christian leads a godly life in the world means that in the world God is hidden. It may seem difficult to believe that God's love is hidden in his wrath, that God humiliated Christ, and that the believer in the world must be humiliated. But this is the nature of God. He has "concealed his power only under weakness, his wisdom under foolishness, his goodness under austerity, his righteousness under sin, and his mercy under

[85]Luther, *Lectures,* p. 103; see also pp. 98, 417.
[86]Luther, *Lectures,* p. 263.
[87]Luther, *Lectures,* p. 255.
[88]Luther, *Lectures,* p. 262.
[89]Luther, *Lectures,* p. 331; see also p. 328.

wrath."[90] By the same token, "our wisdom and righteousness are not at all apparent to us but are hidden with Christ in God. . . ."[91] They are hidden in the sense that "there is none who is not sometimes confounded in his conscience (otherwise, Christ died in vain), but everyone must strive to violate or wound his conscience as little as possible and to keep it as clear and honorable as he can, and he must see to it that *what is then left over or remains hidden is covered and excused and forgiven by faith and hope in Christ.*"[92] Thus, Christ transforms the hiddenness of God from a wrathful to a merciful presence of God. And the believer, once fearful of the hidden God, can be assured that the God who remains hidden is, through Christ, *for* him rather than *against* him.

Erasmus again holds a more moderate view. The Christian is indeed a new man; his allegiance has been transformed from the flesh to the spirit, from the world to God. His old self, however, is not cancelled out; he does not become a man for the first time, though he becomes a better man.[93] "Better" here means a man capable of expressing love for his neighbor. In this expression of love, which is the true emulation of Christ to which all Christians are called, he may suffer as Christ suffered. But the result will not be that he casts himself into hell or damns himself for God's sake. Rather he brings a blessing upon himself, for which God praises him even if mortals deny him his due praise.[94] More-

---

[90]Luther, *Lectures*, p. 246. See also p. 242: "For God's working must be hidden and we cannot understand it when it happens. For it is concealed so that it appears to be contrary to what our minds can grasp." And again, p. 264: "For our good is hidden and that so deeply that it is hidden under its opposite. Thus our life is hidden under death, self-love under self-hatred, glory under shame, salvation under perdition, the kingdom under banishment, heaven under hell, wisdom under foolishness, righteousness under sin, strength under weakness. And our faith may be anchored in God, who is the negative essence and goodness and wisdom and righteousness and whom we cannot possess or attain to except by the negation of all our affirmations."

[91]Luther, *Lectures*, p. 264.

[92]Luther, *Lectures*, p. 418, emphasis added.

[93]See above, p. 153.

[94]LB, VII, 785B.

over, he may through his actions overcome the evil of the world to such an extent that he persuades men (even as God persuaded him) to forsake their evil ways and turn to true piety. Instead of damning other men by his own faith, he may enable them to be receptive to faith. In this respect, he may be an agent of the reform of Christendom.[95] Finally, while it is true that God is hidden in the world, this has to do, not with contradictions between God and the world, but with the fact that his ways are past finding out.[96] The task of the Christian is not to understand everything, but to believe that God is good and wants the best for him, and to act on this belief.

> If it is unnaturally arrogant for the clay to argue with the creator, is it not much more arrogant for man to dispute about the purposes of God which are so far above us that we are scarcely able to understand a shadow or a dream of them? Begin to believe and cease to debate and then you may understand more quickly. And the potter can make a mistake, God cannot. It is enough for you to believe that God, since he is omnipotent, can do whatever he wishes. But at the same time, since he is the best, he does not desire anything but the best.[97]

Erasmus' emphasis on the limitations of human understanding has the same religious function as Luther's doctrine of predestination. In both cases what remains central is the primacy of faith and the power of God in human life and destiny.

Conclusion

Erasmus and Luther are very much alike and at the same time very different. For Erasmus man is basically good, though finite, and the question is how man acts; for Luther man is a sinner, and the question is the conditions under

---

[95]See above, pp. 152-53.
[96]See above, pp. 112-13.
[97]LB, VII, 808D-E.

which he can act. It follows that for Erasmus there is a continuity between the old and the new man, as there is between Christ and Moses and between nature and grace. For Luther there is a radical discontinuity: the new man is a man for the first time, Christ abrogates the Mosaic covenant, and grace annuls rather than perfects nature. Further, for Erasmus God is a kind father and Christ the perfect exemplification and pattern of the virtues derived from a kind father. For Luther God is a father who shows his kindness only through his wrath, but once we have passed through the fire of God's wrath we find Christ who is indeed the perfect exemplification of the kindness of God. For Erasmus, faith in Christ renders us righteous or potentially so; given this faith, the choice of action is up to us. For Luther, faith in Christ *is* our righteousness, and there is nothing we can do either before or after that righteousness to make it manifest. Nonetheless, we will do so, for a man *does* as he *is*. The sign of his doing will be suffering in the world, for the man of grace is so unlike nature that he can only relate to it by opposition. For Erasmus also a man does as he is, but when he has faith in Christ and therefore is (at least potentially) righteous, then he has the power in himself to act righteously, and when he does so he may help bring about the righteousness of his neighbor and of the world. Nature, in other words, may become more and more like grace.

In the prefaces of their later debate on free will, Erasmus said that in discussions of dogma, "I would willingly persuade the man in the street that . . . it is better not to enforce contentions which may the sooner harm Christian concord than advance true religion." At the same time, he adds, "there are other things which God has willed to be most plainly evident, and such are the precepts for the good life. . . . These truths must be learned by all, but the rest are more properly committed to God, and it is more religious to worship them, being unknown, than to discuss them, being insoluble."[98] Luther responds that to take away assertions is

[98]E. G. Rupp, *et al., Luther and Erasmus: Free Will and Salvation,* pp. 38, 39-40.

to take away Christianity. And he adds: "You prescribe our actions, but forbid us first to examine and measure our powers, or to find out what we can and cannot do, as if that were inquisitive and superfluous and irreverent."[99] This initial salvo by each reflects theological visions already present in their respective commentaries on Romans in 1516 and 1517. One sought the reform of life, the other the reform of doctrine as the basis for the possibility of the reform of life. On various secular counterparts of these two standpoints we are still—perhaps more than ever—impaled today.

[99]*Ibid.*, pp. 106, 115-16.

INDEX

NOTE: In the following entries, reference to a page number includes footnote references; footnotes are mentioned only when they refer to items not in the text. Further, contemporary scholars are mentioned only when their interpretations of Erasmus are discussed in the text or footnotes.

About the Author:

Albert Rabil, Jr., a native of North Carolina, holds the B.A. degree from Duke University, the B.D. degree from Union Theological Seminary, and the doctorate of philosophy from Columbia University. His singular academic career has been recognized by a number of awards, including: a Fulbright Grant to Paris, where he studied under Paul Ricocur and Jean Wahl (1961-62); the Ansley Award from Columbia for his doctoral dissertation on Merleau-Ponty (1964); Senior Class Award for Outstanding Teaching, Trinity College (1966).

Professor Rabil has published one book, *Merleau-Ponty: Existentialist of the Social World* and numerous articles and book reviews. Two of the most significant studies are "An Interpretation of Marshall McLuhan," *Soundings,* and "Historical Study and Contemporary Moods," *The Chicago Theological Seminary Register.* In addition, he is editor and co-translator of Erasmus' Paraphrase and Annotations on Romans and Galatians, to be published by Toronto University Press in 1975.

Now an Associate Professor of Humanities at the State University of New York, College at Old Westbury, the author lives on Long Island with his wife and two children.